Kim Il-song's
NORTH KOREA

Kim Il-song's NORTH KOREA

HELEN-LOUISE HUNTER

Foreword by
STEPHEN J. SOLARZ

Westport, Connecticut
London

Library of Congress Cataloging-in-Publication Data

Hunter, Helen-Louise, 1934–
    Kim Il-song's North Korea / Helen-Louise Hunter ; foreword by
Stephen J. Solarz.
        p.   cm.
    Includes bibliographical references and index.
    ISBN 0–275–96296–2 (alk. paper)
    1. Korea (North)—Social conditions.   2. Korea (North)—Economic
conditions.   3. Kim, Il-song, 1912–   I. Title.
HN730.6.A8H86   1999
306′.095193—dc21   98–24560

British Library Cataloguing in Publication Data is available.

Library of Congress Catalog Card Number: 98–24560
ISBN: 0–275–96296–2

First published in 1999

Praeger Publishers, 88 Post Road West, Westport, CT 06881
An imprint of Greenwood Publishing Group, Inc.
www.praeger.com

Printed in the United States of America

∞™

The paper used in this book complies with the
Permanent Paper Standard issued by the National
Information Standards Organization (Z39.48–1984).

10 9 8 7 6 5 4 3 2 1

Contents

Illustrations

TABLES

CHART

Photographs follow page 128

Foreword

"If the Soviet Union," as Winston Churchill once observed, was "a riddle wrapped in a mystery inside an enigma," what is one to say of the Democratic People's Republic of North Korea?

When I was asked this question, as I often was after my first visit to North Korea in the summer of 1980, I would reply by saying that if my interlocutors really wanted to understand the DPRK, they should read the best book ever written about the subject, George Orwell's *1984.* To be sure, Orwell's masterful fictional depiction of the inner workings of a totalitarian society never mentioned the political and social realities of North Korea. But in the absence of any books about what life is really like in the "Hermit Kingdom," it came closer than anything else to conveying the comprehensively claustrophobic character of what is without question the world's most repressive regime.

Those who are interested in gaining a better understanding of the DPRK no longer have to rely on the fictional imaginings of George Orwell. With *Kim Il-song's North Korea* they have an opportunity not only to obtain a penetrating understanding of what life is really like in the Communist half of the Korean peninsula, but to learn once again that truth is stranger than fiction. What the Rosetta stone was to ancient Egypt, this book is to North Korea. It illuminates, as nothing like it ever has before, not only the politically repressive and psychologically crushing realities of daily life in the DPRK, but the operative mechanisms through which the regime keeps its people in a state of existence somewhere between subservience and slavery.

I first met Helen-Louise Hunter in the spring of 1980 at a "working" dinner at my home in McLean, Virginia. I was about to embark on a trip to North Korea in my capacity as a member of the Foreign Affairs

Committee of the United States House of Representatives. My impending journey was the result of an invitation I had received from Prince Norodom Sihanouk of Cambodia, who was then living in exile at a palace Kim Il-song had built for him on the outskirts of Pyongyang. I hoped to have an opportunity once I got there to meet with "The Great Leader," Kim Il-song, and to discuss with him the ways in which it might be possible to diffuse tensions on the Korean peninsula. But before I went I wanted to get a better understanding of North Korea's internal politics and foreign policy. So it was that I found myself with Ms. Hunter, the chief analyst of North Korea for the Central Intelligence Agency, and some of her State Department and Pentagon colleagues that spring evening in McLean.

I'm not sure what someone who works for the CIA is supposed to look like, but she certainly bore no resemblance to the legendary Mata Hari, perhaps the most famous female spy of all time. Of course, Ms. Hari was an operative and Ms. Hunter was an analyst, so perhaps I shouldn't have been surprised to find an attractively but conventionally dressed middle-aged woman who looked as if she would be more at home in a suburban country club than the inner sanctum of the CIA.

There was, however, nothing conventional about her analysis. It was immediately apparent that in her own low-key way she was better informed by far than the rest of her colleagues combined about what I might expect once I set foot on the *terra incognita* of North Korea. At the time, however, my main focus was not on what life was like for the ordinary people living in the DPRK, but on the views of its political elite and what might be done to maximize the prospects for peace on the Korean peninsula.

After I returned from my trip to North Korea, where I did meet for four hours with Kim Il-song at one of his retreats in the coastal city of Hamhung, I met again with Ms. Hunter and shared with her some of my observations about North Korea. It wasn't until a few years later, when I read a classified study of North Korea she had just completed, that I realized how little I had understood, even though I had been there, of what life was really like in the "Hermit Kingdom."

During my eighteen years in Congress, I had read many classified studies and reports about countries all over the world. But never before had I seen anything like Ms. Hunter's stunning sociological analysis of North Korea. This was a brilliant and breathtaking dissection of the inner workings of a country about which we knew virtually nothing. It would have been an extraordinary achievement if it had been written about a society to which she had access and about which there was an existing corpus of knowledge and information on which she could draw. But to have authored this study without being able to visit North Korea was nothing short of miraculous.

I was so impressed by her work that I immediately commenced an effort to have it declassified so that others who had an interest in North Korea, but who did not have the necessary security classifications, could read it as well. I thought that if people really understood how truly evil the North Korean system was, it would help to shore up support for South Korea which, whatever its shortcomings, was infinitely freer than North Korea. I also felt that were Ms. Hunter's analysis given a much wider circulation it would help to dispel any illusions about the willingness of the DPRK to agree to the kind of confidence building measures that, precisely because they were designed to reduce tensions on the Korean peninsula, would diminish the ability of Pyongyang to justify the massive repression that is the ultimate guarantee of its power.

Alas, in spite of the fact that Ms. Hunter had relied primarily on defectors, who had already fled North Korea, for the bulk of the data on which she based her report and was not using "sources and methods" that would have been compromised had her analysis been made public, my efforts to persuade the CIA to de-classify her analysis were consistently unavailing. From William Casey onward, I wrote or spoke to every CIA Director from the early 1980s until I left Congress in 1993, urging them to permit the publication of Ms. Hunter's monumental study.

Perhaps because it's not just in Pyongyang that officials like to keep reports written for their benefit confidential, it took well over a decade to finally convince the CIA that it wouldn't be jeopardizing our national security if it permitted the publication of this book. Now that it is in the public domain readers will have an opportunity to judge for themselves whether this analysis should have been suppressed for so long. But whatever conclusion they come to about the timing of its publication, I am sure they will come away with a far better understanding than they ever had before of exhibit number one in the museum of totalitarian repression.

Eventually, and probably sooner than later, the DPRK will end up in the dust bin of history, as have so many other Communist regimes whose political, social, and economic systems have been so antithetical to the human spirit. When that day comes, there will be unlimited and unending confirmations of what Helen-Louise Hunter has so brilliantly described in this volume. In the meantime, let no one ever again say that we don't really know anything about North Korea. The key to the mystery of the "Hermit Kingdom" is now in print.

Stephen J. Solarz

Introduction

It may come as a surprise to many that an earlier version of this book was originally written for the U.S. intelligence community and was only recently declassified for publication to a wider audience. What is surprising is that it is not the typical analysis of foreign military, political, or economic developments that U.S. policy makers are generally interested in, but a sociological study of everyday life in North Korea, a small Communist country that is today one of the four surviving Communist nations in the world.

That such a study was considered to be of sufficient national security interest to warrant an investment of considerable time and effort is noteworthy in itself. In this sense, the book is unique. It is probably the most in-depth sociological study of another country ever undertaken by the U.S. government.

Why was everyday life in North Korea of special interest to U.S. policy makers? The answer assumes, of course, that North Korea was of special interest to the United States, despite such obvious disqualifiers as its small size and small population, its underdeveloped economy, its geographical location, its hermit-like existence with virtually no foreign trade with other countries, its political ostracism from the world community, and its utter lack of any major contribution to the world in the arts, sports, culture, science, or technology.

Despite these constraints, North Korea has engaged the attention of U.S. policy makers for almost fifty years. Since its Communist forces invaded South Korea in June 1950, it has maintained one of the largest armies in the world, poised in a state of combat readiness along the length and breadth of the demilitarized zone separating North and South Korea, the last flashpoint of the Cold War. Its nuclear capabilities and penchant for promoting terrorism around the world add to its threatening posture. Finally, its potential for creating unrest in its export of military equipment to Third World countries threatening the stability of their regions has merited constant attention.

What little has been known or written about North Korea has focused on strategic issues such as its internal power structure; its changing policies toward South Korea, the United States, and the nonaligned world; its evolving relationship with its former Communist allies; and, of course, its military developments. The one constant over the years was the amazing staying power of Kim Il-song, the unchallenged leader of the country for almost half a century until his death in 1994, assuring his place in history as the longest ruling leader of the twentieth century (unless Fidel Castro outlasts him by living another five years or more). Yet precious little was known about Kim, considering his long tenure in power.

What was totally missing from our picture of North Korea was any sense of the people and their life under Kim Il-song's Communist rule. The Democratic People's Republic of Korea (DPRK), as the regime is officially known, had allowed few foreigners, mainly Communist officials and technicians from China, the Soviet Union, and Eastern Europe, entry into the country. The few Westerners who had been admitted, mainly technicians involved in the construction of some of North Korea's early industrial enterprises, had not been allowed to travel freely or extensively around the country or to talk privately with its citizens. For the most part, they were confined to the capital city of Pyongyang or the immediate vicinity of the industrial projects they were supervising. Some who entered North Korea from China had seen a limited view of the country from the train but nothing more. None of these foreigners ever lived in North Korea for any appreciable period of time. No foreign correspondents, a major source of information on the Soviet Union in the early days of communism, were allowed to live in the country and report on events from inside the country.

There was no freedom of expression within North Korea. No voice had ever spoken out in dissent—no Alexander Solzhenitsyn, Andrey Sakharov, or Milovan Djilas—from whom we might have gleaned some knowledge of the true state of affairs. No citizens were allowed to leave the country except on official business, and those officials, when living or traveling abroad, were forbidden to establish personal contacts or relationships with foreigners. They were never alone, in their hotels or on business, traveling always in pairs, to minimize the possibility of their defecting.

Thus, the scant information that was available on life in North Korea came essentially from three different sources, all flawed in one respect or another. There were the official North Korean materials, carefully censored to present the most favorable impression. There were the observations of the foreign visitors mentioned above—foreign diplomats and technicians, businessmen, journalists, members of international sports and trade delegations, Korean residents of Japan who were allowed to visit their relatives in North Korea, and private visitors of one sort or another, usually sympathizers but, in any case, persons selected and approved by the regime for travel to North Korea for purposes that served the DPRK's national interests. While these visitors provided a more or less objective account of life as they saw it, they saw only a narrowly prescribed view and, in nine out of ten instances, exactly the same view. They were able to collect data on prices and wages, observe the quality of food, clothing, and other consumer goods, and note the general health and morale of the people. Some took pictures of factories and housing complexes rebuilt after the war, and others described the lavish government homes where they met with Kim, usually late at night. However, they never had any meaningful contact with North Korean citizens that might have afforded some true understanding of the people's thinking.

The crucial information about life in North Korea obviously had to come from its citizens themselves. Reliable defector reports that gradually became available to the U.S. government in the late 1970s began to fill the void. Try as hard as it might, the regime had not been able to prevent the defection of some North Koreans to South Korea and a few to other countries, including the United States. Given the pressing need for a much better understanding of North Korea, the paucity of information about North Korea in the academic community, which had few of the sources available to the U.S. government, and the sudden availability of those new and reliable sources of information, it was only natural for government specialists to take the lead in writing the first comprehensive sociologial study of North Korea.

This task was made somewhat easier by the relatively small size of the country and the population, the unusual homogeneity of the North Korean people, and the egalitarian practices of the regime. Although there obviously are differences from one area to another, from one city to another, these differences are minimal compared to most countries.

Hopefully, this book conveys something of the natural diversity that might be expected of a society of some 20 million individuals. However, the main impression is likely to be that of the uniformity of North Korean society under Kim Il-song. A uniquely homogeneous country always, North Korea is even more so today after almost fifty years of Communist rule. But though more homogeneous, it is, if anything, more fascinating. Indeed, the most interesting aspect of North Korean society may be its uniqueness as neither the typical Communist society nor the typical Asian society. More isolated from the rest of the world than any other society, it is its own unique blend of a traditional Asian culture, a Communist society and the most extreme of cult societies.

It is hoped that this book will bring the North Korean society alive in conveying a feeling for what North Koreans are really like, how they raise their children, how they feel about the work they do, the limited leisure they have, the political study sessions that dominate their lives and the compulsory, so-called volunteer labor they perform, how they felt about Kim Il-song, how they see their country today and what their hopes are for the future.

The picture of the society that emerges from the book has surprised even the more informed observers of the North Korean scene, who have tended to concentrate on the larger issues of national policy without a full appreciation, perhaps, of the human quotient—of Kim's dynamic personality: his personal rapport with the North Korean people who literally have worshipped him as a cult hero, his palpable pride in the dazzling capital city of Pyongyang which he created and adored, his dread of another war that might destroy it again, his hopes for the future of his country, and his absolute hold over his people in a totalitarian state that more closely resembles George Orwell's *1984* than any other society yet conceived. That one of the master totalitarian leaders of all times, who controlled virtually every aspect of his people's lives, was regarded by the people as benevolent and worshipped as a cult hero may seem unbelievable; indeed, it is one of the fascinating truths about Kim Il-song's Korea.

No effort has been made to relate the sociological findings of the book to North Korea's policies—past, present, or future. However, certain observations are inescapable, such as the incredible ability of the regime to cope with natural disasters, such as the devastating floods and droughts of recent years, by mobilizing most, if not all North Korean students for indefinite periods into shock troops to work alongside military units, diverted from their military duties to perform so-called volunteer labor lasting as long as the crisis dictates. Scarce supplies of food resulting from poor harvests during these times can easily be rationalized to the people's satisfaction by the creation of a diversionary crisis—such as a deliberate provocation or incident with South Korea, raising the specter of imminent hostilities, carefully controlled so as not to escalate into war but justifying the phantom stockpiling of food. Only with some understanding of the regime's complete control over the population and the people's total ignorance of events outside North Korea could one possibly imagine the regime's amazing ability to survive economic crises by making major adjustments of this kind, on a moment's notice, in the society and in domestic and foreign policies, with absolutely no worries about public opinion.

Hopefully, such insights will confirm the practical value of a sociological study like this to present-day policy makers. However, the true value of the book almost certainly lies in its documentation of so strange, unique, and abhorrent a society that it might never be believed to have existed except for reliable accounts of people who actually lived in North Korea in the second half of the twentieth century and others who traveled there for shorter periods of time. Aside from documenting life in so thoroughly a totalitarian state, the book provides a fascinating view of life in a cult society that should be of general interest to sociologists not necessarily focusing on Korea.

No effort has been made to update the book in terms of information available since the book's original publication as a classified study. In all essentials this current published edition is unchanged from the original classified version except for the deletion of classified sources, the rewriting of the book in the past tense to account for the passage of time between its writing and current publication, and the addition of an Epilogue several paragraphs at the end of this introduction. With Kim's death in 1994, references to him obviously had to be put in the past tense, but nothing of substance in the text was otherwise altered. The deletion of classified sources prevents the citation to particular defectors and foreign visitors to North Korea who are quoted in the book. There is no question about the reliability of these sources, however; in every instance, the individual who is quoted is judged to be a reliable source of the information provided. With these caveats, then, this study represents the most objective synthesis of the information available to the U.S. government at the heyday of Kim's long rule. New information available since then may well justify a new look at this most fascinating of societies.

In the long run of history, Kim Il-song's North Korea may scarcely be remembered, a footnote at best to the history of a war that left an indelible impression on American military history and the history of the international Communist movement in the twentieth century. Hopefully, this book will keep alive some memory of what life under Kim Il-song was really like. It is dedicated to a courageous young man who lived that life—and dared to escape it for a much better life. It is his life story that inspired the book and gives it the imprint of authenticity against the backdrop of other reports from countless sources that confirm his experience.

With thanks to William B. Brown, who contributed to the grand design of the book, and to Barbara Barry, who completed the final task of preparing the manuscript for the publisher. But above all others, to Congressman Stephen J. Solarz, who worked so diligently to gain a true, objective, unbiased understanding of North Korea and its enigmatic leader Kim Il-song and who has shared my enthusiasm for this book and its publication outside government circles, I extend my heartfelt gratitude and respect.

HLH
February 1999

To John

PART ONE

The Twin Pillars of Society

RUSSIA

CHINA

Sŏnbong

Najin

Ch'ŏngjin

Hyesan

Kanggye

NORTH KOREA

Kimch'aek

Sinŭiju

Hamhŭng

Korea Bay

Hŭngnam

Sunch'ŏn

Wŏnsan

Sea of Japan

PYŎNGYANG

Namp'o

Kosŏng

Songnim

Sariwŏn

Kaesŏng

Haeju

P'anmunjŏm

Yellow Sea

SOUTH KOREA

1

Songbun

One has only to talk to a North Korean for a few minutes to get a sense of what is important in his life. Two phrases are likely to dominate any conversation, regardless of the subject under discussion, just as they dominate every aspect of life in North Korea. They are *songbun*, or "socio-economic" or "class background," and *Kim-Il-song sangsa*, or "The thought of Kim Il-song." It would be impossible to understand North Korea, its people or its policies, without having some understanding of these two concepts, which color the thinking of every North Korean about himself, other people, his country, and the rest of the world.

In North Korea, one's *songbun* is either good or bad, and detailed records are kept by party cadre and security officials of the degree of goodness or badness of everyone's *songbun*. The records are continually updated. It is easy for one's *songbun* to be downgraded for lack of ideological fervor, laziness, incompetence, or for more serious reasons, such as marrying someone with bad *songbun*, committing a crime, or simply being related to someone who commits an offense. It is very difficult to improve one's *songbun*, however, particularly if the stigma derives from the prerevolutionary class status or the behavior of one's parents or relatives.

The regime has tried to convey a different impression—that any person can easily overcome his or her social origins. At various times, it has launched campaigns to erase bad social origin, promising to remove unfavorable designations for people who perform extraordinary service over a protracted period of time. The people concerned are not told that their names are still kept on a separate black list for secret surveillance. Whether they realize it or not, there is really no way to escape one's *songbun*.

In the early days, *songbun* records were spotty, and some people were able to survive by concealing the fact that a father, uncle, or grandfather had owned land or was a doctor, Christian minister, merchant, or lawyer. However, in the late 1960s, a major effort was made to conduct exhaustive secret investigations of the background of all North Koreans. Periodically after that, additional investigations were carried out by the public security apparatus whenever Kim Il-song had reason to believe that there was any substantial opposition to his rule. Because of suspected corruption of earlier investigations, the regime felt the need to conduct repeated investigations to the point where everyone has now been investigated and reinvestigated, and investigated yet again.

Since the only "good" people, in the Communist view, in Korea in 1950 were factory workers, laborers, and poor farmers, they and their descendants are the privileged class of today. The highest distinction goes first to the anti-Japanese guerrillas who fought with Kim Il-song and second to the veterans of the Korean War; next come the descendants of the prerevolutionary working people and the poor, small farmers. Together, these favored groups constitute from 25 to 30 percent of the population. Ranked below them in descending order are forty-seven distinct groups in what must be the most class-differentiated society in the world today.

Perhaps the only touch of humor in this otherwise deadly business of ranking people according to *songbun* is the party's terminology for the chosen versus the unchosen: the "tomatoes" versus the "grapes." Tomatoes, which are completely red to the core, are considered worthy Communists; apples, which are red only on the surface, are considered to need ideological improvement; and grapes are considered hopeless.

Although different sources might use slightly different percentages, it would seem that North Korea's population can be broken down into three main groups, roughly equal in size. The preferred class, consisting of some 30 percent of the population, is given every advantage; with hard work, individuals in this group can easily rise to the top. The middle 40 percent of the population—the ordinary people—hope for a lucky break, such as a good assignment in the military that will bring them to the attention of party cadres and get them a better job. There is no hope, however, of a college education or a professional career. The bottom 30 percent of the population—the "undesirables"—are treated like a pariah class; all doors to advancement, the army, and higher schools of education are closed to them. They can expect little except assignment to a collective farm or factory.

Although one might have broken down pre-Communist Korean society into roughly these same three groups, it must be remembered that the elite of today are yesterday's poor working class and their descendants, while those discriminated against are the former privileged class and their descendants—the educated, sophisticated elite of pre-Communist days. The implications, in terms of the educational level and experience of the top leadership, are overwhelming. North Korean leaders of Kim Il-song's generation were not likely to have been educated beyond middle school. Their children—the younger leaders of today who have received a privileged education through college and a few through university—are a first-generation educated elite, schooled in Kim Il-songism more than anything else.

In a very short period of time, the Communists managed nothing less than the complete remaking of the social structure. While Kim Il-song's methods may not have been as dramatic or as violent as those of the Soviet Union and China, his success in effecting fundamental social change would seem to have been much greater. The changes reported in North Korea go far beyond anything reported in other Communist states. Although the North Korean society of 17 million people is far smaller and less complex than the societies of either the Soviet Union or China, it was presumably no less resistant to change. Thus, Kim must be judged to have accomplished one of the most successful and intensely coercive social engineering feats of modern times.

The potential for opposition should not be overlooked, however. In denying social advancement to more than one-quarter of North Korea's population, the regime has created a potentially explosive situation in which one-fourth of its people have good reason to be dissatisfied with their lot in life whatever the improvement in their living conditions. They can hope for nothing more for their children than that given to them: the opportunity to improve their material standard of living. There is no opportunity to advance up the social ladder or to seek a higher education, a job of their choice, a place of residence of their choice, or a husband or wife of a higher class. Thus, when we consider the progress that has undoubtedly been made in North Korea since 1953—the good reasons for many people's unquestioning loyalty to Kim Il-song and his son, Kim Chong-il, and the lack of any sign of real opposition—we need also to consider that a social system based on *songbun* has created widespread, albeit latent, dissatisfaction. In actively discriminating against one-fourth of the population, the *songbun* system, as it is now practiced in North Korea, has created a hopeless minority class that must be a constant worry to the regime.

LIVING WITH *SONGBUN*

Everyone in North Korea seems to know pretty much what his *songbun* is, although there are no precise gradations and no official notice is ever given. At every important juncture in life—at the end of middle school and high school, with admission or nonadmission to college, entry or nonentry into the army, admission or nonadmission to the party, approval or nonapproval for marriage, assignment to a job, or transfer into or out of the city or into or out of a collective farm—it is fairly obvious whether one's *songbun* is good or bad. Just how good or how bad becomes clearer over time, with the more subtle changes in a career.

By the time they are twelve years of age and in middle school, North Koreans have a firsthand knowledge of the system and some appreciation of their own place in society. It is apparent that neither intelligence nor ability is the prime consideration in getting good grades or positions of leadership in class. *Songbun* comes first.

Popularity in school depends on such factors as personality or the ability to play a musical instrument or excel in sports; however, if a student's *songbun* is bad, he will not be popular, no matter how musical or athletic he may be. Everyone knows he will never amount to anything, and close association with such a person will bring no advantage and can lead only to trouble. A person with bad *songbun* who is really outstanding in sports may be selected for further athletic training, but the talented musician will never go to an advanced music school unless his *songbun* credentials are good.

The ideal or dedicated student, *mobomsaeng* or teacher's pet, who meets the twin criteria of having good *songbun* and being dedicated to the thought of Kim Il-song, is not likely to be popular either and may even be secretly ridiculed by his peers for his excessive zeal. The tension between this kind of student and the really popular students is apparent in every class. It is rare to see a person who is both popular and dedicated. Out of a middle school class of thirty students, there might typically be five or six *mobomsaeng* and seven or eight popular students; the rest are hangers-on. Fairly tight informal subgroups with strong bonds of friendship form among group members. It is possible for people with respective good and bad *songbun* to be friendly with one another, but it is almost inconceivable that the dedicated students at the top of the class would be friendly with the troublemakers at the bottom. A friendship between students with good and bad *songbun* would be broken off immediately if there was any hint of subversion or if any criticism of the regime was voiced.

As students get older, they resist the system less and less; there is a marked difference between middle and high school in this respect. However, this is more a reflection of the natural selection process in weeding out students with bad *songbun* than a reflection of a change in the students over time. Middle school students with bad *songbun* go directly to work, no matter how well they do in their studies. Only about 10 percent of the middle school graduates (those who have completed eleven years of free compulsory education) go on to high school, and fewer than 10 percent of these go on to college (including those who go into the army after middle school or after high school but eventually go on to college). All college students are dedicated students of the very best *songbun*; they are a homogeneous group of the strongest supporters of the regime. The career tracks of these students who go to college and those who do not diverge sharply; there is little chance of recouping a career by going to college later, after discharge from the army, for instance. One's career is irrevocably determined early on, at the major crossroads in life from which there is no turning back.

The exclusiveness of higher education is clearly a major source of dissatisfaction within the society. Roughly a third of middle school students (those with good *songbun*) have some hope of continuing their education through college, but only one-third of those eligible actually go to college. The other two-thirds are understandably disillusioned.

In short, the regime has not been able to satisfy the educational hopes of even its most politically reliable group, much less the other 70 percent of the population. Among the 70 percent of middle school students who have no realistic hope of attending college, there are two potentially disaffected groups: the good students with bad *songbun* and the habitual troublemakers. In providing a universal system of free education through middle school, the regime has raised the expectations of its population for higher education well beyond its capability to provide that education. It has added to its problems by making that education available only to the politically reliable rather than to the educationally gifted. In the long run, this is likely to lead to social unrest; it tends to reinforce the support of the inner group, those with good *songbun*, but it is hardly calculated to maximize political support among the population at large.

It is not surprising, understanding how the *songbun* system works, to discover just how lazy and unmotivated many North Korean students are, even those at the finest schools. The system has a negative effect on the incentive, ambition, and diligence of the privileged as well as the nonprivileged. The former feel they are guaranteed success in life, whether they work hard or not, and the nonprivileged have a sense of futility that eventually kills all incentive to work hard and do well. Lacking any hope of significant advancement, people with bad *songbun* tend to act the way the party describes them—lazy, diffident, and sometimes obstructionist—in a kind of self-fulfilling prophecy. The regime has created something of a vicious cycle: in discriminating against people with bad *songbun*, it encourages antiparty behavior that, in turn, justifies the party's labeling them class enemies.

School is only the beginning of a lifetime dictated by *songbun*. Entering the army, which is considered a stepping stone to a better job, is not an option for those with bad *songbun*. In the spring of every year, the local military mobilization departments notify each middle school of the number of students to be conscripted, and the school recommends the students with the best *songbun* (except those with the very best *songbun* who are selected for high school and college and are therefore exempt from military service). The remaining students are assigned to work. After from eight to ten years of army service, roughly 5 percent of those with the best *songbun* have a chance to attend high school and college. The very small percentage afforded this opportunity is a source of great disenchantment, especially after a long tour of military service. After ten years in the army, without seeing their families, a good many enlisted men are discharged from the army only to be sent to a coal mine or collective farm. Generally, the discharged veterans get better jobs than their middle school classmates who did not enter the military, but few get the opportunity they may have been hoping for—to attend college.

Many sources have reported the importance of *songbun* in such social institutions as marriage. People with bad *songbun* are plagued throughout life, not just in being denied a higher education or a better job but also a spouse of superior *songbun*. They are subjected to a host of other inconveniences and difficulties as well. In a society that allows very little freedom of movement, those with bad *songbun* are afforded virtually none. Having been assigned to a factory or cooperative farm immediately after middle school, they are likely to spend the rest of their lives in the same place, in the same job. They will probably find it difficult to get approval for travel to visit family even in emergencies such as illness or the death of a parent.

When people with bad *songbun* are moved to a new place or a new job, it is usually the result of a wholesale relocation of a large group of people to a more secure location. Around 1960 the party initiated a relocation program, referred to as the Residents Project, which moved large numbers of unreliable people to collective farms and other sites located in remote areas, where police surveillance was simpler and it was easier to prevent dissidence from spreading to the population at large. Several sources reported the resettlement of people from the Kaesong area near the demilitarized zone (DMZ). The relocation was done in a secretive manner, with no forewarning to the individuals involved, who were apprehended during the late evening hours, packed up, and moved before daybreak. The were not told where they were going, and other villagers in the Kaesong area were unaware of their new whereabouts. Their relocation served the dual purpose of providing labor for collective farms and factories in undesirable areas of North Korea and controlling political dissidence. More than 1,500 families were forced to leave the Kaesong area in 1974 and another 3,200 families in 1975. They were reportedly sent to mines or collective farms in the mountainous areas of Yanggang, Chagang, and Hamgyoung Pukto provinces. For obvious reasons, only people with very good *songbun* are reported to live near the DMZ now, where they might have a more reasonable possibility of escaping into South Korea if they were so inclined.

One lives with the reality of *songbun* all during one's working career. It can be the reason for suddenly losing a job or for being passed over for promotion. In 1967 and 1968, when there was a general tightening of internal security controls to prevent defections and control political dissidence, all persons with bad *songbun* were abruptly removed from jobs on boats. The captain of the North Korean fishing boat that was sunk in South Korean waters in June 1978 had just lost his job, but he was later promoted because of an acute shortage of captains.

One of the surprising findings is the effect of *songbun* on the morale of the relatively privileged as well as the underprivileged. One source, who had been given every advantage in life, schooled in the finest schools, trained for the Foreign Ministry and given an overseas assignment, was preoccupied with the unfairness of a system that allowed his friends, sons of higher-ranking party officials than his father, to escape volunteer labor, vacation at seaside resorts, and obtain choice assignments abroad despite their poorer grades and inability to speak a foreign language. There is no question that the system breeds discontent all along the line, except perhaps at the very highest level. Competent people constantly "find themselves working for people who are their inferiors in knowledge and intelligence." They see incompetent people, trusted by the party because of their good *songbun*, getting ahead, while the more competent are blocked from advancement on account of their *songbun*. People are still secretly admired for their own worth, despite their lower status in life, but being held in good repute by others is no substitute for being deemed politically reliable by the party. For instance, one defector reported that his father, who had been demoted from a teacher to a collective farm office worker, was still very much respected by his former students, some of whom held important positions; nevertheless, they could not help him get a better job.

In the final analysis, the system hurts more than just the people themselves. In the words of one defector:

> Workers with a good family background neglect their work and are not pushed by their supervisors because of their family background. Workers with a poor family background do not work hard because there is no hope for promotion. Workers with neutral family background have little motivation, considering the attitudes of the others.

Thus, among its other evils, the *songbun* system clearly has a negative effect on labor productivity.

A promotion system based on *songbun* is, by its very nature, antithetical to the industrialization process, which prospers when people are promoted on the basis of merit, rather than class background or ideology. If the *songbun* system is as much the main operating principle for upward mobility in North Korea as available information suggests it is, it is a major anthropological finding that has great significance for the future industrialization of the country.

The ever-widening disparity between North and South Korea has borne this out. In South Korea, where less importance is attached to class background and more emphasis is given to money and ability, the economic boom in the 1970s and 1980s left North Korea far behind. In North Korea, loyalty to Kim and a good family background are all that count. The regime is simply not interested in bringing others,

whatever their talents, into positions of leadership. No effort has ever been made to use the talents of gifted people who have been classified as hostile elements, simply because their grandfathers were doctors or merchants or landowners, who, given a chance, might, in fact, become loyal supporters of the regime.

2

The Cult of Kim Il-song

In addition to having a rigid class structure based on *songbun*, North Korean society is very much a cult society, organized around the cult of Kim Il-song. This is immediately apparent upon first meeting a North Korean. His every sentence is peppered with the words *Kim Il-song sangsa* (the thought of Kim Il-song), *Kim Il-song chui* (Kim Il-songism), *Kim Il-song ege ch'ung song henda* (dedication to Kim Il-song), *Kim Il-song chuija* (Kim Il-song man) or just plain Kim Il-song. The phrases all amount to the same thing.

The Kim cult flourished in the special conditions of a relatively small country with an homogeneous population, a charismatic leader with a personal style of leadership, and an unusually long rule by one leader, which, combined with his penchant for giving on-the-spot guidance, allowed him to become personally familiar with virtually every town and village, every factory and farm, in North Korea. Over the years, most North Koreans saw Kim at close hand on one or another of his routine visits to their provinces.

Kim is reported to have spent an average of from ten to fifteen days each year in each of North Korea's fifteen provinces, making a total of from 150 to 225 days a year that he was away from Pyongyang traveling around the country. From 1954 to 1961 he is reported to have made more than 1,300 on-the-spot inspections throughout the country, averaging 190 days a year outside Pyongyang. He is said to have traveled more than 318,000 miles in thirty years, from 1950 to 1980, averaging approximately 32 miles a day.

At the Industrial Museum in Pyongyang, there is a twenty-foot-high map of North Korea which is dotted with flashing red lights that show all the places he ever visited. He is reported to have provided on-the-spot guidance to 706 agricultural sites 3,943 times. There are plaques in all the rooms that he visited, recording the date of his visit and what he said. He is reported to have visited the Hwanghae Iron and Steel Complex more than thirty times, the Children's Palace in Pyongyang over fifty-five times, and Kim Il-song University many times each year.

If one thinks of North Korea as approximately the size of Pennsylvania with approximately the same population, one can get a sense of the familiarity that a governor of such a state would have for his constituents, the major institutions in the state, and the well-known places after forty-five years in office, especially if he has traveled extensively throughout the state for more than one-third of each year.

Persons and places and objects associated with Kim's life are treated with reverence, as if hallowed by their connection to Kim. His parents, grandparents, wife, and oldest son are still worshipped, as extensions of Kim. Objects that he touched on his visits to collective farms or factories or universities are covered with glass or draped with a veil. Usually, these objects are set aside in a special room at each factory, farm, school, or kindergarten, and visitors are taken to that room to see the displays of Kim's on-the-spot guidance. Invariably, the guide will begin his lecture with an account of the teachings delivered there by Kim. The numeral identification of a factory or collective farm is derived from the date of Kim's first visit. For example, the 18 September Nursery School in Pyongyang is named for the day when Kim first visited it. Although this name for the most prestigious nursery school in North Korea, which caters to the crème de la crème in Pyongyang, seems unimaginative and unimpressive, it establishes Kim's personal connection with the school. In North Korea that is all-important.

Kim's visits to various places are marked in other ways, too, most commonly by a plaque mounted over the door of the rooms in which he slept (such as in the Guest Villa at the International Friendship Museum) or rooms that he visited; in some cases, as at the Kim Il-song University, there is a plaque over almost every door. The Pyongyang subway hallowed the seat in which Kim took his first ride by permanently setting it aside as a memorial, not to be used by subway commuters. In other places, the ground where Kim stood is marked with a plaque or some other marker. According to one source, there are raised sections in the road from Panmunjon to Pyongyang, marking the various spots where Kim gave on-the-spot guidance during the construction of the road. "These raised sections of the road are an obstacle to traffic and liable to cause accidents. But that does not matter. They are considered sacred spots."

On his constant inspection tours to every collective farm, factory, nursery school, or construction site, Kim was surrounded by groups of local party officials who recorded his every word. The news reporters who traveled with him were an elite corps of newsmen permanently assigned to cover his activities. Pictures of Kim at his on-the-spot inspections were given front-page coverage in the Party newspaper; the only pictures that appeared on page one of the party newspaper, *Nodong Sinmun*, were pictures of Kim, either greeting foreign guests or talking with North Koreans in various parts of the country. Kim's words of instruction on these inspection trips were usually printed in bold-face print or in darker print, much like Jesus's words in some editions of the Bible. He was the only person ever directly quoted in North Korea.

During the course of his long rule, North Koreans coined a dozen or more honorific titles reserved exclusively for Kim. Normally, he was referred to as the "Great Leader" but other titles, such as the "Respected and Beloved Leader," were also used. Visitors to North Korea were literally dumbfounded by the incredible frequency with which the names and titles of Kim Il-song were invoked by cadres and guides. The record may well be held by the stationmaster of the Pyongyang subway who referred to Kim no fewer than 100 times in about fifty minutes! Some guides were known to mention Kim three times in one sentence. An American scholar, who visited North Korea in August 1981, reported:

In the briefings by the heads or deputy heads of various institutions we visited, the average frequency of mention (of Kim) was once a minute.

The visitor is told that it is the Great Leader who selects the site for a museum, a youth palace, or a hospital; who lays down the basic guidelines for its building and operation; who bestows gifts of various kinds; and who makes periodic "on-the-spot guidance" visits to ensure that all goes well.

It is when North Koreans are playing their public roles that references to Kim occur with ritualistic frequency. When we talked with them in less formal contexts, we seldom heard about the leaders. Even at banquets, of which I attended four, the only time the Great Leader was mentioned was during the obligatory toast to his health at the end.

In addition to his honorific titles, Kim was always referred to in honorific verb forms. Although traditionally used for everyone in authority, honorific verb forms were reserved exclusively for Kim during his lifetime, setting him apart from all other people in authority in a major break from the past.

Certain semireligious aspects of the cult include the making of Kim's birthplace, Mangyongdae, into a shrine for worshipping Kim and, to an ever-increasing extent, his family. North Korean students and workers are taken on annual pilgrimages to Mangyongdae from all parts of the country, often walking miles to get there. They go in large groups from their schools and factories rather than as individual family groups. On a typical day, there are some 10,000 visitors to Mangyongdae, including foreign visitors who are taken there as a routine first stop in their tour of Pyongyang and vicinity. According to North Korean guides, as many as 120,000 people have toured Kim's birthplace on a busy summer day. The religious mystique of Kim's life includes an association with Mount Paektu, the "holy mountain of revolution," where Kim lived in hiding during the war years. In North Korean embassies abroad, in most factories and homes, and at all institutions of higher learning little rooms were set aside as chapels for worshipping Kim. His pictures were hung beside lighted candles.

For years North Koreans began and ended their day with a bow to Kim's portrait, hung as the only picture on the most prominent wall of every home. The state issued portraits of Kim to each household. Portraits of Kim were hung in offices, school classrooms, shops, public halls, factories, hospitals, and other indoor locations, as well as on the front of trains and the deck of ships. Below many of these pictures was a small box containing a dust cloth used to wipe the picture glass; the cloth was not to be used for anything else. People were not required to bow down to Kim's portraits in public locations, but North Koreans were known to carry their own picture of Kim, take it out, and bow to it, sometimes ostentatiously, for example, when a North Korean diplomat returned home after an overseas assignment.

All pictures of Kim, including those in books and magazines, are still treated with the same reverence as they were during his lifetime. Negligence displayed toward a Kim picture is punishable as a crime. Parents of children showing disrespect to a Kim portrait are officially reprimanded. An unknowing foreigner who once threw a newspaper picture of Kim into a trash basket was lectured to by local party officials for several hours.

In 1972, when Kim's sixtieth birthday provided the impetus for a major intensification of the cult, North Koreans began to wear a portrait badge of Kim on their left breast pockets. The badges were introduced gradually. Only some North Koreans wore them at first, but by 1980 everyone was reported to be wearing them. The badges were distributed free to North Koreans by schools and other organizations. There were three different types of badges: one for party members, one for other adults, and one for students. Unlike Mao pins, these badges were not for sale to foreigners; to North Koreans, the idea of such a thing was said to be sacrilegious. People are reported to have been very much afraid of losing their badges.

Foreigners visiting Pyongyang were conspicuous for their lack of a Kim badge. After everyone started wearing a Kim badge, foreigners were suddenly allowed to walk around Pyongyang unescorted, something unheard of a few years before. It would seem that the Kim badge provided a new security control; the regime could give foreigners a seemingly greater freedom of movement, yet make them readily identifiable as outsiders. A Korean American who visited Pyongyang in the summer of 1981 experienced this feeling of isolation:

> Since virtually all North Koreans wore a Kim button and it is not available for purchase by foreigners, the latter stand out among the North Korean crowd, no matter how inconspicuous their clothes, how unmistakably Korean their appearance, and how flawless their spoken Korean. Whenever we ventured out into the back alleys of Pyongyang or to the park near our hotel, we were immediately recognized as outsiders.

The value of the badge as a means of security control, while not immediately obvious and not the least detracting to the cult of Kim, may be as important to the regime as its value as a political symbol. Those accused of anti-Kim behavior can easily be deprived of their Kim badges, resulting in their identification, at first glance, as an untrustworthy element in society. The lack of a Kim badge notifies all others around them to be circumspect in their presence. Small wonder that people are so afraid of losing their badges, either temporarily or permanently, and being marked as outcasts.

Besides the Kim badges, likenesses of Kim are found everywhere. There are statues and sculptures, murals and mosaics of Kim in every village, in front of every public building. By one count, there were over

500 life-size bronze statues of Kim in 1980; by the time of his death in 1994, that number had increased dramatically. The most famous statue, a sixty-five-foot bronze statue that dominates the monumental Korean Revolutionary Museum in Pyongyang, was gilded in gold in 1977 as part of the elaborate celebration of Kim's sixty-fifth birthday. Defectors have spoken of the feeling of pride and, even more than that, the actual thrill that they experienced in seeing Kim Il-song's towering presence in gold.

Their feelings were not reciprocated by foreigners, however, who were appalled by the excesses of the Kim cult, symbolized in the garish excess of a sixty-five-foot gold-plated statue. In one of the few concessions to foreign disapproval and a rare admission to having exceeded acceptable limits in their national idolization of Kim, the North Koreans quietly stripped the statue of gold in late 1978. Smaller statues of Kim in Nampo, which foreigners are less likely to see, are reported still to be gold-plated.

The International Friendship Exhibition Hall in Myohyangsan, a two-hour drive from Pyongyang, has perhaps the most impressive statue of all—a huge white marble statue of Kim seated, very reminiscent of Abraham Lincoln's statue in the Lincoln Memorial in Washington, D.C. It is illuminated day and night by huge floodlights. The statue is located at the far end of a gigantic entrance hall, covered by one of the largest, most beautiful Oriental rugs to be seen anywhere in the world. The effect, although different, is every bit as arresting as entering the Lincoln Memorial. Imagine the effect on the populace, and on the leader as well, of a majestic national shrine like the Lincoln or Jefferson Memorial constructed *during the lifetime* of the leader himself. Imagine it all the more in a small country like North Korea where all schoolchildren can easily be brought on school trips to visit the shrine whose monumental excesses, financed out of the meager resources of a bankrupt nation, simply emphasize the gap between the leader and the led.

In Pyongyang, where Kim statues abound, one literally cannot walk a hundred feet without encountering his likeness—in statues, mosaics, wall paintings, on belt buckles, telephone dials, billboard posters, or even hundreds of feet underground on the walls of subway stations. In murals and mosaics Kim always stands somewhat elevated, although he actually was of medium height by Korean standards. He is pictured with godlike qualities; his soldiers may be sinking up to their knees in the snows of Mount Paektu but he hovers light-footedly on top.

It is customary for foreigners, as well as for local residents, to place wreaths on Kim statues on national holidays; two of the four national holidays are the birthdays of Kim Il-song and Kim Chong-il. North Koreans celebrate Kim's birthday with extra food rations and new clothes, given out once a year on Kim's birthday to reinforce the idea, taught in nursery school, that Kim is the source of all material, as well as spiritual, gifts to the people. The children sing songs of praise on receiving their new school uniforms.

Political meetings, including the morning and evening study sessions, begin and end with songs glorifying Kim and his son, the two most famous being "The Song of General Kim Il-song" and "The Song of the Comrade Beloved Leader." Growing up amidst such a chorus of praise, it apparently seems only natural to North Koreans that even the parrot in Pyongyang Zoo should have been taught to say "Long Live President Kim!" North Korean defectors have said that they saw nothing unusual or amusing about that. When it comes to Kim Il-song, North Koreans take everything seriously.

All of the arts, not just music, are used to promote the cult of Kim Il-song. The arias from well-known operas, such as the *Song of Paradise*, are literally hymns of praise:

> Heaven and earth the wise leader tamed;
> Repelled the cold front and brought in good harvests
> We shall live forever in the land of bliss
> With his care and happiness in our heart.

Contemporary poems are no less extravagant in their praise:

> We will follow you, dear Leader, to the limit of the Earth
> Loyally attending you 'til end of sun and moon.
> Oh, your blessing we'll convey, to this forever true,
> We'll remain forever loyal, all our faith in you.
> To our leader we pray, with all that's in our hearts,
> To our great dearest father, long and fruitful years.

On the occasion of Kim's sixtieth birthday, when this poem was written, more than 400,000 people from all over the country participated in relay teams to bring this and other poems to Kim in Pyongyang. The poems and letters were reported to express "the feelings of burning loyalty of the party and people to their great leader."

Traditional Korean art has been largely replaced by a contemporary school of socialist realism in art, typical of Communist societies, but, in this case, one that serves the cult of Kim above all else. In the Museum of Fine Arts and the Central Art Museum, the works of famous Korean artists of prerevolutionary days are relegated to the back section of the museum. Bold oversized mosaics and paintings depict the story of Kim's life and the development of North Korea since the revolution. Most paintings bear gold plaques inscribed with the words of Kim Il-song upon first seeing that particular painting; nothing is said about the artist.

Most of the plays and movies produced in North Korea since 1948 are variations on the theme of Kim's life, especially his life as a guerrilla leader fighting the Japanese. The plays are highly emotional and on the sentimental side. North Korean men and women who have seen these plays over and over again have been observed crying throughout the entire performance. In this and other respects, North Koreans appear to be a highly emotional, sentimental people, as Kim Il-song himself was reported to be.

Foreigners who have spoken to North Koreans about Kim Il-song have been struck by this same display of emotion. It is not uncommon for young people to cry as they speak about the "unbounded goodness" of Kim in caring for them as war orphans. Visitors to North Korea have had so many encounters of this kind that it raised suspicions that they were carefully planned in advance—even the acting. However, there is good reason for thinking that such displays of emotion are not unusual even when there are no foreigners present. That is not to say that they are not contrived; they are not contrived to impress foreigners. The regime seems to use orchestrated displays of emotion to propagate the cult within North Korea, as well as abroad.

For instance, when South Korean fishermen were captured by the North Koreans in 1980, when their boat allegedly trespassed in North Korean waters, they were "forced to cry" while describing North Korea's humane treatment of them at a press conference held on November 7, 1980. After their release, the fishermen told how they had been prepared for the conference in all-night rehearsals instructing them "how to shed tears, make appropriate body gestures and facial expressions." Those fishermen who were unable to perform as directed were criticized as being "emotionless and expressionless." No doubt, government officials in North Korea are also carefully rehearsed in the art of crying; their careers demand emotional expression of their dedication to Kim as well as practical devotion in the performance of their jobs.

On a more serious, less emotional level are the hours and hours North Koreans spend studying Kim's life and teachings. Apart from academic courses, which in themselves contain a large ingredient of Kim Il-songism, there are nightly study sessions—three or four evenings a week—beginning in middle school and lasting for life. Generally, the time is spent in self-study of Kim's teachings, with one or two evenings being devoted to group discussion. The most noteworthy aspect of Kim study, and apparently the most tedious aspect as well, is the rote memory of long passages and trivial details. At a very early age, schoolchildren can recite long essays written by Kim on revolution and national reunification. They can also reel off the exact date when Kim did such-and-such, the specific factory where he delivered particular on-the-spot guidance, or the precise words that he used.

As for the substance of the cult, it is both simplistic and exaggerated—and tiresome on both counts. The history of the anti-Japanese struggle and the formation of the North Korean state has been distorted and falsified to glorify Kim's revolutionary record to such an extent that Kim emerges as the only true revolutionary of any consequence. He alone defeated the Japanese, carried out the revolution, constructed the North Korean state, rebuilt the war-torn economy, relieved the people from poverty, and protected the state from hostile, aggressive enemies. All progress since 1948 is attributed to him personally. He is responsible for everything positive and agreeable about the DPRK; everything bad is blamed on someone else—the bureaucracy, the enemies of the people, or foreign powers. Kim is credited with having solved every difficulty, planned every good. Some of the examples border on the ridiculous. As the director of the Pyongyang zoo explained it, "There used to be serious problems with the animals' food until Kim came to the zoo and instructed the caretakers how to take care of the animals. Thanks to Kim's insights, the animals are now thriving."

Foreigners, disturbed by the distortion of history, have mentioned this to North Korean guides at the Korean Revolutionary Museum where Kim is portrayed as the only Korean revolutionary. Interestingly, the guides have admitted that Kim, himself, criticized the museum displays on this very same point; however, "the North Korean masses who are boundlessly loyal to the Great Leader and love and respect him from the bottom of their hearts will not allow the museum to make any changes." When questioned why they would display documentary evidence that obviously has been doctored to eliminate any trace of Kim's affiliation with the Soviets in his revolutionary days, the guides replied that "the displays are primarily intended for the education of the North Korean populace." There is apparently no compunction about doctoring history when it comes to Kim.

For years North Koreans have been systematically misled as to how foreigners view Kim. According to an American visitor in Pyongyang in August 1981, roughly 90 percent of the international news shown on television each night consisted of reports of the "publication" of the "immortal works of the Great Leader" in various foreign newspapers and magazines and videotapes of the meetings of study groups, seminars, or conferences devoted to Kim Il-song's *chu'che* philosophy. Pictures of Kim in foreign publications, which almost certainly were published as full-page advertisements paid for by the North Korean government, were replayed in North Korean media as straight news items. The fact that these activities were funded by the North Korean government was never explained to the people. Even the most well-informed North Koreans appeared to be unsuspecting of this, as the following observation suggests:

> Even our guides, who were well-informed about the events outside of their country, expressed genuine surprise upon hearing that their diplomatic missions in Western countries periodically place paid advertisements containing the speeches or articles of Kim Il-song, complete with portrait, in major newspapers. Insofar as the overwhelming majority of the North Korean people are concerned, the pictures of foreign publications carrying Kim's "articles" and of foreign groups studying his thoughts are tangible proof of the international stature of their Great Leader.

That impression of the international fame of Kim Il-song is reinforced in other ways. In the impressive International Friendship Exhibition Hall at Myohyangsan, mentioned earlier as housing the grand marble statue of Kim in its spectacular entrance hall, a dazzling array of gifts presented to Kim from 130 different nations conveys the calculated impression of the great love and respect for Kim Il-song in other countries. The visitor is told that the gifts constitute "proof of the endless love and respect toward the Great Leader."

The guide proudly states that, whereas Korea used to send tributes to China in the old days, it is now China and other nations of the world which bring tributes to the Great Leader. Since most North Korean visitors, of whom there is an average of 500 a day during the summer months, are not familiar with the diplomatic protocols of reciprocity and ceremonial exchanges of gifts, they are bound to be impressed by the self-serving explanations offered to them.

In a similar vein, the North Koreans are reported to have asked the Japanese to rush an order for the carpeting for the new museum's study center and "to reduce the price of the carpet by 50 percent as a gift to President Kim." Apparently insensitive to foreigners' feelings about the excesses of the Kim cult, the North Koreans have exposed themselves to much foreign ridicule in expecting foreign respect for the cult to be no less than their own.

It is a sobering thought indeed to consider the fact that Kim Il-song has probably had more buildings built in his honor than any other national leader in history, certainly any other leader still living while the buildings were dedicated. The Korean Revolutionary Museum, built in 1972 in honor of Kim's sixtieth birthday, has a floor space of over 50,000 square meters and more than ninety rooms. It is probably the largest structure dedicated to the glorification of any political leader of modern time. In front of the two-story structure stands the largest of the literally thousands of Kim Il-song statues that decorate the North Korean landscape. Not far away is the beautiful Korean-style Kim Il-song Library, dedicated to Kim on his seventieth birthday in April 1982. The North Korean people devoted hours and hours of volunteer labor to the building of the library, as they did to the building of the Revolutionary Museum in 1972. They are reported to have been "inspired" by the thought of such a grand national project as a personal gift to Kim on his birthday. On his seventieth birthday Kim was presented with a complete amusement park also in his honor, and most impressive of all, a grand arch modeled after the Arc de Triomphe in Paris. An impressive obelisk located in the center of Pyongyang is another of the grand projects built that year, all in honor of Kim's seventieth birthday.

North Korean Foreign Ministry officials are reliably reported to have engaged in black market operations abroad to finance some of these grand building projects in honor of Kim's sixty-fifth and seventieth birthdays. Relatively sophisticated diplomats have said that they felt privileged by the opportunity to make a personal contribution toward the people's gifts to Kim. It was easy for them to rationalize whatever scruples they may have had about engaging in illegal activities in terms of greater service to Kim Il-song.

During the spring and summer of 1980, every village, commune, town and city in North Korea was reported to be constructing something to honor President Kim on the occasion of the convening of the Sixth Party Congress. Bridges, theaters (in Pyongyang), hotels (in Kumgang-san), and other structures were built. Most of the volunteers were reported to be females between sixteen and thirty-five years of age. Few men and no military personnel were engaged in the projects. The laborers, who presumably were volunteering as a special gift to Kim, above and beyond their normal jobs, were observed to look "tired and drawn." They worked around the clock, using artificial illumination during the night. Loudspeakers were used to encourage people "to work harder and make better contributions on behalf of their great leader." Foreign observers were impressed that "the people seemed willing to undergo any personal sacrifice to honor Kim Il-song." They appeared to be quite willing to do extra work out of genuine love and respect for Kim. They seemed to derive a real sense of satisfaction from having worked on the grand national monuments constructed in honor of Kim—a satisfaction not found in the drudgery of most volunteer labor jobs: transplanting rice, resurfacing roads, or building embankments.

An anthropologist who interviewed a number of North Korean defectors compared the impression conveyed by defector reports of people working on these grand national projects in North Korea with the building of the pyramids in ancient Egypt. In both cases, the people who worked on those projects looked up to the leader as a kind of god and thought of the magnificent building that they were constructing as reflecting the personal glory of their leader even more than the national glory of the state. Although the national monuments that the North Koreans have constructed will certainly last nowhere near as long as the pyramids of ancient Egypt, they are likely to be around for a good many years. In the sheer number of monuments to Kim, if in nothing else, the Kim cult may prove to be one of the most remarkable cults of all time.

One can read about the personality cult in North Korea and apparently still not fully appreciate its profound psychological impact. Even well-informed visitors to North Korea are shocked by the intensity of the people's feelings. Though they may be impressed with other things, such as the improvement in living conditions, the beauty of Pyongyang, the vitality of North Korean agriculture, or the determination of the country to reunify Korea, these impressions are always overshadowed by their sense of awe in the midst of the world's most intense personality cult.

B. C. Koh, a leading Korean American scholar, is typical of many foreign visitors, both American and otherwise, who have been virtually stunned by the overpowering aspects of the cult. His comments are particularly meaningful because of his status as perhaps the foremost American scholar of the Kim cult. After his first visit to North Korea, he wrote,

> If one phrase can sum up the myriad impressions I gained during my 19–day visit to North Korea, it is the cult of personality surrounding its supreme leader Kim Il-song. As a longtime student of North Korean affairs, I was no stranger to the phenomenon. My prolonged exposure to the North Korean press and publications had made me amply aware that it was the single most important characteristic of North Korean society, and I had read the accounts of a number of American and Japanese visitors to North Korea in which both its intensity and pervasiveness were described and emphasized. What is more, I had previously written a couple of articles which explored the dimensions, sources, and consequences of the Kim Il-song cult.
>
> None of this, however, had prepared me for what I actually saw, heard, and felt in North Korea. Never before had I experienced such an overwhelming presence of a mortal human being or, for that matter, of a divine being in the daily routine of life: Kim Il-song was literally omnipresent.

The most distinguishing feature about the Kim cult, then, is not its more extreme outward manifestations, extreme as they may be, but the intensity of the people's feelings. Even allowing for all the contrived displays of emotion and the feigned dedication of those who go along with the cult for reasons of self-interest, one cannot but be amazed at the overwhelming evidence of the people's strong emotional attachment to Kim.

With all the instruments of control at their disposal, North Korea's leaders could never have created so intense a psychological phenomenon had it not been for Kim's own unique personality and his incredible success in establishing a personal relationship with his people. By all accounts, he was an "engaging . . . charismatic . . . compelling" man of native intellect and ability, though not formally educated. He conveyed a deep personal interest in the lives of the people, worked tirelessly for the national good (as he saw it), and maintained the image of a man of the people. Moreover, his particular style of leadership, featuring endless tours of the country, kept him in close touch with the population, where his personality was used to the fullest. The people's emotional response to his presence among them reinforced the teachings of the cult, learned since childhood, and transformed the cult from a national creed into a national religion.

The stories of Kim's special appeal to young children, women, and old men are legendary—and convincingly confirmed. On visits to elementary schools, Kim often took a polaroid camera and had his picture taken with the schoolchildren; he would then autograph a picture for each student to take home. In the course of his constant tours around the country, he had a particular penchant for getting on a bus or subway during morning rush hours and walking long distances with collective farmers and factory workers, giving him ample time to converse with the people about their everyday life.

There is no question, from this and other accounts, that seeing Kim at close hand was an emotional experience for North Koreans:

> Since we were young we had heard about Kim, seen pictures of Kim, talked about Kim, sung about Kim, and read about Kim. I believed that he was omnipotent. . . . It was with great excitement that I hoped to see him. After I had seen him, I resolved to strive very hard to become some kind of model and thereby gain another opportunity to see him.

The relatively small size of North Korea obviously made it easier for Kim to establish a personalized relationship with the people than it was for Joseph Stalin or Mao Tse-tung, who were remote by comparison. However, much more important than the size of the country or the homogeneity of the people, Kim's particular personality and his special genius for establishing personal rapport with his people were the core of the cult. According to no less an authority than Prince Norodom Sihanouk of Cambodia, a charismatic figure in his own right, a foreigner who came to know Kim Il-song well during his long exile in North Korea, "Kim has a relationship with his people that every other leader in the world would envy." When asked how that relationship compared with his own relationship with the Cambodian people, Sihanouk responded that "it just doesn't compare. Kim's is so much closer."

Visitors to North Korea all comment on the depth of the people's feelings for Kim. Individuals are unable to talk about the state, the party, the institutions of government, morality, their own aspirations, or practically anything else without constantly referring to Kim Il-song. Studied at a distance as an abstraction, the cult may appear ludicrous but, up close, its hold over the perception and thought patterns of North Koreans is awe-inspiring.

Apparently, one rarely hears anyone speak ill of Kim in North Korea. The people always use honorific terms when referring to Kim, even in private conversations with close friends and family. There may be some criticism of Kim in the intimacy of some families, and defectors have admitted to having secret doubts about the infallibility of Kim, though they never voiced these criticisms in public or, for that matter, in private.

As well as we can determine, then, it would seem that the cult of personality in North Korea rests on a genuine belief of the vast majority of the people, if not all the people, in the greatness and goodness of Kim Il-song. Whatever criticism of Kim there is—and there is surely some—it is rarely voiced, even in private; people are afraid to criticize the regime, especially Kim. These two factors—the great popularity of Kim and the fear of voicing criticism—combine to produce an overwhelming psychological pressure on people to believe. In this sense, most people are believers. Their faith and their fears go beyond their doubts. Like many religious believers, they may have their doubts, but they hold fast to the faith in spite of these doubts.

The most convincing reason for accepting the depth of the people's love for Kim comes from defectors who have absolutely no reason to exaggerate their true feelings for Kim. Having made the courageous and highly dangerous decision to defect from North Korea and having no thought of returning to a dreaded existence from which they have narrowly escaped, they still express a certain reverence for Kim in spite of the reservations they may have about the excesses of the cult. Their admiration for Kim as a person and leader is clearly deep-seated, genuine, and unshakeable; the hold of the cult over them is not to be understated. While they can—and do—renounce the cult intellectually, expressing abhorrence at its excesses, they retain an almost religious feeling toward Kim as a semi-god of the North Korean people.

Ironically, the cult of Kim, which has succeeded in creating a society of believers, seems also to be one of the major sources of dissatisfaction within the society. One wonders if the regime is aware of the feeling against the cult's excesses and, if so, why it allows these excesses to continue. From available evidence, it would seem that the dissatisfaction, avoidable and correctable, is not threatening the regime. The regime may calculate that it can afford such a nonthreatening level of dissatisfaction, that it is safer to err on this side than to let up on the personality cult and thereby risk some lessening of its hold on the people. Having once allowed the cult to reach certain proportions, moreover, whether planned in advance or not, it is difficult to back away from its excesses without undermining its authority. Many senior party officials are associated with the development of the cult and to curtail it would jeopardize their own political careers.

Of particular interest is the fact that the cult seems to offend the more educated and privileged rather than the ordinary North Korean of lower status. In other words, it alienates the very people who are the regime's most loyal supporters. The less privileged have other sources of dissatisfaction—the denial of higher education or a better job with higher income; they may not be as disturbed or as deeply affected by the excess of the personality cult. Other than being more easily bored with the emotion and trivia of the cult, the better educated have to suffer greater exposure to it. The higher one's education, the more hours spent in studying the life and thought of Kim. Thus, the paradox of the cult is that the more privileged one is, the more necessarily involved one is in the cult. Yet the more educated and sophisticated one is, the more likely one is to be turned off by the cult. The very people who do the most to promote it are very likely the ones most disenchanted with it.

If indeed this is true, it has significant implications for the future. It suggests that opposition to the cult may well come from the top leadership rather than the ordinary people, just as Teng Hsiao-ping and other Chinese leaders are known to have been disgusted by the excesses of the Mao cult (though they gave no indication of it at the time). In a revealing interview with a foreign visitor to China, Teng Hsiao-ping admitted to "hating the Mao cult." He disliked Mao's "feudal, patriarchal style" of leadership, by which Teng explained that he meant Mao's failure to ask the opinion of his top leaders and his inclination to do whatever he wanted without regard for others' opinions. Another feature of Mao's patriarchal style that Teng strongly objected to was his grant of power to his wife, Chiang Chang. (The parallel with Kim Il-song's delegation of power to his son Kim Chong-il, is interesting.) One would never have suspected Teng's feelings, judging from outward appearances at the time. It was Teng, after all, who defended Mao's cult of personality against Nikita Khrushchev's attack on personality cults, specifically Stalin's cult of personality but, by implication, Mao's cult, as well. The same fawning obeisance to the Mao cult was obvious with Lin Piao, who used to carry Mao's little Red Book in the most obvious manner in the days and months, as we were later to learn, that he was actually plotting Mao's downfall. The simple fact of life is that in a cult society, like China in the late 1960s and early 1970s and even more so in North Korea during Kim's lifetime, one has to pay lip service to the cult to survive. The higher up one is, the more committed one must appear to be. So, too, may some of North Korea's leaders be repelled by the excesses of the cult of Kim and of his son and one day may seek to undo the damage, even though they give the opposite impression now.

In the meantime, although they may be repelled by the excesses of the cult, there are pressures operating on North Korea's leaders that will not only perpetuate these excesses but intensify them. In a society that promotes people on the basis of political loyalty, it is only natural that people, especially those aspiring to high positions, should try to outdo one another with ever greater displays of fidelity. There was obviously an element of this in the diplomat's ostentatious display of bowing to Kim's portrait in the Pyongyang airport. One constantly has to prove one's loyalty to ensure one's position; the higher the position, the more proof is required.

Thus, the most important factor contributing to the intensification of the cult, and arguing against any curtailment of it, is the natural competition among North Koreans for promotion on the accepted grounds for promotion, namely, professed loyalty to Kim Il-song and his son.

3

The Kim Il-song Man: Good *Songbun* and Dedication to Kim

Second only to *songbun*, then, loyalty to Kim is the key element of success in life. Promotion or demotion within one's social class is determined on that basis. Dedication to the thought of Kim Il-song cannot erase class origin, but it can improve one's lot in life, within established limits. The son of a former wealthy landowner will not go to college, however dedicated he may be, or however smart. However, proven dedication to Kim is likely to get him a job as a factory worker rather than as a cooperative farmer. Dedication to Kim's teachings might give an ordinary citizen the chance to live and work in a city rather than in the countryside or allow him to be a fisherman or office worker rather than a factory worker. Among the privileged class, it could spell the difference between a top career in government, education, management, or the arts and a middle-level career in these same fields.

Less than zealous devotion to the teachings of Kim is grounds for demotion, again within clearly established limits. A person of good *songbun* is not likely to be sent to a collective farm or to the coal mines except for the most serious offense, such as the defection of a close family member or some other treasonable act. Normally, he will be demoted several notches within the range of occupations reserved for his social class. A top party official in the government might be demoted to some low-level party position on a collective farm; a high-level factory manager might be reassigned to office work; or a middle school teacher might be demoted to a factory worker or, worse still, a collective farmer.

Myriad case studies bespeak the influence of one's political attitude as a contributing factor but not the main factor (*songbun*) in one's success in life. The case studies provide a fascinating study of the interplay between one's *songbun* and one's dedication to Kim. It is easy to get the wrong impression from some of these stories, which typically focus on one or another of the two factors but do not take both factors into account. Promotions and demotions operate within certain prescribed limits; *songbun* determines the range, the upper and lower limits. Political loyalty is the key factor in promotions and demotions within that range.

Everyone in North Korea understands the twin criteria for advancement. No one seems fooled that intelligence, ability, or technical expertise count for much. Since there is absolutely nothing that can be done about one's *songbun*, which is all-important in determining the parameters of one's life, and since the only factor that matters in terms of advancement within the limits set by *songbun* is dedication to Kim, the only thing one can do to get ahead is to convey the impression of complete dedication to the Great Leader.

Dedication to Kim is judged from a very early age, certainly by the time one is in middle school. The *mobomsaeng*, or dedicated student, will have been faithful in attending political meetings as early as primary school; he is not likely to have missed any meetings during middle school except for the best of reasons. In high school and college, mere attendance would not be enough; enthusiastic participation would be required. He is likely to have used the criticism sessions, dreaded by most North Koreans but manipulated by the more ambitious, to put down the competition while obtaining high marks for his own dedication. He is also likely to have far exceeded the normal requirements for volunteer labor, working on economic construction projects on Saturday afternoons, Sundays, during school holidays, and on weekday evenings. As noted earlier, such a student is not likely to be popular, but that does not matter; he is obviously interested in getting ahead, first and foremost.

In his early twenties, the upwardly mobile young man or woman must be sure to join the party before he or she gets married. Advancement to the top—that is, to the upper limits of whatever *songbun* category one is in—is impossible (except for a few artists and scientists) without party membership. Everyone knows this. Once in the party, one's advancement will be determined much more by one's display of devotion to Kim's teachings than by one's technical or administrative or substantive skills. Thus, the constant pressure, even among high-level officials such as ambassadors, is to outdo one another in public displays of fidelity to Kim, long hours of study of Kim's thought, and zealous criticism of oneself and others in falling short of Kim's ideals.

Dedication to Kim (with its promise of promotion) can be expressed in hard work as well as enthusiastic study of Kim's thought. The media are full of stories of "revolutionary heroes" who have improved the quality or increased the quantity of production by devising new or better ways of performing their jobs. The extraordinary production records they set are likely to become tomorrow's accepted norm, much to the dismay of their fellow workers, and to lead to higher and higher production quotas in the future.

It is interesting to consider the implications of a promotion system based so exclusively on political and class origin considerations. The negative effect of the *songbun* system on the ambition, hard work, and morale of all but the top 15 or 20 percent of the population has already been discussed. We know from defectors that many people are repelled by the blatantly political nature of advancement in North Korea, especially very bright people of good *songbun*. They could compete on any basis, but they would prefer a system of advancement based on merit, rather than dedication to Kim. Not surprisingly, they were not so disturbed by the *songbun* system (which placed them in a very favorable competitive position) as they were by the political requirements of total loyalty to Kim Il-song's teachings.

On the other hand, there must be those, presumably the less bright who are less able to compete on merit, who do better in a system demanding complete political loyalty. In this sense, the North Korean system tends to promote the less gifted over the more gifted to the extent that the more gifted are unwilling to go to the absurd lengths of slavish obedience to the Kim cult. The system gives an advantage to the political sycophant over the nonsycophant. This tends to reinforce the negative effects of the *songbun* system in promoting the politically reliable rather than the more able people in North Korea. Thus, on both counts, the criteria for success would seem to run counter to the criteria for promoting the most able in North Korea.

Moreover, to the extent that the Kim cult monopolizes the time and energy of the people, it would seem to detract from their productive energies. There is ample evidence that the people are overworked, overfatigued, and worn out and exhausted by the combination of long working hours and endless study of Kim's thought. The average man's work day is extended by three or four hours and the average woman's work day by two or three hours of political study each day. There is no question that the regime has paid the price of an exhausted workforce by demanding heavy political chores on top of a strenuous work day. It may not fully appreciate the economic costs involved, but they have been heavy, indeed. There may also be political costs involved. At the heart of the people's dissatisfaction with the Kim cult, which existed in spite of their genuine devotion to Kim during his lifetime, is the exorbitant time involved in the perpetuation of the cult. It is only natural that they would resent the time spent in endlessly proving their dedication to Kim, especially when it leaves virtually no time for themselves. Although the resentment may be directed at the party bureaucracy, rather than Kim, it is a negative force that detracts from the populace's enthusiastic support of the regime, just as it saps its physical energies.

Some have observed another effect of the cult on the North Korean people—a heightening of the emotional and a lessening of the intellectual personality of the people. Whether the cult has produced a genuinely more emotional people in the north than in the south is difficult to judge. Certainly, it has produced a far less intellectual people, who are used to following orders without asking questions. To many people, this has raised the possibility of North Korea's acting irrationally, in attacking South Korea, for instance. It does not necessarily follow that the top leadership will act irrationally, but it does suggest that the people can be expected to do exactly what the regime orders, to preposterous lengths at times, just as the followers of Jim Jones or Charles Manson or other cult leaders have done what their cult leaders ordered, including killing and suicide.

Even if one accepts the basic rationality of those in control, there is a distortion in one's thinking that arises from extreme cult worship. One would have to admit that the cult of personality in North Korea, more extreme than perhaps any other national cult of personality in history, introduces a note of irrationality, all other signs of rationality notwithstanding.

There is one final observation to be made about the effects of the cult on North Korea. In contrast to pluralistic societies where wealth and power are shared by the political elite, successful businessmen and professionals, popular athletes, writers, artists, and entertainers, in North Korea there is only one way to get ahead economically, socially, or any other way, and that is through politics. Those in the political elite are also the economic elite and the social elite. They have reached the top through a promotion system that puts a premium on one thing only—political loyalty to Kim Il-song and his son Kim Chong-il. The society has been politicized to the point where politics dominates all aspects of life.

PART TWO

Kim's Blueprint for Life: From the Cradle to the Grave

4

Family Life

Every North Korean over the age of six is a member of a unit of some sort. Outside of the family, that unit is the basic social grouping of North Korean society. It can be the school one attends; the factory, collective farm, or government office where one works; or the military unit to which one is attached.

The unit provides housing, as well as food and clothing. Normally, a father's work unit provides housing for his family. Thus, wives and children do not usually live with the people they work for or go to school with, although some students do live at school. With the exception of housing, women and children do everything with their work unit.

It is to the unit that one applies for permission to marry, to travel, to stay at out-of-town hotels, or to eat at public restaurants. It is the unit that authorizes vacation time and arranges for one's stay at government-owned vacation retreats. It is the unit to which one must apply for permission to see a doctor or have an operation. If a person has saved enough money to buy a watch or a bicycle, he must first get his unit's permission to purchase it. Finally, it is with fellow members of the unit that one attends all party meetings, militia training, self-criticism sessions, morning and evening study sessions, and cultural events such as concerts and museums and social events such as movies and dances.

Sociologists who contend that the complexity of an individual's personality derives from the number of social groups to which the individual belongs could only conclude the personality of North Koreans must be relatively simple. There is no evidence to refute this. To the contrary, it seems that North Koreans probably do know many fewer people in their lifetimes than the average person in almost any other country. Moreover, the people they know all share basically the same life experience, sometimes from birth to the grave in the same collective farm or factory community.

While Westerners almost certainly would find such a narrowly prescribed social grouping intolerable, North Koreans may not necessarily see it that way. The work unit affords a sense of security and belonging. Available evidence suggests that people also like the sense of equality promoted by the system. Some may object to the management's criteria in making decisions, but they do not necessarily object to the system, per se. Their grievances are more likely to center on the blatantly political basis of decision making and the intrusion of politics into a few highly personal matters, such as the choice of a marriage partner.

This social grouping of people into work units applies to all North Koreans—not just the physically handicapped or mentally retarded—from the age of six to sixty (for women) or sixty-five (for men). It includes both men and women. Women, like men, go to school until the age of sixteen, unless they are lucky enough to go on to high school or college, and then they work until they retire at age sixty.

Unless husbands and wives belong to the same work unit, a not uncommon occurrence, they do not share many of the experiences that families in the United States normally share together. Nor do they do as much with their children as parents in the United States do. For instance, children in Pyongyang visit Kim's birthplace (Mangyondae) and other museums in the city in outings arranged by their schools. They get tickets to the theater and musical concerts through their school. Meanwhile, their parents go to these same events, at different times, in the company of fellow members of their work units. Tickets are distributed to members of a work unit as a group; they are not sold separately to individuals or families at a time of their own choosing. Thus, though family members may be exposed to many of the same experiences, they do not share these experiences with their brothers, sisters, mothers, and fathers.

Parents are much less directly involved than American parents in other aspects of their children's upbringing, such as their education and medical care; family vacations are virtually nonexistent. Children see the doctors assigned to their school; their parents consult other doctors assigned to their work units. School authorities, working with local party officials, arrange the volunteer labor schedules of students during vacation times, with little or no coordination with parents' volunteer labor schedules. Teachers accompany students to collective farms during rice transplanting and rice harvesting; parents are likely to be assigned to different collective farms for, perhaps, the same or, perhaps, different two-week stints of volunteer labor.

The only time that parents and children are regularly together after 7:30–8:30 A.M. and before 10:00–10:30 P.M. is on Sundays, the one true family day in North Korea. Generally, families spend the day together at home, most often doing household chores or resting. In Pyongyang, parents and children may go for walks in parks or visit an amusement center or, possibly, the zoo. The more affluent might eat Sunday dinner at a local restaurant as a special treat, not a common occurrence, something they would probably do no more than a few times each year. In the countryside, children can be seen playing outside while their parents relax inside, reveling in the leisure day at home despite all the household chores to be done. There is pleasure simply being at home, together as a family. Engaged in work, study sessions, self-criticism sessions, militia training; and other activities for most of their waking hours, six days a week, North Koreans long for leisure moments at home with their families. Women especially resent the activities that keep them away from home in the evenings and separated from their children most of the week.

There is much in this picture of family life in North Korea to suggest that the family is no longer the basic social unit of society, that it has been supplanted by the work unit, which controls virtually every aspect of an individual's life. Some observers of the North Korean scene, convinced that the Communists are out to destroy family life, have found enough evidence to convince themselves of this truth. They believe that Kim and his cohorts actually succeeded in replacing the family with a new Communist unit of society, much as the Chinese and Soviets were all too often given credit (or blame) for destroying the family in their Communist societies. Certainly, much has been written to this effect about all three societies.

It may be that this view of the success of the Communist system in destroying family life is not altogether accurate. Sociological studies made of the Soviet Union and China suggest that this may well be the case—that the family was never really as threatened as many Western observers thought. John Fraser, for instance, writing about the Chinese, observed, "If the Chinese people heard [Western commentary about the dissolution of family life in China] they would laugh out loud in scorn. The family is stronger in China today than anywhere else in the world."

Furthermore, there is no compelling evidence that shows that the North Korean leaders ever intended to destroy family ties. Indeed, one of the distinguishing features about the leadership has been its strong familial aspects—up to and including Kim's blatant nepotism in giving his relatives high party and government posts and his even more extraordinary and eventually successful efforts in promoting his son as his successor. Kim's sense of family was always central to his life and leadership. He would hardly have promoted such an aura of familial closeness if that worked to undermine party policy to the contrary. Lest there be any misunderstanding about how the regime feels, North Korean officials constantly stress the importance of the family, in public and in private. Concerned that separating babies of only a few months of age from their working mothers and putting them in daytime nurseries, a practical solution to the pressing need to keep women in the workforce, might be interpreted as a move against the family, officials have always been at pains to deny any such intention.

Another argument, often advanced, is that the Kim cult, with Kim as the father figure, has substituted a new sense of family—that of all North Koreans belonging to one big family—for the old sense of family. Proponents of this thesis see the regime's efforts to play on the emotions of the people in inspiring loyalty to Kim as an effort to destroy conventional family ties, as if the two were incompatible. There is no reason to think that they are necessarily incompatible, however, and the evidence suggests that they can be used to reinforce one another, rather than act in conflict. North Koreans did look upon Kim as a father figure, which promoted a sense of national family, but they have always felt a keen sense of family, in the conventional sense, a traditional Oriental value. The time spent with one's parents or one's children may be limited, but the time is treasured and the feelings are intense.

From all evidence, parents in North Korea dote on their children, no less than parents elsewhere. In fact, an interesting finding about the Soviet Union and China that seems to be true about North Korea as well as other Communist societies is that parents seem to live for their children, perhaps because their own lives offer little but the hope of future improvement. Whether this is mainly a reflection of the sacrifices they are forced to make and the hope that these sacrifices will result in a better life for their children or whether it is a reflection of the few other pleasures in life and the lack of opportunity for self-fulfillment in other areas is unclear. But it does seem to be true. The regime makes a big point of all that it does for the children of North Korea, "the hope of the future" as the official propaganda calls them, whom it openly describes as "living like Kings and Queens." Parents make sacrifices gladly, saving as much as they can all during their lives to secure the best for their children.

North Koreans may be much more reserved than Americans in expressing their feelings, partly because the constant fear of appearing disloyal to the regime chokes the free expression of one's innermost thoughts. Nevertheless, parent-child relationships appear to be very close despite the limited opportunities for sharing.

Most Koreans grow up with a strong sense of loyalty toward both their parents and the state. They are taught to love and respect their parents in the traditional Asian way. The regime does nothing to distort those natural family feelings. The concern is only to incorporate such feelings into a broader love for Kim and the North Korean state, much as traditional religions have incorporated family love into a broader love for God and other people. Contrary to much that has been written, the authorities do not act to undermine parental authority.

Long separations of sons from their families while they are in the military are very much a part of the North Korean scene—one that both parents and sons find difficult. It is not unusual for a young man to serve his entire eight years in the military without a home leave, except for emergency reasons, such as a death in the family. The long separation from family and deprivation of female companionship are probably the two major factors contributing to low military morale. Soldiers are reliably reported to be very lonely and melancholy after being separated from their families for long periods of time. This is particularly true if their careers are blocked by bad *songbun*. A few even have nervous breakdowns, although this is rare. They are not looked on with sympathy. Everyone has the same hardships. "I am tough enough to endure it, why can't he?" is the typical attitude. The family of such a person not only suffers from public shame but the *songbun* of all family members is likely to be lowered as well.

An American visitor who once established a rare (and forbidden) secret dialogue with an elderly peasant woman outside Pyongyang was touched by the woman's deep sorrow at the prolonged separation from her two sons serving in the army. She seemed to accept this as a fact of life—a sorrowful one—but not one to destroy well-established close family ties. She certainly did not see it as a Communist plot to destroy the family, but rather as a military necessity to defend the country. She wanted to know how long American boys are away from their homes while they are in the service.

North Koreans do resent the regime's arbitrary assignment of jobs which sometimes takes young people away from their families. Usually, however, people are assigned to jobs in their own neighborhood areas. Their resentment is directed against the lack of free choice in a career rather than the separation from loved ones. Generally, it is the people who are upwardly mobile, with good careers in the party, army, government, or economic management who are transferred around the country. Their success in life compensates for their separation from family. Otherwise, the society is still characterized by the traditional tendency of families to remain in the same general area where their ancestors lived for generations. Marriages between people from different geographical areas are discouraged, which contributes to the stability of the population. Marriages between urban males and rural females are particularly discouraged, as a means of limiting migration into the cities. Thus, daughters as well as sons of collective farmers have little chance of moving out of the countryside into the cities, unless they truly excel in school and are given the rare opportunity of a higher education, with the possibility of a good job in the cities.

The stability of the family is reinforced by attitudes toward divorce. As in traditional times, marriage in North Korea is still viewed as an alliance between families, suggesting something much more permanent than the union of two people. Although the Family Law of 1946 liberalized divorce (no longer requiring the consent of both families involved), marriage as an institution has been idealized by the Communists and divorce criticized. This is one area in which the attitudes in North and South Korea are very similar, reflecting traditional values. According to one poll, three out of four South Koreans find divorce objectionable "whatever the reasons." If anything, attitudes in North are even more conservative.

In actual practice, there are a number of restrictions, not explicitly stated in the law, that make it very difficult to get a divorce in North Korea. All divorce cases must be decided in a people's court, located only in cities and in county seats. It is difficult to get permission to travel in order to institute legal proceedings. Divorce application fees are high, except in cases involving a wife's political background, in which case the fees are much lower and the proceedings much less complicated.

The law actually favors women over men in obtaining a divorce. Usually, if a husband seeks a divorce, it will be denied, except in cases involving his wife's political background. A wife's chances of being granted a divorce are much better.

Besides being considered immoral, divorce is harmful to one's career. Most people holding high positions, especially in the Party, would be deterred from seeking a divorce. At a minimum, it would ruin the chances for advancement; more likely, it would result in a demotion. There are exceptions of course, and there is corruption in the system. In some cases, high-level party officials have filed for divorce on the grounds of their wives' political background where other grounds were obviously involved, and Party officials have promptly granted the divorce. Although rare, such instances of corruption are well documented.

On the whole, divorce is not a common occurence. When there is a divorce, the property is shared equally. Custody of the children is decided by the court, after discussions with both families. In one case, a father was given custody of the sons and the mother custody of the daughters. In another instance, a grandmother was granted custody of a three-year-old boy when both his parents and his mother's parents refused responsibility. Serious consideration of the child's best interests may be one of the finer features of the North Korean legal system. It would be very much in keeping with the society's general interest and emphasis on children. It is also a consideration that is more easily weighed in a society where parents do not have clearly established legal rights to custody of their children. The fear of losing one's children is a serious deterrent to divorce, all the more so because it is viewed as a shirking of one's duty to the state in bringing up one's children. It carries official opprobrium, as well as personal censure.

5

Children: "Living Like Kings and Queens"

One thing that North Koreans do not hide behind the veil of secrecy that shrouds their country is their love of children. People's affection for little children is one of the easily observed hallmarks of the society, and the exigencies of life are momentarily forgotten with the birth of a child. Babies are cuddled by their mothers, doting grandmothers, and devoted fathers. Fathers idolize their children and show them more overt affection than fathers on the streets in most Western cities. One sees fathers strolling in the parks of Pyongyang with their young children on Sundays. Sometimes the mother comes too, but most often she is at home doing the week's household chores on her one day off from work.

Love of children has become a national dogma, following the example set by Kim Il-song, who easily surpassed even the most consummate Western politician in his seemingly endless joy in kissing babies and hugging young children. He visited state nurseries constantly, usually taking a polaroid camera to have his picture taken with youngsters who were then given the picture as a priceless memento of his visit. He referred to the children of North Korea as the "Kings and Queens" of the country, the "hope of the future." Perhaps there were ulterior purposes in his use of children to focus people's attention on the future, with its promise of better things to come and its rationale for accepting things as they are; however, it was not all pretense. Kim seemed to genuinely delight in young children. It was part of his personality and appeal, and it captured the North Korean spirit and attitude perfectly.

Drab and uniform as adult clothing may be, children are dressed to the teeth. They are showered with other material things, too, like toys and games, to the limit of their parents' and the state's power to provide them. An example of this is the fancy equipment—playground equipment, sports equipment, and musical instruments—on which state nurseries spend an inordinate amount of their money. The epitome of state nurseries, the 18 September nursery in Pyongyang, sets the lead in this regard in its extravagant display of playground equipment, including an electrified train, a ferris wheel, electric cars, and a heated swimming pool—all for the enjoyment of a select few of Pyongyang's five- and six-year-olds.

The earliest recollections of North Koreans are of nursery school, which all North Korean children attend from the age of four months, if not earlier. There are day nurseries in every village, large cooperative farm, or major workshop, where the children go home every evening with their parents; and there are three-day nurseries at the county level, where the children go home on Wednesday evening and again on Saturday through Sunday; and there are weekly boarding nurseries in Pyongyang and other big cities, where the children either go home on weekends or where they live permanently while their parents are serving abroad. The size of these nurseries varies; most day nurseries accommodate from 20 to 100 children, and most county and boarding nurseries accommodate from 60 to 200 children. The equipment, the routine, and the teaching are all standardized, which makes the experience a universal one for all North Koreans.

Depending on the size of the nursery, one or more rooms are filled with cribs and look like a maternity ward in a hospital. Usually, there is one nurse for every fifteen children. Children over two years of age move from one room to the next, every three months, as they grow older. All nurseries provide the same comprehensive care, including medical checkups by doctors or nurses and regular barber service of haircuts and shampoos. Thus, parents are freed from many of the routine child-care chores that would otherwise keep a working mother from work.

Children are taught discipline and love for Kim, the state, and their parents from the earliest age. The first words many of these youngsters learn is "Comrade Kim." They are taught that Kim is the source of everything good and that they should love, honor, and obey him. They are taught respect for their elders, which is expressed in the custom of children bowing to their parents, teachers, and others in authority. Visitors to North Korea who are recognizable as VIPS, because they are being driven around in Mercedes Benz cars, report "receiving salutes from children all along the route; in certain parts of the countryside some children even bowed as the cars passed by." All young people, well into their twenties and thirties, are accustomed to bowing whenever they meet others in authority, including their parents. The system teaches love and respect for one's parents and reinforces the idea of love and respect for Kim and the North Korean state. Teachers never belittle parents in front of their children.

Informed observers of the Communist societies in both China and North Korea have noted that authority relationships between children and adults in North Korea are, if anything, even more structured and unambiguous than in China. In schools, classroom discipline is very tight, and the role of the teacher is supreme. Spanking children, as a form of discipline by teachers, is forbidden. A teacher would lose her job if she spanked a child, although parents are allowed to spank them. (Sticks and belts are still used by some parents to discipline their children, but not as much as in earlier times. The party encourages parents to use other kinds of punishment.) Generally, as a form of punishment, children are sent to the principal; are forced to stand up in front of the class; or are asked to stay after school to clean up the classroom. They are never made to wear dunce caps, as they were in China.

Violations of school discipline, such as not paying attention in class or leaving the school grounds, are quickly addressed. First, the school notifies the parents. If the student does not quickly improve, his or her ration is cut. If these measures still do not work, the police are notified. By now the *songbun* of both the student and the parents has slipped several notches. If, after the warning and further discussions with the police, the student remains out of control, he or she is simply picked up, and no one sees the student again. The parents may lose their jobs and be sent to the countryside too.

The good manners and discipline learned at an early age tend to become reflex actions that North Koreans actually find difficult to abandon later, in adjusting to life in another country. South Koreans, raised in a much more permissive atmosphere, can easily spot North Korean defectors living either in South Korea or elsewhere on the basis of their mannerisms, such as their tendency to bow when meeting others, the upright way they sit in a chair, their military walk, or just the way they act in the presence of others in authority, a kind of learned disciplined behavior. Aside from the difference in accents, North Koreans also betray themselves in their formal, ritualistic manner of speaking, also learned in nursery school. All of these characteristics—so typical of North Koreans—are learned by an early age; they become inbred, and contribute to the impression that North Korean children are robots, all acting alike.

Although this robot quality is unmistakable, there is also a lively, high-spirited, happy, self-confident attitude in North Korean children that foreigners immediately notice. As one American noted,

> While children are very deferential, bowing to visitors whom they meet, they are also lively, talented, and, a particularly striking impression, very forceful and self-confident. Middle-school students questioned off-the-cuff seemed to have a very clear idea of what they were doing and where they were going.

This may derive from their acceptance of Kim's *chu'che* philosophy, basically a mind-over-matter view of the world in which all things are possible if people work hard enough to achieve them. The self-confidence of this national *chu'che* philosophy which promotes both the individual's worth and North Korea's own national superiority in such slogans as "We have nothing to envy in the world," is bound to have a supportive effect in developing self-confident, self-assured, happy North Korean children.

The social atmosphere in which children grow up may also have the effect of making them more outgoing, adjusted members of a group. Almost from the moment they are born, North Korean children are thrown together with other children of their own age. Except for the relatively few hours they spend at home with their families, they are surrounded by their peers in a much more social environment than most children in the world experience at such an early age. Presumably, they are more at home in a group than the average American child of the same young age. Moreover, they are taught a variety of skills at a very early age—singing, dancing, athletics, and instrumental music—which may, in fact, put them ahead of most other children in these skill areas. There is no denying the fact that foreigners are often amazed at the musical and gymnastic abilities of young North Korean children who perform in these areas with great poise, self-confidence, and maturity.

Visitors to North Korea inevitably comment on the "happy smiling faces" of children, compared to the "grim, unsmiling expression" of adults. Compared to later life, childhood is indeed a happy time.

Interestingly, when questioned about the highpoints in their childhoods, North Koreans have difficulty remembering any particular special day or occasion, except the memorable occasion of their becoming

Young Pioneers. Childhood seems one happy continuous experience, uninterrupted by many moments of special elation but unmarred by times of stress or tension. Birthdays are not celebrated in any special way. Families do not have the money for parties and the government discourages expensive celebrations. Some families might have a family dinner together, though the foods would not be memorably different. Traditionally, the big birthdays in Korea are the first, tenth, and sixtieth. Parents might have a few friends in for dinner to celebrate the milestone of a child's first birthday, and they might also plan something a little bigger on the child's tenth birthday. A man's sixtieth birthday is a major celebration, in keeping with the traditional Korean custom. A father might simply give a teenage son a little extra money (two or three won) on his birthday to take his school friends out to dinner or invite them home for dinner. There is no custom of giving presents.

The one day that does seem to stand out in every North Korean's memory as the most exciting day of childhood is the day he or she becomes a Young Pioneer, at the age of nine to eleven. The day has the feel of a birthday, Christmas or Hanukkah, and confirmation or Bar Mitzvah rolled into one. It has a quasi-religious feeling in the sense of one's joining Kim's brotherhood, the Young Pioneers, the first step toward party membership. It holds tremendous excitement for a child to get and be able to wear the bright red scarf of the Young Pioneers, the national uniform. It marks the only gala celebration of a child's life up to that point. The children receive their red ties and Young Pioneer buttons at a ceremony held at school attended by their families. The occasion usually takes place on a national holiday, such as Kim Il-song's birthday (15 April) or National Day (9 September) or Army Day (8 February). After the ceremony, everyone goes on a picnic, either in a local park or, perhaps, at Mangyondae (Kim's birthplace) if they live near Pyongyang. The schools provide buses for the occasion. The new Young Pioneers receive presents from their families, such as a new pen, notebook, or schoolbag. These were the only gift-wrapped presents one North Korean defector ever remembered receiving.

The excitement of the day is compounded by the sense of satisfaction one feels at having met the first important test in life. One has to qualify to become a Young Pioneer. Although the standards are not set too high and every boy and girl can be expected to join by the time he or she is eleven, some are able to join earlier than others. One defector remembered being very disappointed when he was not selected by his teachers to join when he was nine and quite relieved when he made it the next year, at age ten.

The mission of the Young Pioneers is to prepare children mentally, morally, and physically to be Communist builders of the *chu'che* (self-reliant) type. If one child is more prepared than another, he or she is admitted earlier. There are about 3.3 million Young Pioneers and nearly 2.7 million teenage members of the League of Socialist Working Youth. The goal of both organizations is the same: admission to the party, the final rung on the ladder to influence and material well-being. One does not have to look far in North Korea to spot a Young Pioneer. They can be seen everywhere marching two by two, with yellow epaulets on their bright blue uniforms and red scarves tied around their necks.

Young Pioneers receive two hours of ideological training every day and give a full day of volunteer labor on Saturdays. This is nothing compared to later demands on their time when they become members of the League of Socialist Working Youth between the ages of fourteen and sixteen. At this time of their lives, political reality has not yet infringed on the happy times of childhood.

Typically, North Korean children do not visit one another's homes, certainly not for overnight visits. Their fun consists mainly in playing outside with neighborhood friends on weekends and those afternoons when they are not involved in organized extracurricular activities. Rural youngsters appear to spend more time in such unsupervised play with their friends than urban children. The latter are much more programmed into extracurricular activities at their local "children's palaces," the center for all extracurricular activities of the young people through high school. Children appear to enjoy these state-provided extracurricular activities, which enable them to engage in sports, drama, musical productions, or perhaps the study of science, as well as socialize with friends.

Children also enjoy a number of regularly scheduled school outings, organized primarily as learning experiences but enjoyed mainly as social occasions. Schools all over the country organize trips to Mangyondae and Mount Paektu, the holy mountain associated with Kim's guerrilla exploits. Sometimes the students are bused to these places but often they walk incredible distances, camping out along the way.

Visitors to Pyongyang often find themselves surrounded by groups of school children, marching two by two in orderly fashion, always singing on their way to the museums and art galleries in the city. Foreigners have been surprised to see these groups of children, as young as nine, walking along the streets of Pyongyang as late as 11:00 P.M. No doubt, they were returning home from a school-sponsored trip to the theater or opera. Adults in the group are likely to have been their teachers, not their parents.

One rather surprising finding about the life of young children is the amount of time they spend at home without parental supervision. This would include every afternoon that they do not have organized extracurricular activities and every evening from about 5:00 P.M. to 9:00 P.M. or even later. Children growing up in the countryside, where there are fewer organized extracurricular activities at the local children's palaces, are often home alone from 3:00 P.M. to 9:00 P.M., although their parents could be nearby, working on the collective farm or at a local factory.

One can appreciate the regime's concerns about the lack of parental supervision, especially in the cities, during the late afternoon and evening, when both parents are at work. The mushrooming of children's palaces all over the country has clearly represented a practical solution to a serious social problem, traceable to the economic necessity of both parents working. In promoting the children's palace concept, which has attracted favorable attention in many Third World countries as an original, creative social contribution of Kim Il-songism, the regime has actually been motivated much less by ideological considerations than by practical concerns.

The lack of adequate supervision of young people, especially those in the cities, is one of the most serious problems confronted by the regime. As children get older, this lack of supervision has contributed to the rise of teenage gangs who, with free time on their hands, have gotten into trouble by breaking windows or otherwise destroying public property. Generally, these problems involve teenagers, rather than younger children, as discussed in Chapter 9.

6

The Teenage Years:
A Rude Awakening

Happy childhood days do not last long. From all accounts, they end fairly abruptly and painfully at about the age of fourteen to sixteen when teenagers move on from Young Pioneers and become members of the League of Socialist Working Youth. The political pressures of the adult work would quickly engulf them.

If any one event can be singled out as marking the end of childhood, it is entry into the League of Socialist Working Youth. With that comes many of the pressures and responsibilities that differentiate adult life in North Korea from the somewhat surrealistic existence of childhood. There is a new seriousness about everything in life, a new sense of responsibility to the state, tremendous new pressures to conform, and endless new requirements for work, study, self-criticism, dedication, and service to the state. The symbolism involved in joining the league, giving up one's bright red Young Pioneer scarf in exchange for the much more somber league button, seems to catch the mood exactly. Although teenagers may be eager to move on to the next stage in life, they almost certainly do not appreciate the pressures that lie ahead.

Teenagers become eligible for admission to the league on their teacher's recommendation. It is hard to join at age fourteen, but by age sixteen almost anyone can become a member. One does have to pass an exam, but it is easy and almost everyone eventually passes it even if they fail several times at first. It is very embarrassing to be one of the last among one's peers to be selected for admission to the league. Sometime between the age of fourteen to sixteen, then, North Koreans face pressures that might be comparable to the pressures of getting accepted into college in the United States, except that North Koreans are younger and the stakes are higher. Certainly, the chagrin of failure is greater, publicly advertised as it is by what one is allowed or not allowed to wear.

There is no celebration when one joins the league as there is when one becomes a Young Pioneer—another symbol of the change in mood. There is simply a meeting at school attended by the students and teachers, but not families. There is definitely a feeling of excitement and pride on the part of the new members and, perhaps, also a sense of relief. Not knowing the changes that are in store for them, they have no real sense of the significance of the event. Only when one looks back, defectors say, can one appreciate entry into the league as the watershed in life that it really is.

At this point in their lives, having completed primary school and moved on into middle school, most North Koreans have had a chance to observe the workings of *songbun* in society. They have seen some of their classmates get good grades, class offices, exemptions from volunteer labor, special opportunities to study at prestigious schools, and vacations at plush government resorts because of their good *songbun*; and they have seen others discriminated against because of their bad *songbun*. They should have gained some insight into their own standing in the rigidly class-conscious society. At this point, they begin a lifetime of adjustment to the unhappy fact of their having been born with bad *songbun* and thereby deprived of any chance of great success in life; if they have neither particularly good or bad *songbun*, they begin to feel the tremendous pressure for superior performance in the tough competition among those with average *songbun*; or they begin to relax somewhat in the comfortable feeling of having the breaks on their side, having been lucky enough to be born with good *songbun*. In any case, their childhood of happy innocence is over.

STUDENT VOLUNTEER LABOR

By this time in life, there are many pressures to contend with, one of which is practical economic work, the so-called volunteer labor, that must be done in addition to schoolwork. There is always pressure to do more volunteer labor than is required; one of the criteria for party membership is the amount of volunteer labor one has done as a member of the league.

Several visitors have commented on the amazing construction activity in Pyongyang late at night. They have described huge construction sites of several city blocks in size, swarming with thousands of workers, poorly dressed, laboring for long hours into the night, the whole scene lighted by a series of lightbulbs strung up above. Foreigners have understandably, but incorrectly, assumed that these are regular construction workers on the night shift; their shabby clothes and wan appearance suggesting their poor standard of living. They do not realize that these workers are really middle school and college students, unused to hard labor and wearing their oldest work clothes, performing their yearly month's stint of nighttime volunteer construction labor.

Certain projects are known to have been constructed by student volunteers, as opposed to adult volunteers, who generally are recruited for the larger projects of greater renown. University, college, high and middle school units in the Pyongyang area built the highway between Kaesong and Sinuiju. Presumably, they were bused to these areas for construction during school vacations. Middle school and high school students in the Kangtong area, working with the Kangtong Construction Office, played a major role in road construction. This must be remembered when one considers the poor quality of many North Korean roads, which are a stark contrast to the good-quality roads in and around Pyongyang which were built by professional construction workers and crack military engineering units. Volunteer laborers are reported to do most of the road repairs in North Korea, as distinct from road construction, which also contributes to the general poor appearance of many roads. Foreign observers have commented on the poor repair of most roads, including ill-fitting patches of concrete poured into potholes.

Student volunteer labor is typically used in the unskilled stages of construction, such as excavating, rather than in more technically complex areas. Students played a major role in the construction of three grand national monuments dedicated to Kim Il-song on his seventieth birthday on April 15, 1982: the Kim Il-song Library, an impressive memorial arch modeled after the Arc de Triomphe, and an imposing obelisk structure reminiscent of the Washington Monument. People are reported to have been "inspired" by the thought of donating their labor to these projects. In addition to these major projects, there were hundreds of other commemorative projects built around the country in 1982—bridges, theaters, hotels, museums, and sports complexes. The celebration that year for Kim's birthday was the most elaborate and impressive ever. As part of the celebration, there were mass games, expensive to stage and involving tens of thousand of people, mostly students, who spent more than a month rehearsing their marches and drills. Education clearly took second place to the overriding need for massive amounts of volunteer labor that year.

Officials of the League of Socialist Working Youth are responsible for organizing student volunteer labor. They are given the number of volunteer laborers needed for each project, and they see to it that all students in their jurisdiction are assigned on an equitable basis. Depending on where one lives, one might be assigned to work on national monuments in the cities; others, living in more remote areas, are assigned to road repair work; others, living near the seacoast, might help with the fish catch; still others, living in mountainous areas, might do forestry work. It is hard to generalize except about the total number of hours involved. League officials oversee the preparations for the job and execution of the work. During work on each project, students participate in meetings organized by the league to discuss the successful completion of the job.

Some volunteer labor, such as work on the nighttime construction projects in Pyongyang, has a certain excitement for teenagers. Students enjoy seeing friends whom they have not seen for awhile. There is a sense of camaraderie and esprit de corps as they work together through the night. Girls are there, as well as boys, so there is something of a party atmosphere which lightens the work and helps to pass the time. Free bread and soft drinks are usually served. Students get extra credit for doing night volunteer labor, which improves the chances of their being accepted into the party. The work is not strenuous and requires no special skills.

Most volunteer labor jobs are not that entertaining, however, and one quickly tires of them, even with the enthusiasm of youth. Adults, after many years of volunteer work, become quite jaded. The range of activities was described by one high school student who used to work on the roads in Pyongyang helping to move heavy equipment damaged by floods and setting up new equipment in farm tractor stores. He often polished stone floors in newly constructed buildings in Pyongyang and did clean-up work after renovations. One summer he spent almost two months helping with the construction of a swimming pool. Twice a year he was sent to a collective farm to help farmers transplant rice (in April and May) and then harvest it (in August and September). He hated that, above all else. All the students camped out on the front porch of the farmers' homes in crowded conditions. They generally received inadequate food, certainly much less than they were used to getting at boarding school in Pyongyang. Apparently, farmers, who find it difficult to put up with the students who live temporarily in and around their homes, appear to be irascible to the students. The students, at least the privileged urban youths who are attending college or university, probably think of themselves as superior and are not always cooperative. The work is hard for many students not used to farming; some have difficulty surviving the four to six weeks on a reduced food ration, working ten to twelve hours a day with no break.

Virtually all North Korean students in upper middle school, high school, and college help with the spring transplanting and fall harvest. Schools are essentially closed during these periods, as are many offices and factories, whose workers also do volunteer labor on the farms. There is considerable travel involved for some urban youths.

Students are required to give thirty to forty-five days of volunteer labor during rice transplanting season, fifteen to twenty days during the harvest, and an unspecified number of days during the monsoon season to repair flood damage. In addition, they must do other kinds of volunteer labor during their summer vacation (June and July), during winter break (December), and on school afternoons, including Saturdays, and on Sundays. This can easily add up to more than 150 days a year, on the basis of two hours a day, three or four days a week, on school days and four hours on Sundays (see Table 6.1).

Male college students normally participate in a sixty-day military training program during their summer break in lieu of volunteer labor. Female students in all grades and male students in upper middle school and high school are involved in volunteer labor projects during this period.

Table 6.1
Average Annual Volunteer Work of Students

Days of Service		
	30–45	Rice transplanting
	15–20	Rice harvest
	10–15	Winter break
	40–50	Summer vacation, June–July
	15–20	Sundays
	35–40	School afternoons
TOTAL	145–190	

All in all, this amounts to an incredible amount of volunteer labor per student per year. It has profound implications, not only on the contribution that it makes to national production, but also on the limited time left for studies and leisure activities.

None of the volunteer labor is paid for, of course. College students in North Korea do not have paid summer jobs. Because it is not renumerated, volunteer labor is probably not accurately reflected in Communist statistics on national income or gross national product. To the extent that student and adult volunteer labor contributes to the production of rice or to the value of new construction, it may be counted in production statistics of these foods and services. However, many volunteer labor jobs, such as the repair of roads and repair of flood damage, are probably not calculated in official production statistics and where they are, they are probably undervalued. It is difficult to arrive at a fair value for volunteer labor, especially in those areas where most of the work is done by students for whom there is no typical wage. Generally speaking, student labor is not as valuable as adult volunteer labor, especially the labor of office workers and skilled factory employees who are pulled off their jobs to do emergency volunteer labor. For this reason, volunteer labor is doubtlessly inaccurately reflected in the regime's production statistics. Western economists with little understanding of the true extent of volunteer labor in the economy, or the quality of that labor, are at a loss to compensate for the built-in biases in official statistics. They have tended to overemphasize the shortage of labor in the economy not recognizing the regime's amazing ability to commandeer volunteer labor in the amount of 150 days or more a year from students, plus additional volunteer labor of adults.

In crises, such as droughts or floods, students are mobilized for indefinite periods, putting in more than the average 150 days of work per year. In August 1967, for instance, when Pyongyang was heavily damaged by floods that were reported to have killed several thousand people and to have caused approximately one billion won in property damage, all high school and college students were mobilized on a full-time basis.

Similarly, in March 1975, all students above the age of sixteen, as well as all single workers, were mobilized under the slogan of "a speedy war to complete the Six Year Plan (1970–1976) a year ahead of time." Again, all classes were discontinued. The six-year plan, as it turned out, was not fulfilled by the end of 1976, and 1977 was declared a year of adjustment before the new seven-year plan (1978–1984) was introduced in 1978. Kim Il-song's son, Kim Chong-il, is thought to have played a major role in organizing students into "Youth Shock Troops of the Speed Battle" in this campaign. On his instructions, students were organized into platoons, companies, and battalions. They were drafted to work on major construction projects, such as revolutionary museums and large factories. One source heard that 10,000 youth shock troops were mobilized for the construction of one revolutionary museum in Samjiyon, Yanggang-do. They were given various kinds of medals and citations for their work and given preference in joining the party. As a result, there were many applicants for the shock teams.

In other years, such as 1972, students and adults were asked to give additional volunteer labor time because of the special national celebrations held in honor of Kim's sixtieth birthday, in Korea traditionally the most important holiday in a man's life. Many national monuments, including the impressive Revolutionary Museum in Pyongyang, were built with volunteer labor. According to defectors, the people were more than willing to do extra work that year out of genuine love and respect for Kim Il-song. Most people supported the regime's efforts to make 1972 a special year for Kim.

According to inside sources, most students probably would not object to volunteer labor if they did not have to do so much of it, especially so much rice transplanting. Besides the sense of pride in having contributed to major construction projects, they enjoy learning something about a wide variety of jobs.

The comments of those who have participated in many of the student volunteer labor projects say it best: "There is too much work"; "it takes too much time from studying"; "much of it is wasted effort since there are too few experts directing the work, consequently much of the work is done wrong." On the other hand, it is "refreshing" occasionally to leave school with one's classmates and be driven by bus to some nearby location to work on some volunteer labor project. Some work is more satisfying. For instance, there is a "real sense of satisfaction" in having worked on a grand national monument versus the "drudgery" of working on a collective farm.

With these pluses and minuses, then, North Korean students seem to accept volunteer labor as part of life. They derive satisfaction from what they do—for free—for their country. Most are probably willing to give a lot. They only resent being asked to give so much, and the pressure is always there to give more, even when they have given a lot. It is the pressure that is so bad, not the work itself, a pressure that is "unrelenting" and unabating. There is social pressure to keep up with everyone else, and there is political pressure to do more than other people to get into the party. Since one of the main criteria for party membership is the amount of volunteer labor that one has done as a member of the league, there is always the feeling that one must do more and even that might not be enough.

POLITICAL STUDY SESSIONS
AND SELF-CRITICISM MEETINGS

On top of the obligatory volunteer labor, North Korean students must participate in political study sessions three or four times a week and self-criticism meetings once a week. The study sessions are separate from academic studies, though the latter include a strong ideological content, as well. Generally, study sessions focus on contemporary issues and events. They may be devoted to the latest editorial in the party newspaper *Nodong Sinmun*, the current party line on economic construction, new directives from Kim Chong-il or guidance from Kim Il-song's teachings, or current events in South Korea and other countries. There is continual study of Kim Il-song's life and teachings, of course, much of it repeating what students are taught in school.

Students tend to study certain aspects of Kim's works, such as his teachings about education and Communist morality, whereas farmers concentrate on his speeches on agriculture, party officials his teachings on party guidance, and factory workers his teachings on the Taean work method. By the time they have graduated from college, most students have read all of Kim's works and have taken detailed notes on them.

Self-criticism sessions begin when one joins the League of Socialist Working Youth, at the age of fourteen to sixteen. In the 1960s those sessions were held monthly, but in the early 1970s Kim Chong-il made a number of changes in the system, including a change to weekly meetings. It was felt that weekly meetings of shorter duration would be less of a strain on the people. Apparently, tremendous pressure used to build up between the monthly meetings, as people lived for weeks with feelings of guilt or fear of being criticized. In another change intended to lessen the pressure, Kim Chong-il sanctioned criticism of less serious offenses—such as smoking or staying up too late—whereas previously people felt pressured to discuss more weighty problems. Apparently the pressure is much less under the new system, although North Koreans admit to dreading these meetings.

Each school and factory sets aside a particular afternoon or evening each week for criticism meetings. It was common for students to joke about its "being Monday." If asked how they felt, they might respond, "Well, pretty good, considering tomorrow's Monday," or "Terrible, of course! It's Monday!"

Criticism sessions consist of both self-criticism and criticism of others. According to a reliable source who endured many such sessions, it is a "terrifying thing to stand up in front of others and be criticized" and almost as upsetting to be under constant pressure to criticize others. People are encouraged to keep a notebook and write down all the things that they and their friends and neighbors have done wrong during the week. They use these notes as talking points in the criticism sessions.

Apparently, it becomes easier to criticize others, as well as take criticism oneself, as one gets older. One gets more expert at playing the game, as it were, learning to avoid dangerous subjects while still seeming to take the idea of criticism seriously. One learns, for example, certain innocuous criticism—such as criticism of smoking or criticism of staying up too late—that one can document with many references to Kim's speeches. As one gets more familiar with his speeches, one can think of more possibilities for criticism.

There is also a knack to analyzing one's own behavior. In criticizing oneself or others for staying up late, for example, it is important to explain that such behavior not only makes one lazy and sleepy the next day but is suggestive of a bourgeois attitude. Then one can go on to cite Kim's warnings against other kinds of bourgeois behavior, deflecting the focus of the criticism from one's own transgression to a broader discussion of bourgeois behavior in general. In this way, one can blow up one's sin to large enough proportions to justify the party's criticism but not large enough to deserve total condemnation. The trick is in making oneself and others seem guilty but not dangerously so and, in the process, to score points by citing Kim Il-song constantly.

One defector became quite adept in using smoking to good advantage. He periodically criticized himself for smoking, explaining that it was not only bad for his health but a problem for the school authorities. "By continuing to smoke, I am contributing to the problem of the school authorities, which shows that I do not have regard for Kim's teachings." At this point, the secretary of the meeting would invite others to criticize him. They would feel pressured to join in the criticism figuring that they had to criticize about three out of five people under discussion at any one meeting. The other students could be expected to suggest that the confessor give up smoking, and he would do so for a month or so. In about three or four months, however, he would start smoking again, and in about six months he would use it again as the basis for another self-criticism, and the whole process would be repeated.

There are safe subjects, in other words, and others that are more provocative. Skipping class to go to the movies or watching too much television are safe subjects. One can develop various analyses of the evils of watching television that fit different circumstances. One student who had used it for years as "a sign of his laziness and desire to avoid studying" switched his story in later years to explain how it had caused him "to become Westernized and corrupted and, if [he] did not stop, how it might lead him to become a dangerous element in the Korean revolution." He would write these tortured explanations out ahead of time, looking up relevant passages from Kim's speeches to document his confessions. It became purely an intellectual exercise, without sincerity or remorse.

Students are expected to have a written self-criticism prepared for every meeting. Generally, not everyone is called on to give his self-criticism, but the secretary of the meeting checks all written notes to make sure that everyone is prepared. Thus, it is not possible to use the self-criticism one prepared the week before if one is not called upon that week. According to Kim Chong-il's instructions, everyone is supposed to speak at each meeting, either in self-criticism or in criticism of others. This does not always happen owing to lack of time. However, if one does not speak during a meeting, he or she will feel pressured to speak up at the next. It is safe to assume that most people speak at least every other week.

Sometimes, self-criticism sessions can get very tense, especially if political subjects are discussed. In the books used by North Korean students, Kim's speeches are divided into two sections: one concerns politics and the other, Communist education or behavior. Although subjects are not indexed, any student would know that smoking, for example, is discussed under Communist education. Whenever a speech dealing with politics is mentioned in self-criticism sessions, the atmosphere immediately becomes more tense. If it is a political course that a student has skipped, rather than a math or science course, it is treated as a far more serious offense. One student remembers a friend of his who never again spoke to a student who criticized him at great length in one session about how awful it was for him to have cut a political class. At the next criticism session, the criticizer upbraided his friend for not talking to him: "Ever since I criticized you last week, you haven't even said 'Hello.' Why won't you talk to me? My criticism was meant to help you, not hurt you." At this point, the secretary of the meeting called the student's friend up front and asked the others to criticize him for overreacting to his friend's criticism!

Usually the meetings are deadly serious, and no one would be expected to laugh. "It is much too serious for that." One student does remember several instances "when someone said something so absolutely silly or outrageous" that people did laugh. Once, in the midst of serious criticism of Student X, the secretary turned to Student Y and said, "Y, why are you so silent? Don't you have anything to say about your good friend, X?" at which point Y replied, "Yes, he has been getting up late." Everyone laughed. Such lapses are infrequent, however. Nothing about criticism sessions is meant to be funny. North Koreans quickly learn that the party has no sense of humor about some things.

There is no set length of time for criticism meetings. Sometimes, they go from 2:00 P.M. to 2:00 A.M., with a break for dinner, if serious charges are involved. For students, such charges can involve "participating in teenage gangs, romantic involvements, continual skipping of classes, or being reported by the police or party for wandering around aimlessly during the day or night." Actual disciplinary action for these offenses is taken by school authorities, but the discussions at criticism sessions serve as the basis for a student recommendation of appropriate punishment. The authorities are free to decide on more severe or less severe disciplinary action, but they generally take student recommendations into account.

As would be expected, most students, like most adults, hate criticism sessions. It is one of the few things that friends admit to one another. As one way of blocking it all out, one student said he never really listened during the meetings. His mind was always on other things. "Nothing [he] heard would have changed [his] mind about anyone anyway," knowing it all to be so fake, or at least exaggerated. He and his friends would plan ahead of time to criticize one of their group, never other people whom they did not know so well. That way the person would be prepared for the criticism, no one would seem to be more critical than the others, and all would seem to be participating equally—with the result that no one really got his feelings hurt and no one was seen as promoting his own advancement over that of his friends.

While this student was not prepared to think ill of anyone on the basis of criticism made during a meeting, he did form an impression of people on the basis of the way they criticized others. He and his friends intensely disliked those who obviously used the criticism sessions to advance their own careers at the expense of others. He knew some students who actually had asked to be transferred to other schools because they "could not stand certain students in the school because of the way they criticized others."

Although students may get more used to criticism sessions and learn to hate them less, they continue to find them "boring," "a waste of time," and "basically disgusting." They do not see them as being particularly useful, either, in changing people's behavior. "Occasionally, some student may change his behavior if he is constantly criticized for something. However, most students do not stop smoking, cutting classes, or wearing dirty clothes nor do they do more homework or any of the other things they are encouraged to do." The only things that really influence students' behavior are the school rules and the willingness of the school authorities to enforce the rules. Social pressure in criticism sessions seems to have little effect.

So long as criticism sessions focus on basically unimportant behavior, they are not in themselves threatening. What is more important to the regime is the behavior that students are persuaded to avoid for fear of being discovered and criticized. In this sense, criticism sessions are very effective instruments of control, not in changing behavior in unimportant ways, but in directing behavior in very significant ways. Any behavior that is too dangerous to confess is too dangerous to risk. Most students will eschew it out of the fear generated by the system of controls in which criticism meetings play an indispensable role. The psychological climate that they create is enough to deter most people from most antisocial behavior, as the regime labels all undesirable activities. What keeps North Koreans in line is the knowledge that they are being watched and reported on by all their friends and neighbors, not just security personnel. Criticism sessions establish that climate of watchfulness in conditioning North Koreans, even as young students, to notice their fellow students and to report on their behavior. The fact that most of the reporting is on activities of little consequence misses the point; that it acts to deter negative behavior of much greater significance is what really matters.

According to those who have lived with the system for years, it has the effect of encouraging some of the worst human traits—a disregard for other people's feelings, a willingness to use others to further one's own career, disloyalty, lying, moral superiority, and a supercritical attitude toward others. Although one may not actually succeed in promoting one's own career by criticizing others (it can, in fact, hurt one's career), the system nonetheless tends to promote a fault-finding personality. At the other extreme, it hurts people who are not psychologically inclined to criticize others. It makes their life intolerable and puts them at a disadvantage in the competition of a system that demands criticism of others.

In the view of one thoughtful, thoroughly disgusted veteran of endless criticism sessions, the safest thing to do is to be neither the most critical nor the least critical but to take the middle road. Many ambitious North Koreans who have been all too ready to criticize others, thinking that it was what the Party wanted, realized all too late that the kind of person who fares best in North Korea's bureaucratic Communist society is not the caustic critic of others so much as the slavish follower of Kim Il-song's teachings, espousing Kim's teachings rather than criticizing others for not following them.

Remembering that these self-criticism sessions begin when a student is only fourteen to sixteen years old, one can appreciate that young people in North Korea are subjected to social and political pressures far beyond their capacity to handle them. The maturity that is called for in walking the thin line between overzealous criticism of others, with the risk of losing one's friends, and a lackadaisical attitude toward criticism, with the threat of party censure, is beyond the skill of most fourteen-year-olds. Small wonder that childhood in North Korea ends abruptly when one joins the league and is exposed to the deadly business of self-criticism sessions.

7

Leisure Activities

With all the demands made on their time, North Korean students have little to spend by themselves, with their friends, or at home with family. Their days are programmed: from thirty to forty hours a week in class (including organized extracurricular activities), from one to five hours a week of militia training, from twelve to twenty hours a week of volunteer labor, from six to eight hours a week of political study, and from three to six hours a week of criticism meetings. That leaves precious little free time, some of which must be spent on homework. Essentially, students have Saturday evenings and Sundays free. During school vacations, they are involved in military training or volunteer labor, with probably even less free time.

The regime, which believes that people ought to "do away with the slightest indolence and relaxation in life and work and live with revolutionary morale, always in a strained and mobilized posture," provides little in the way of recreational facilities, except for movie theaters, city parks, some amusement centers, and sports events. Public restaurants are generally beyond a student's budget, and there are no coffee houses, bars, or cabarets in North Korea. Students might have ice skates or simple fishing equipment. Otherwise, their only recreational equipment is likely to be a soccer ball, basketball, volleyball, or Ping-Pong equipment.

North Koreans are sports minded, almost to the point of an obsession. Students are required to participate in after-school sports as an extension of their normal school day. Most schools offer soccer, basketball, volleyball, handball (European style), Ping-Pong, boxing, gymnastics, and track. Most North Koreans have never played tennis, football, lacrosse, or golf, and baseball is apparently played only at some colleges and Kim Il-song University. North Koreans would have no inkling of the fact, well established by inside sources, that some of the elite homes and country clubs have tennis courts. Kim Chong-il is reported to love tennis. There are a few golf courses in North Korea, for instance in Pyongyang and Wonsan, but they seem to have been constructed primarily, if not exclusively, for the use of foreigners.

All sports are played outside, including basketball, handball, and gymnastics; schools generally do not have indoor gyms. The few indoor gyms in North Korea are found in the children's palaces, such as the one in Pyongyang, or in local sports clubs, reserved for expert players who are admitted to the clubs. The Ministry of Culture runs the gyms. The average North Korean has no access to an indoor gym and therefore cannot play basketball or do gymnastics in the winter when it is too cold to be outside. Because of the weather, the only winter sports are soccer, ice-skating, and track. Since after-school sports are required of all students, they are included in the thirty-five to forty hours a week of classroom activities and are not regarded as leisure activities. Most students, except possibly those who dislike sports but are required to participate in them, enjoy the emphasis placed on sports.

North Koreans, especially students, are intensely interested in the national competition between North Korea's professional sports teams, especially the men's soccer teams. There are at least twenty professional soccer teams, which represent each of the fifteen provinces, Pyongyang, and certain national ministries and organizations, such as the Police, Army, Labor Ministry, and Ministries of Culture and Transportation. Students in larger cities, where the soccer games are played, would have an opportunity to attend these games. Tickets are not expensive (0.5 won) but are very hard to get. Often, the games are televised. Popular interest in spectator sports is one of the main escapes from the political pressures of life in North Korea. Students talk about professional sports a lot. According to a reliable source, Kim Chong-il, an avid sports fan, "stole away" professional soccer players from other teams when he assumed his position in the Ministry of Culture. Previously, the ministry had no soccer team. He started one and built it into the best in the country. Fans of other teams were reportedly angry at his willingness to politicize one of the few leisure activities that really mattered to them.

Ping-Pong deserves special mention as a traditional Asian sport at which North Koreans excel. The game is played on cement Ping-Pong tables permanently installed all over North Korea in public places such as school playgrounds and city parks. Children learn to play at an early age and continue through school and into adult life. It is one of the most popular pastimes in North Korea.

In winter, ice-skating is the most popular recreation. By mid-October, the rivers, canals, lakes, ponds, and even the rice fields begin to freeze; by mid-November, they are completely frozen for the next three or four months. Korean children and young people can be seen ice-skating all over the country. In Pyongyang, foreign visitors have observed many skaters on the Taedong and Potonggang rivers. The Potonggang, which is not very deep, has several ice-skating rinks. The Taedong River, which is quite deep, is the scene of several drownings every year. Foreign visitors who observed the drowning of two skaters were amazed at the casual attitude of the bystanders. Either it is not that uncommon an occurrence or more likely, most North Koreans do not know how to swim and are therefore quite helpless in such a tragic situation.

While skating is by far the major winter sport in North Korea, skiing is also popular in the north. Students borrow skis from their schools on weekends. Very few people have their own skis.

As for other leisure activities, students can go to movies on Saturdays and Sundays. Movies are inexpensive (0.3 to 0.5 won), if not free. They are not popular, however, since almost all are North Korean movies with a predictable propaganda theme. One defector who saw only ten or twelve movies during his student days in Pyongyang said that

every one had exactly the same plot. They start with a family split up by the Korean War, some of its members ending up in North Korea and others in South Korea. While the family members living in the North are portrayed as having a bright and happy existence, those living in the South suffer the torment of the damned— partly because of the American exploitation of the country and partly because of South Korean capitalists' mistreatment of the family. Finally the family is reunited at the glorious day of reunification of the two Koreas, the dream of all North Koreans. The movies end with homage to Kim Il-song and the expressed hope that reunification will occur soon.

Students quickly tire of this story line and go to see only those movies that feature their favorite movie stars.

Students have no choice but to see some movies as part of their required political study. No one would go to these movies, according to defector sources, of their own free choice because the message is so tedious.

The only movies that are really popular are foreign, shown once a year during foreign movie month. Schools and other organizations do not sell tickets to foreign movies, as they do to those domestically produced movies, operas, plays, and sports events; nor do they provide transportation, as they do for all state-supported events. People buy tickets at the movie theater. Since there are no advance sales, there is no guarantee of getting a ticket. There are always long lines, and many people are turned away. The movies, mostly Russian but sometimes East European, are generally war movies or adventure or detective stories. There is great interest in the romantic scenes, a taboo subject in North Korean movies.

On Sundays, students occasionally go for walks in parks, always in a group. A boy and girl would never go alone. In Pyongyang, the amusement center in Taesong-san Park is popular with students, as well as with families with young children. There is a roller coaster and other rides which, like the movies, are very inexpensive. Amusement centers are generally crowded on Sundays but virtually deserted every other day of the week.

The circus is also popular. Students in Pyongyang have the advantage of a very fine resident circus that performs all year long. Foreigners are uniformly impressed by the Pyongyang Circus; many of them say it is the best they have ever seen. It features acrobatic acts and magic tricks. There are no pretty girls and animals. Students in other parts of the country are bused to Pyongyang to see the circus, along with the museums and other national institutions in the city. They arrive in droves. As noted earlier, field trips to Pyongyang are part of every North Korean's education. Much organization is involved in these carefully planned and regimented school excursions.

The major recreation at school and at home seems to be card playing, traditionally a favorite Asian pastime. Students play in their rooms at night, sometimes enjoying an illicit smoke in the process. There are no organized dances or concerts, and students appear to spend little time reading for pleasure. Outside of Kim Il-song's collected works, school textbooks, and official propaganda, there are literally no other books available. Almost no works of Western origin have been printed in the NPRK, and none appear to have been smuggled into the country, as they were in the Soviet Union, where they were eagerly read and passed on in a kind of literary underground. In North Korea, there are no dissident writers, like Solzhenitsyn or Djilas, whose works strike a responsive chord in a literary-starved society. From all available evidence, it would seem that North Koreans have been discouraged from reading by the turgid, boring propaganda they are forced to read. The inadequate lighting in homes and schools, which effectively rules out reading at night, may also be a factor. Whatever the reason, North Korea is clearly not a nation of readers.

The implications of this for North Korea are interesting to consider. It would seem that the society is unlikely to produce many creative writers or literary scholars for a considerable time to come. Nor is it likely to have an educated audience who will appreciate good literature. A nation of nonreaders will affect all areas of learning and development.

An amusement and joy of young people the world over—pets—are not a part of the Korean lifestyle and never have been. Dogs are thought of not as pets but as food. They are never kept inside as housepets but outside in fenced yards with other livestock. No dogs are allowed in the cities. The only pets in cities are aquarium fish and birds, both of which can be bought at local pet stores. They are quite popular but expensive. Only the privileged can afford to buy birds, usually canaries, which are considered a prestige symbol. Not accustomed to having pets, North Koreans apparently do not feel deprived on this account. Parents who typically can hardly afford to raise two children are not interested in the extra expense of pets.

8

Romance

Another of the pleasures of life, usually associated with student days, that does not figure in a North Korean student's life is romance. With little leisure time, life being so totally committed to study and volunteer labor in the service of the state, students are deprived even of a romance that might brighten their lives.

This is not as depressing to North Koreans as it might seem to others. Arranged marriages are still very much accepted and apparently preferred. Traditionally, young men and women have had no dating or courtship experience prior to marriage. Kim Il-song held fast to these traditional values, finding no need to preach a new puritanical Communist dogma. Western notions of courtship and marriage now accepted in South Korea, China, and other Asian countries would still be viewed by most North Koreans as a corruption of traditional values rather than as a release from outmoded strictures.

Even though young people apparently do not have major differences with the regime on these matters of long-established custom, there must be pressures arising from the changed conditions of today, compared to pre-Communist years, that unmarried youth of pre-Communist days never experienced. In traditional times, young people married at a much earlier age. However, the Communists have prohibited marriages of men younger than twenty-nine and women younger than twenty-five, and they strictly enforce these new marriage laws. In traditional times, girls did not pursue higher education or work outside the home. In the radically changed social times of today, the Communists mix the sexes in coeducational schools at all levels and leave no choice but for all able-bodied women to work together with men in factories and offices and on the farms. Only a few schools, such as the elitist

Mangyondae Revolutionary School and Pyongyang Foreign Language School in Pyongyang, still have an all-male student body. Other schools, including all colleges and Kim Il-song University, are coed, with separate dormitories for girls and boys. In such dramatically changed times, there are inevitably pressures on young people thrown together in everyday life but prohibited from marrying until they are in their late twenties.

There is little information about how serious these pressures are and how young people cope with them. It is not a subject that North Koreans discuss even with their closest friends. It would seem that they simply accept traditional values, even in the changed circumstances of today. Their puritanical behavior seems to be the natural consequence of a general acceptance of the social norms long practiced in Korea. They have no knowledge of different social customs in other countries that might influence their thinking; their only point of reference is the Korean past, which they do not seem to question, even with the changes in lifestyle today.

Foreigners who have visited both North Korea and China are invariably struck by the contrast between the familiar scene in China of young couples strolling together in the parks and the absence of any such sight in North Korea. "Occasionally, pairs of two girls or two boys can be seen walking along, but never a couple. Usually, young people are seen in groups of three or more. They never get closer to each other than an arm's length. The most they would ever do is to sit down for a few moments to talk confidentially. After a very short time, they would get up and walk along, looking very shy and modest." Not even married couples walk arm in arm; as in Arab societies, there is no public display of affection, even between a man and his wife. Unmarried boys and girls would never dare to hold hands.

From all accounts, premarital sex is rare. There might be one or two cases a year on a cooperative farm, and they usually result in marriage. Once in a while a soldier will get together with a farm girl while doing agricultural work. At school, boys and girls have friendships, even romantic friendships, but sexual relations are taboo. The girl would never be able to marry if her reputation were damaged in this way, and the boy's prospects would be severely damaged, even if his family *songbun* was good. One's career, the standing of one's family in the community, and the girl's future are all endangered. Special friendships are acknowledged in the exchange of notes or love letters, but private meetings are rare.

Illicit sex is a serious business in the sense of the strict punishment that is meted out. It is grounds for dismissal from school, expulsion from political organizations, and sometimes discharge from the army. Individuals punished by expulsion from a political organization are also held for criminal charges. If a girl becomes pregnant out of wedlock, abortions can be performed up to five months. Illegitimate children are very rare. When such a baby is born, it falls under the care of the state. The mother is forced to surrender the child to the authorities who are given full responsibility in deciding what is best for the child. This view of the state's responsibility to children of undeserving parents is in keeping with its attitude toward the custody of children in divorce cases. The legal system gives little weight to parental rights compared to children's rights. The authorities have total discretion in determining what is best for the child.

Whether because of their own sense of morality or fear of punishment, the fact is that most North Korean males forego sex entirely until their late twenties or early thirties. This generally includes the eight-year period while they are in the army; it also applies to students in college and at Kim Il-song University. (Very few students at Kim Il-song University are married.) The problems that one might expect are manifest in the social problems the regime confronts with soldiers who come into contact with young girls, usually those living in the countryside, when military units are brought in to help with economic construction projects. Some military units engage in agriculture in support of the military's need for food. Most military units, except those along the DMZ, participate in rice transplanting and rice harvesting, as well as other economic construction jobs. These occasions provide the opportunity for chance encounters between young men in the military and girls living in the countryside in the narrowly prescribed social grouping of people with whom they work or study. In the normal context of life, young people are very careful. However, in those chance encounters, soldiers may feel they have less to lose or perhaps less chance of being caught. They certainly have no thought of marrying these girls. Upon discharge from the army, they have no choice but to accept the assignment to civilian work that they are given, usually back in their home district. They are not likely ever to see these girls again. The situation is fraught with potential heartbreak for those couples who do fall in love. Naturally, the regime takes a very dim view of any and all secret liaisons between soldiers and young girls whom they meet while in the service, and the risks can include discharge from the army and disgrace.

In short, there is simply no place for young couples seeking private moments together, except possibly in the movies. There are no bars, dance halls, discos, or coffeehouses. What is left for those who establish romantic friendships at school or in the army are a few shared private moments together after class, after criticism sessions, or during volunteer labor stints. Even a walk together in the park or in the countryside, the epitome of a romantic interlude, is accompanied by risk; one must always be careful. Students are constantly on their guard, knowing full well that their behavior with members of the opposite sex is a prime topic for criticism. Social behavior in this and other areas is closely regulated through the control mechanism of endless criticism sessions.

Aside from a few moments of private conversation together, couples can express their feelings for one another by writing of letters. This seems to be the primary romantic outlet. These romances are not taken seriously, however. It is understood that young people will eventually marry a person selected by their parents and approved by the party, someone with a similar background and comparable *songbun*. Marriage is simply out of the question at this time in life. For men, there is the matter of military service to be performed and then assignment to a civilian job. Marriage is part of the next phase of life, at the appropriate age, with no variation from Kim's pre-ordained plan of life for all North Koreans.

9

Hoodlums

The structural environment of school, volunteer labor, and endless political study sessions and self-criticism meetings has not eradicated one major social ill faced by the regime: juvenile delinquency.

Students with free time on their hands, limited as it may be, sometimes leave school without permission and roam around town. Although this occurs fairly frequently, it generally does not get out of hand. Occasionally, however, students roaming around the streets of Pyongyang and other cities get into trouble, breaking windows and destroying public property. These individuals may form gangs, organized around school or neighborhood associations, which naturally leads to gang competition. Several students from distinguished families are reliably reported to have been involved in these gangs, much to the embarrassment of their families.

According to reliable reports, this kind of juvenile delinquency is a major problem in the larger cities. There have been instances of youths running away from home and embarking on organized robbery. In some instances, the youths were the sons of high-ranking officials, and security department officials have not dared to arrest the leaders. Once a youth has taken part in the activities of a gang, it is practically impossible for him to get out of the organization. If he betrays the members of the gang, he may be subjected to severe disciplinary action by the gang or even murdered.

In the mid-1970s, at a time of mounting food shortages, students in the countryside sneaked onto farms, stole crops, and put the stolen food into knapsacks strapped to their backs. A law was promulgated that anyone found touching farm crops would be forced to work for three months without compensation. Parents of such culprits were also ordered to work for three months without pay, receiving only basic food rations. In other reported cases, students, acting together in a group, raided private homes to steal rice.

A "hoodlum" is defined as anyone who "engages in larceny, picking pockets, physical violence, fraud, lewdness, and other socially unacceptable behavior." The main reasons that are cited for young people becoming hoodlums are poverty, family trouble (many are orphans or are being raised by a single parent or stepmother and lack parental guidance), a desire for adventure (many individuals with privileged family backgrounds enter hoodlum society in search of adventure), bad friends, and frustration (young people who are unable to go on to college or senior technical school, those who receive undesirable employment after school, and those considered politically unreliable because of their parents' bad *songbun*).

Hoodlums are usually between seventeen and twenty-five years of age. According to one report, there were about 10,000 hoodlums in North Korea, including all the major cities. Most were in Pyongyang and Wonsan; smaller numbers were in Hamhung, Sinuiju, and Ch'ongjin. In Wonsan, gangs of as many as 200 or 300 young people were reported to have defined areas within the city; they did not operate in other gangs' territory. All stolen articles and money were brought to the gang leader, who divided the loot into equal shares for all gang members. Target areas for picking pockets were waiting rooms of train stations, theaters, stores, and restaurants. Stolen items included money, food coupons, wristwatches, and fountain pens. Other items stolen from homes included clothing, clocks, and bicycles. If convicted of stealing more than 10,000 won worth of goods, a person could be sentenced to death. Reportedly, an average of three hoodlums were executed every year in Wonsan up until 1962, when the executions began to be carried out in secret. For lesser offenses, hoodlums are sent to reformatories and eventually given work as factory laborers or miners.

Often hoodlums appear to fellow students or workers to be model students or laborers. At school or their factory, they would be recognized as hoodlums only by fellow hoodlums. During their off-duty time, they gather at appointed meeting places to pursue an altogether different life as members of a gang.

If, as teenagers, children are too unruly or are suspected by their parents as being members of a gang, parents may insist that they join the army or, as a last resort, go to a local labor education center or reformatory. Many high-level families, with much to lose if their children get into trouble, have sent their sons to these labor education centers where they are confined with thieves and robbers in a life of hard work and no school. Apparently, there are two or three of these reformatories in the suburbs of Pyongyang; several sons of influential families have gone there. The experience does not necessarily rule out a good career later, especially if the parents choose to send their sons there before they get into trouble, instead of the authorities sending them there after arrest.

Involvement with a student gang is the most common reason for students being expelled from school. Romantic involvements and skipping classes are other reasons. In matters involving the breaking of school rules, such as skipping classes, school authorities have the final say. However, when a law is broken, public security officials take the lead, in consultation with the school.

In either case, students at the school are consulted, and teachers and other school authorities apparently listen to the recommendation of students, often deliberated in criticism sessions, before deciding on disciplinary action. Teachers have been known to change their minds after students have challenged their decision. In one instance, where the authorities decided to give a student a warning but the students thought he should be expelled, the case was reopened and a harsher punishment agreed upon. The authorities listen to the full range of student opinion expressed at several lengthy meetings on the subject. There is a kind of collegial rule, in other words, with something of a democratic flavor, that outsiders may not appreciate. Whether the authorities seriously consider student opinion or just pretend to, the procedure obviously accomplishes the purpose of making students believe they have a real voice in disciplinary matters.

The unjustness of the system is not so much the lack of a fair hearing by one's peers, as well as the authorities, as the unjustness of the criteria by which students are judged. Here, as in every situation, the operation of the *songbun* system undermines any true sense of fairness. There are major discrepancies in the punishment meted out to students based on their *songbun*, and there is further corruption in the system because some fathers of privileged status can block the execution of a judgment, once rendered. In one case, five students at Pyongyang Foreign Language School were accused of the same offense. One student, who was the student president of the school's English department and who had very good *songbun*, was given a light warning, even though his classmates thought he should be expelled. Three other students were given heavy warnings; the fifth student was expelled ostensibly because he had broken other rules (going out with girls) but actually because his *songbun* was not good enough to protect him. In North Korea, justice, like other things, is dictated by *songbun*.

The existence of hoodlum gangs and other forms of juvenile delinquency would probably never have been suspected by outside observers of North Korea without inside information from defectors. With such insight, one can read between the lines of North Korean propaganda railing against hooliganism and teenage gangs. From the propaganda, it is clear that the regime finds it difficult to comprehend the problems it has with its youth, given the favored position of young people in the society. Ironically, the students so often involved are the sons of the elite who, as privileged students in Pyongyang, have more free time than other young people of their age who are assigned to full-time labor right out of middle school. The ability of their fathers, because of their high position, to extricate their sons from these difficulties is one of the major corruptions of the system.

While engaging in unlawful activities of this sort might be ascribed to the natural exuberance of youth, especially a youth proscribed from most other kinds of rebellion, it reflects a deeper unrest and frustration. According to one defector, the situation stems from the boredom of students who are sick of studying Kim Il-songism and are not sufficiently challenged by the intellectual content of the state-prescribed education. In the view of this student, authorities simply do not appreciate the reasons for such boredom or "turn-off" on the part of students lucky enough to be receiving a privileged education. They seem to be baffled as to how to deal with the situation, being unwilling to admit the basic cause of the problem, unable to do much about it in terms of lessening the ideological content of education, and having to be very careful about how they deal with it because of the people involved. The situation does not seem to have improved significantly, judging by the continued reference to hooliganism in the North Korean press. Despite the government's constant efforts to suppress it, hooliganism is reportedly on the rise.

Acts of sabotage and other examples of open dissent by the adult population are nowhere near as widely known or publicized as instances of juvenile delinquency. It may be that the regime has greater problems with its youth than with the population at large or it may be that it is much more careful to keep the latter secret, thinking it a more serious threat to internal security. Although one cannot be sure, it seems that students present the most persistent, troubling problem for the authorities, and ironically, it may be the most educated, privileged group of students who are the most disenchanted who are the biggest problem. Only the promise of their own favored future and the fear of losing their privileged status, keep them from venting their frustration with a system that dictates their every thought and action.

10

The Long Years in the Military

For most North Korean young men, military service follows middle school or, in some cases, high school as a matter of course. Of the physically fit, only the privileged few and, at the other extreme, those disqualified by their bad *songbun* manage to escape it. Kim Chong-il is typical of the elite group, sons of the top leaders, who go from high school to college to leading positions in society—in politics, the arts, or sciences—without ever serving in the military. The son of the Army Chief of Logistics, who showed special aptitude for languages and was given a prestigious education at the Foreign Language School in preparation for a career in the Foreign Ministry, is typical of a somewhat larger group who, through a combination of good *songbun* and prized talents, are exempted from military service to pursue a career right out of school. A younger son of the Logistics Chief, of equally good *songbun* but not as good a student as his brother, is typical of the majority of North Koreans who go into the army at sixteen or eighteen years of age right out of middle school or high school.

Most young men are anxious to join the military, if only to avoid the stigma that is attached to those who do not, either because of a physical handicap or bad family background. There are few cases of deliberate draft evasion. For most, the military offers the promise of a better future. At a minimum, it improves the chances of getting a better job after discharge from the army. Soldiers trained as radio operators can expect to be assigned to the same work in a civilian capacity, perhaps as the radio operator of a fishing boat. For a lucky few, the army may open the door to greater things, including party membership and possibly even college. Although one's career is essentially blocked out by one's *songbun*, a young man's performance in the service can alter its direction within certain prescribed limits. It definitely has a more profound effect on the rest of his life than in other countries where the military is not the main testing ground in life. Most North Koreans go off with high hopes, only to be sorely disappointed in many cases when, after serving eight years in the military, they are still assigned to a collective farm or mine.

Parents are generally happy to have their sons in the military, not only because of the long-term possibilities but also because of the short-term advantages. Parents are likely to be much better off with a son in the military. They can save on food and clothing, both of which soldiers receive free of charge, on a preferred basis.

There are intrinsic advantages, too. In a country that has traditionally liked to place categories of people in neat rankings within the society, the military ranks high in North Korea. Parents are proud to have their sons in the army, and others hold them in high regard, too. For soldiers, there is the psychic income of being a member of a privileged group. Practically every family has at least one member of the family on active duty, in the reserves, or retired from the military. This adds a personal dimension to the close feeling between the military and the population, which is further reinforced by the army's close support of the civilian population in nonmilitary ways. Incidents of wrongdoing to civilians by members of the armed services are rare, although not unprecedented. Instances of the military helping civilians, on the other hand, are legion. The population is well aware of the debt it owes the military.

The major disadvantage of being in the military is the long separation of sons from their families. Most young men do not see their parents during the entire time they are in the service. Although officially they are eligible for two weeks' leave after three or four years, few seem to get it, for any reason. Even in times of family crisis, such as the death of a parent, they are often denied leave. In some cases, individuals have been notified that a family member has died only to arrive home long after the funeral. Should they ever take leave, soldiers know they will never get another one. This is a major source of discontent in the army and a major sorrow for parents.

In the spring of each year, the city or county military mobilization department (MMD) arranges a physical examination at a local hospital for all school students who have reached the age of sixteen. The results of the physical are forwarded to the MMD at which time the names of the individuals are officially added to the conscription rolls. Individuals who fail the physical exam but who could pass with proper medical treatment are issued a certification for priority medical treatment. While completing medical treatment, they either continue in school or are employed at local cooperative farms and factories.

Periodically, usually two or three times a year, the MMD notifies each school of the number of students to be conscripted. The school makes the actual selection of students, generally choosing those with the best *songbun*. Those students are then given a second physical examination, including x-rays. The official notice of conscription is sent a few days before the students are required to report for duty. At one time, notices were sent about four weeks in advance, but the practice was changed, supposedly on instructions from Kim Il-song, to avoid the long, emotional farewells between the conscriptees and their parents, who knew that once their sons were conscripted they would not see them for a long time.

A farewell ceremony is given for the conscriptees at each school on the day of departure. Usually, they are presented with gifts, such as fountain pens, and are highly praised on their selection into the military. Students at the school line both sides of the road from the school to the train station, as the conscriptees walk together to the station. On the train trip to the People's General Hospital in the provincial capital they are escorted by a member of the county MMD, who oversees yet a third physical exam. After this, the recruits are assigned to different training centers, where they are issued their military uniforms. Upon completion of six months of basic training, they are assigned to regular military units.

Normally, an enlisted man remains in the service until he reaches the age of twenty-eight, regardless of his age at the time of conscription. Should he want to stay longer, he can apply for extended service, provided that he has an excellent record. Enlisted men who are selected as long-term "volunteers" serve until the army no longer needs them. There is no set policy. Persons discharged for medical reasons, even after extended service, are said to have a very difficult time obtaining employment. Their grain allowance is reduced to 400 grams per day. However, soldiers receiving an honorable medical discharge for combat wounds are given good pensions and generous food allowances.

Except for the separation from family, life in the military is not that much different or more difficult than ordinary life. Indeed, the major point to be made about military life may be the unusual degree to which it is an extension of everyday life. In part, this is a reflection of the regimented, almost military syle of ordinary life. The distinction between military and civilian life blurs, in other words, in a garrison state like North Korea where the military, which constitutes such a large segment of the population, necessarily becomes involved in economic pursuits and civilians live a regimented life of hard work and political study, leaving little time for leisure. Except for the added feature of soldiers living apart from their families, in an all-male environment, for a long period of their lives, military life is not that different.

It may involve a longer workday, although that is not clear. The average workday for the military is sixteen hours, compared to the average twelve-hour day of civilian workers. However, if one counts the time that civilians devote to volunteer labor, militia training, political study sessions, and self-criticism sessions, most people (including students) put in more than a twelve-hour day. The military simply counts in its regular workday the hours devoted to civilian economic work and political study that students and adults would consider outside activities, separate from their normal work schedule.

The close relationship between the military and civilian sectors of the economy has been attested to by countless sources, in and out of the army. Although this is a feature of other Communist countries and some Third World countries, it appears to take an extreme form in North Korea. Because it is so fundamentally different from the role of the military in the United States and other developed countries, it is often misunderstood by Western analysts who are inclined to think of the military as a separate establishment that is financed by the civilian economy. In estimating North Korean costs in sustaining one of the largest armies in the world, proper allowances must be made for the productive contributions of the military to the economy.

These productive contributions take the form of agricultural services, labor and capital contributions to civilian construction, and human capital formation in technical and management training of civilians by the military. Military units, other than those stationed along the DMZ, routinely engage in agricultural labors that are estimated by some sources to take as much as one-third to one-half of their time. The military participates, along with civilian volunteers, in the all-out national effort made to transplant and harvest rice, usually six to eight weeks a year. Even senior officers are not exempt from this duty. KPA officers assigned to the Korean Military Armistice Commission (MAC) at Panmunjom are also known to have assisted in rice transplanting operations every year.

In addition to their participation in these periodic activities, most military units, except those along the DMZ, are expected to be very nearly self-sufficient in providing their own food supplies. Except for rice and certain other food grains and meats, most units grow most of their own food. As a partial offset to the grains that the military draws from the civilian economy, the army grows more corn than it consumes. The corn is exchanged for rice. Units along the DMZ are supplied with food grown by military units in rear areas.

These agricultural activities regularly bring military personnel into contact with farmers, as well as students and adult volunteers who help the farmers with rice transplanting and harvesting. Sometimes, these occasions provide an opportunity for soldiers to meet local townspeople, including young girls living on cooperative farms; however, the authorities try to keep the two groups apart. Soldiers stay in tents outside the village, and work teams are rotated to minimize the chance of friendships developing.

Occasionally, the participation of the military in agriculture has resulted in major confrontations with farmers. In an area of Ongjin County, where the army had peacefully shared land with the local farmers for many years, fighting suddenly erupted when a severe drought prompted the army to channel water from the farmers' fields to its fields. The farmers fought with axes and the army used guns. Officials had to be sent from Pyongyang to adjudicate the matter. The party chief of Ongjin County sided with the army, but the investigators sent from Pyongyang sided with the farmers. As a result, the party chief's career suffered temporarily when he was transferred to a lesser job. However, after two years, he was appointed party chief of Sinuiju County and then later chief of Pyongyang City. There have been other instances when the army has had less than amicable relations with the local population when soldiers have pilfered crops from farmers.

The military also engages in industrial construction and other civil engineering projects. Soldiers built the Pyongyang-Wonsan Highway and other roads, railroads, bridges, the Pyongyang subway, and many ports. Military units have been given citations of merit for their work on these and other industrial projects, such as the Sinchon Cement Plant, the Hungnam Fertilizer Plant, and the February 8 Vinylon Factory. More than half of the buildings at the Sinchon Cement Plant were built by army units that lived on the site for several months, then were moved out into the surrounding mountains for training, and returned for several more months of work. The February 8 Vinylon Factory was named for the army units that built most of that plant. (February 8 was Army Day before it was changed to April 25.)

When the priority of civil projects warrants it, the military is also used in the construction of national monuments, such as the Revolutionary Museum, the International Friendship Museum, the new "Arch of Triumphant Return," and the "Tower of Chu'che" in Pyongyang. Exiled Cambodian leader Sihanouk told U.S. Congressman Stephen Solarz that his palatial home outside Pyongyang had been built by a battalion of troops that worked full-time on the house for almost a year. Military units have also been involved in the construction of Pyongyang's modern high-rise apartment buildings.

As in the case of agricultural activities, the amount of time devoted to civilian construction depends on the military units. Front-line units work exclusively on military construction, such as tactical roads and hardened military positions. By contrast, military engineering units work on civilian construction all during the year. Rear-area non-engineering military units have about one to five months available for economic support activities other than agricultural labor. In many cases, military units are deployed on civilian construction projects at distances of up to a day's march from their permanent assignment.

Military personnel perform other economic functions, too, such as collecting medicinal herbs, gathering firewood, trucking civilian goods, and repairing irrigation systems. They are also involved in technical training programs, teaching farmers how to drive, how to repair their homes, and how to hunt wild animals. In other words, they constitute a ready pool of skilled technicians who are available to teach a vast array of technical skills to the population at large.

Taken together, these economic activities easily consume more than half of the typical soldier's working hours. For many, they consume much more. One defector spent roughly two-thirds of his time in the military on economic activities, mainly farming. There is no reason to think that he is not typical of most soldiers, except those serving along the DMZ. Since the units are regularly rotated between DMZ duty and rear-area duty, they too participate in economic activities, but not while they are stationed at the DMZ. Only the military units along the DMZ should be exempted in any calculation of the productive contributions of the military to the North Korean economy.

The importance of the military's extensive interaction with the civilian economy from a sociological viewpoint is its reinforcement of the sameness of life, whether one is in the military or not. The military does not provide nearly as different or unique an experience in North Korea as it does in most other countries. What has been said about military life in China cannot be said about military life in the DPRK: that it is, first and foremost, an escape from an otherwise inevitable round of rural drudgery. The North Korean military offers the advantages of travel, superior housing, better food and clothing, and respect, but not an escape from agricultural and industrial construction. It is essentially a more militarized version of everyday life, featuring a mix of economic and military tasks, substituting annual military training exercises of four to six months for civilians' two months of militia training each year.

It offers no escape from political study, either. If anything, soldiers are subjected to more intensive political indoctrination than civilians. They attend classes at least three days a week and self-criticism sessions at least once a week. Political meetings held to launch major campaigns in the KPA have been known to last for twenty-four hours and to degrade unit readiness as a result of sleep deprivation. Officers, all of whom are party members, conduct the study sessions. Soldiers take notes on the lectures and study the notes until they have virtually memorized them; they then destroy the notes. Whatever private doubts the soldiers may have about the party line, the system produces outward acquiescence and in fact a phobia against the expression of even slightly different political thoughts.

Since the early 1970s the power of political officers in the army has been strengthened at the expense of military commanders. Enlisted men are "inclined to comply with political officers' orders, ignoring the authority of commanders whose powers have been reduced." Apparently, this has caused some problems in military discipline because military training periods have been reduced and political education time has been expanded. It is a trend that has been noted in other areas, such as education, as the society has become increasingly politicized during the past decade, largely under Kim Chong-il's influence and direction.

A decline in military discipline could also be explained by the increased burden of economic support functions, as well as the expanded time devoted to political study. According to Western military doctrine, an extensive mixture of civilian with military tasks is fundamentally at odds with military training and skills. Many who have noted the lack of military discipline have also observed how tired North Korean troops appear. According to one foreign observer, the soldiers appeared physically exhausted, weakly disciplined, displaying a high degree of individualism, with no consideration for esprit de corps. Their uniforms were not neat or properly cared for, and their footgear, which was a mixture of slippers, field boots, and regular shoes, was often untied. Officers appeared much better dressed and disciplined.

Apparently, there is a sharp contrast between military units in the Kaesong and Panmunjom area, near the DMZ, where foreigners are apt to see them, and other troops in rear areas. The former have been described as "very military in appearance and bearing; like the sailors and marines we saw in port cities, they appeared well-disciplined with neat uniforms, seeming to have a certain pride that was lacking elsewhere." Other troops were "sloppily dressed, apparently poorly trained, and poorly disciplined." One suspects that the regime makes the same effort to hide the truth about military discipline that it does about so many other things in creating the false impression that what foreigners see in Pyongyang or along the DMZ or in port cities—the only windows through which Westerners are allowed to see North Korea—is true of the rest of the country. What one sees in these places is definitely not typical, according to insiders.

A decline in military discipline, if true and if related to the expanded economic and political activities of the military, has similarities with developments in the Chinese military in the late 1960s and early 1970s during Mao's last, fanatical drive to politicize all segments of the Chinese society and make "revolutionary builders of socialism" of the military, as well as civilian population. It is interesting to speculate whether similar trends in North Korea will produce similar results—opposition from the military to its expanded political and economic role and a drop in military morale, capabilities, and discipline.

Information on military morale in North Korea—scant, to be sure—is contradictory. Inside sources speak authoritatively of a drop in morale due to increased political pressures, and of the resentment and resistance of soldiers to the time spent on political study. They cite disenchantment with the military's economic support role, assumed at the sacrifice of its military training program, and inadequate food and clothing, insufficient sleep, and the long separation from friends and family. From insiders, we have also learned of the resentment of enlisted men with the preferential treatment of officers who are allowed to marry and have family housing and other luxuries denied to soldiers.

The tremendous difference between officers and enlisted men—in pay, fringe benefits, duties, and prestige accorded them—is bound to affect military morale adversely. The comparison between an enlisted man's situation in life—forbidden to marry, paid only a subsistence living, and forced to work hard—with the privileged life of an officer is one of the most unfavorable comparisons that could be made in North Korean society. The fact that these two extremes exist side by side is bound to create problems. Compared to the average civilian, the average military officer lives well, earning 60–200 won per month, depending on his rank (see Table 10.1).

The military pay differentials tell only part of the story; as wages and prices give a very distorted view of the realities of civilian life, they do not begin to suggest all the fringe benefits that officers receive in the way of quality food, superior clothing, and better housing, which constitute their real advantage in life.

In contradiction to these reports of low military morale, there are other reports that military morale is high, in large part because of the favored status of the military. It may be that the psychic income that soldiers derive from being in the military and the prospects of eventual

Table 10.1
Military Pay Scale

Rank	Pay
Enlisted Men	
Private	1 won, 40 chon
Senior private	1 won, 80 chon
Junior sergeant	2 won, 80 chon
Sergeant	3 won, 20 chon to 4.2 won
Senior sergeant	4 won, 20 chon to 5 won
Master sergeant	6 won, 80 chon to 10 won
Officers	
Junior lieutenant	60 won
Lieutenant	60–70 won
Senior lieutenant	70–75 won
Captain	75–80 won
Major	80–100 won
Lieutenant colonel	100–110 won
Colonel	110–120 won
Senior colonel	(Unknown)
Major general	120–150 won
Lieutenant general	200 won

reward in preferred treatment after discharge keep them happy, or at least willing to put up with the disadvantages of military life. It may be that reported high military morale refers to officers' morale as opposed to enlisted men's morale. Military officers are unquestionably a privileged group. Their satisfaction with their lot in life does not reflect the feelings of the enlisted men, however. There is simply not enough evidence to answer these questions. The subject warrants serious study in view of its impact on the question of North Korea's military strength and the ability of the country to sustain the same high level of military effort over the next decade.

In any case, whatever their morale, North Korean young men accept military service as their duty. They are told that young men in other countries, including South Korea and the United States, spend many years of their lives in military service.

All male college students, some of whom have been exempt from military service to go to college and some of whom have already served their eight-year stint in the army, spend two months a year in North Korea's militia training program. Each province operates at least one training camp. It may be that we have overestimated the strength of the North Korean military by counting some of these student military training camps, which look very much like regular military training camps in our estimates of North Korea's military strength. The training camps are manned by regular North Korean Peoples' Army (NKPA) personnel from the local NKPA command. The highest ranking officer in charge of each camp is referred to as the battalion commander; students make up the battalion under his command. The number of companies in the battallion depends on the number of college students. Communications refer to the "battalion commander," "battalion strength," and the "number of companies" as if they were regular military battalions.

Militia training includes an introduction to elementary military doctrine, basic training, mortar training, marksmanship, physical fitness, marching, and bivouacking. Introduction to elementary military doctrine includes familiarization with military organizational structure and basic infantry tactics, basic defense including familiarization with a protective mask, and the theory of unconventional warfare. These topics are taught mostly in the classroom.

Basic training consists of familiarization with a 7.62 AK assault rifle, including assembling and disassembling the rifle, firing practice, close order drill, bayonet drill, and hand grenade throwing. Mortar training consists of familiarization with the 82-mm mortar, including handling and dry firing the mortars. Actual firing with live ammunition was discontinued after 1973 because it was too expensive. Physical fitness includes running, hiking through rugged mountain areas, using horizontal and parallel bars, and some ranger-type training such as rope climbing and rappeling. College students march at least forty kilometers from their training camp once during the sixty-day training period and bivouack for two nights.

Each student is required to take a qualification test at the end of the sixty-day training period. Those who successfully complete the test are qualified to be commissioned as junior lieutenants in the event of military mobilization.

Women do not serve in the regular armed forces but do serve in female militia units. Apparently they can choose between militia training or volunteer civilian work during their summer vacations.

11

The Women Left Behind

With virtually all able-bodied young men in the military, except the elite few in school, it is not surprising that foreigners inevitably note "the conspicuous absence of young men" in the work places they visit. According to one foreign visitor, "over 90% of the civilian work force [was] between the [estimated] age of sixteen to twenty-five. Farmers were either old men or women. Most of the workers at the factories we visited were also women."

According to North Korean statistics, women account for over half of the total workforce (45 percent of industrial workers and 60 percent of agricultural workers). However, with most young men of the same age in the military, it would not be surprising if they do in fact constitute more than 90 percent of the civilian labor force between the age of sixteen and twenty-five.

This represents nothing less than a social revolution, in terms of the role of women in society. In 1947 only 5 percent of industrial workers were women; by 1949 the numbers had jumped to 15 percent. By 1967 women accounted for almost half of the total workforce. In a scant twenty years, then, the role of women changed dramatically from the traditional role of full-time housewife and mother to full-time worker, in addition to wife and mother. It is a radical change achieved over a minimum period of time. It is doubtful that any society has accomplished a more basic change in so short a time.

Another major change has been the increase in women's education; there are now more college-educated women than college-educated men. Including older male students who have served in the army before going to college or university, women probably account for almost 70 percent of college students. The graduates of teachers' colleges and medical schools are almost all women; before long, the two fields should be exclusively the domain of women.

Thus, the regime's claims that women are better educated are true, although the claims are misleading in several important ways. For one thing, the great majority of women go to work on collective farms or in menial jobs directly out of middle school or high school; most do not go to college. Most men go into the military and then into civilian jobs at much higher grades. Women with comparable education clearly do not do as well as men, except in specialized fields such as teaching and medicine and textile manufacturing, where women predominate. Over three-fourths of the primary teachers, over half of the middle school teachers, and more than a third of the advanced middle school teachers are women. Women have done equally well in the public health field. They have also taken over as managers of almost all of North Korea's textile factories and many food-processing plants.

Because so many of the women attending institutes of higher learning are students at teachers' and medical colleges, there are disproportionately fewer women in other fields, such as government, business management, engineering, or trade and finance. The numbers of women in college and university, taken by themselves, create an exaggerated impression of the advances made by women in these other fields.

This is not to say that women have not made significant gains in the past two decades. They are now holding jobs previously held exclusively by men: manning railroad stations from the station manager down, managing restaurants, managing food-processing and textile factories, and running collective farms, government administrative offices, schools, and hospitals. More women than men hold lower and lower-middle offices in the party, as well.

While they compete favorably with men at the low and middle levels, few women have risen to top management positions in fields other than teaching and medicine (excluding women athletes and artists who have achieved success essentially because of natural ability rather than formal schooling). This belies official claims of full equality between the sexes, promulgated as law in the Law of Equality, enacted in July 1946 and later incorporated into the Constitution of 1948. Under the law, North Korean woman are guaranteed full equality "in every phase of life, including political, economic, and cultural life." They are promised the same work privileges, wages, social security, and education as men. In practice, however, they are not paid comparable wages for essentially comparable work, and they are not promoted comparably.

Women's positions in the party are illuminating in this regard. They dominate the party in terms of overall membership and offices held at lower levels; yet, they are poorly represented at the top level. They hold the majority of committee jobs at the factory and neighborhood level but a far lower proportion of party jobs at the city and county level and even fewer party posts at the provincial and national levels.

Women's positions in the government roughly parallel their role in the party. They are very active at lower levels; but many of the jobs would be volunteer jobs in other countries. For instance, in national elections, several thousand women normally participate as election committeewomen and women campaigners for (mostly male) electoral candidates. In its count of all women "active in government," the regime includes the women working in these low-level jobs together with women deputies to the Supreme People's Assembly (SPA) as if the two were comparable.

Official propaganda touts the "great gains made by women" over the past forty years, and there have been dramatic changes to be sure, perhaps more dramatic than the changes in men's lives. The role of women has been fundamentally and seemingly irreversibly changed from prerevolutionary days, when few women worked outside the home and fewer still held management positions—at any level. Today, women are engaged as full-time workers, and they juggle their lives as wives, mothers, and homemakers around sixty-hour workweeks, including volunteer labor work and self-criticism sessions. It is a change that they might not really have wanted and apparently do not regard as an improvement.

12

Marriage

In contrast to other Communist societies that have downplayed the differences between the sexes, in keeping with Communist notions of the equality of all people, the North Koreans have adopted a much more traditional attitude in celebrating the femininity of women. In contrast to the grim appearance and dress of Soviet and Chinese women, North Korean women are very feminine in their use of makeup, hairstyling, and graceful clothing. Although they do not generally wear much jewelry, other than antique wedding rings, they use lipstick, face powder, and other cosmetics, adorn their hair with bright ribbons and bows, and wear colorful traditional dresses. They have maintained their attractiveness as women far more than their Soviet and Chinese counterparts.

In traditional times, young girls in their late teens and early twenties had married. Custom decreed that girls marry before they reached the age of fourteen; often their bridegrooms were even younger. Today the marriage laws prohibit the marriage of women younger than twenty-seven and men younger than thirty. The regime has raised the legal age of marriage at least three times since 1948.

Were it not for these laws, which are strictly enforced, there would presumably be a large age differential between husbands and wives. Whereas most girls have finished school and have started to work by the time they are twenty, most men are almost a decade older by the time they have finished school and military service. As it is, husbands are generally about five years older than their wives, still a larger age differential than is common in most countries that do not legislate social law on the basis of national military needs. Some observers suggest that the regime's purpose in enforcing late marriages has been to control the birthrate. Although this has been a definite side effect of the policy (to many North Koreans a negative side-effect), the main reason for late marriages has been the requirement for all young men to serve in the army until they are twenty-eight. The regime does not want early marriages to lower the morale of recruits in the military. In South Korea, it is usual for young men to wait until after their military service to marry; however, they are required to serve three years, not seven or eight years.

In traditional times, virtually all women married. Although there are no statistics, it seems that there are many more single women in North Korea today as a result of various reasons: there are more women than men due to Korean War casualties, careers offer women a satisfying way to fulfill their duty to the state, and it is difficult for women to combine a full-time career with a family in an Asian context, in which men are not expected to help with household chores. Whereas in traditional times single women were looked upon "with suspicion and lifted eyebrows," they are not looked upon with disdain today. In addition to the unmarried women, there are many widows of men killed in the Korean War. Since second marriages are looked upon with disfavor, much the same as divorce, most widows remain unmarried and devote the rest of their lives to the socialist struggle for which their husbands died. Some have risen to top positions in a variety of fields.

One really cannot describe North Korea's Communists as traditionalists or anti-traditionalists. Where tradition has served their purposes—as in the preservation of the family and the continuance of the practice of arranged marriages—they uphold tradition. Where tradition has contravened their purposes—in the accepted age of brides and grooms or the preferred number of children—they have abandoned tradition. They have acted pragmatically in every instance, taking no stand either for or against tradition, preserving their freedom to pick and choose as suits their purposes.

The tradition of arranged marriages has served their purposes well. It is an excellent control mechanism, which can be used to promote marriages on the basis of any desired criteria. For the North Koreans, the criterion has always been *songbun*. All other considerations, including the personal feelings of the couple involved, count for little; *songbun* is what matters. The system, as it works, tends to preserve the purity of the privileged class, keeping it free of impure elements. Those with bad *songbun* have no choice but to marry others of the same background. The system works against the mixing of the classes, perpetuating the sharp cleavages of a class-conscious society based on political reliability.

As in traditional times, marriages are arranged by the parents of the bride and groom. In pre-Communist days, a go-between or middle-man oversaw the negotiations between the two families. Today, the party acts as the middleman. Personal records, kept by the party secretary of every factory, collective farm, or government ministry, provide the necessary information to match couples of similar background. Permission from the party is absolutely required. If the party does not give permission for a marriage, a couple cannot live together since the husband's or the wife's place of work has to provide accommodations, and it does that only with party approval. In many cases, couples have to wait a long time for housing, especially if they are from different cities. In that case, one of the partners has to apply for permission to move to another city and work at a different factory or collective farm.

Families can ask the party's permission for a young couple to marry or they can leave the choice of a marriage partner to the party entirely. Orphans from the Korean War, who were favored above almost every other group in all things ranging from education to choice assignments in the Foreign Ministry, have been particularly well cared for by the party in this regard. The government assumed full responsibility for finding suitable spouses for these promising careerists.

Interestingly, the better one's *songbun*, the more likely one is to rely on the party in the selection of a spouse. Families of influence in the government usually leave the choice of a husband for their daughters to the party, especially if the daughters are not attractive. At the lower end of the social spectrum, workers on collective farms, miners, and un-skilled factory workers, whose careers are not likely to be materially af-fected by their choice of a spouse, seem to prefer to play a much greater role in the selection of their marriage partners. Their parents generally arrange their weddings, only asking approval from the party for a match that the bride and groom have essentially engineered on their own, hav-ing known each other at work or from living in the same town. The re-gime is mindful of this natural selection process in assigning young men, newly discharged from the army, to collective farms and factories where there are extra single girls. Apparently, young men are tempo-rarily assigned to textile factories, where there are many young female workers. Later, after they have married, they are transferred to other jobs.

On the whole, people seem to accept the system of arranged mar-riages, as it is practiced, with the party exercising totalitarian controls over the most personal of social issues—the choice of one's marriage partner. Whether this acceptance derives mainly from a general acceptance of the traditional custom of arranged marriages or whether it represents some rationalization of the Communist system of career advancement is not clear. The second consideration is obviously involved, however, judging from the many reports of the people's willingness to accept the party's verdict in the interests of furthering their careers. A typical story is that of the party official who wanted to marry a woman whose grandfather had been a landlord in the old days but was refused permission to marry her. In telling his story, the official "showed no remorse or bitterness over the incident." He later married someone with good class background and they had a daughter. Other North Koreans were of the opinion: "If he joined the Party, he should have known better than to pursue the relationship. Party people deserve all the miseries they create for themselves. I don't have any sympathy for him, only for the girl."

The better one's career prospects, obviously the easier it is to rationalize personal disappointments of this sort. With the passage of time, such disappointments may be forgotten, as people go on to marry someone else and their careers prosper. For those with less bright futures, whose choice of a marriage partner matters less, the party can afford to be much more lenient in approving marriages. These people are likely to have fewer disappointments in rejection by the party of their marriage choices; on the other hand, they are likely to have less satisfaction from their careers.

What emerges, then, is a picture of considerable discontent on the part of young men forbidden to marry until they have been discharged from the army, some disappointment on the part of young men and women whose marital choices do not accord with the party's judgment of their career potential, but an eventual acceptance of the party's decision as having been in the best interests of the individual.

The Communists' downplaying of the wedding ceremony has been one of the most obvious social changes in North Korea, considering the elaborate weddings that traditionally involved costly ceremonies, wedding feasts, and gift exchanges between the two families. While South Koreans have continued many of these traditional ceremonies, at a high cost to families, Kim Il-song and the North Korean leaders outlawed costly, showy weddings primarily for economic reasons but also, perhaps, because of the tradition of simple weddings they started during their years as anti-Japanese guerrillas. In North Korea, weddings no longer involve the traditional exchange of gifts between families. Parents give the bride and groom whatever they can afford in the way of furniture, blankets, and other household effects; although it represents a lifetime's savings, it usually does not amount to much.

In rural areas, weddings generally take place after the fall harvest or before the spring plowing when the families have more resources to share. The ceremony is held at home, with a small reception afterwards. Those living in the cities have weddings any time of the year. Again, the ceremony is performed at home, usually with the reception at home or at a restaurant. Most weddings are held on Sundays or holidays because those are the only times that people are not working.

Weddings are small, private affairs. Relatives living nearby and a few close friends of the bride and groom, usually including their bosses, are invited. The wedding ceremony itself is rather perfunctory. The bride and groom simply bow to a picture of Kim, in a Communist update of the traditional bow to the bride's and groom's parents. Then they kiss each other briefly, a North Korean couple's only public kiss. The presiding official, usually a close friend of the bride and groom, gives a congratulatory address. There is no exchange of wedding rings or other jewelry, although there may be an exchange of other gifts, such as fountain pens. After the ceremony, the bride and groom go to the local police department to record their marriage. No medical tests—before or after the ceremony—are required. The bride keeps her maiden name. A man and wife are referred to as, for example, Pak Tok-p'om and his wife Yom Chong-pok. Children take their father's name.

Although simple by traditional standards, wedding receptions are nonetheless joyous occasions for North Koreans. Such receptions offer one of the few opportunities they have to indulge in the social pleasures of drinking, singing, and eating. Only for such occasions can North Koreans buy special quantities of wine and rice cookies and cakes. The major constraint on the number of guests that can be invited is the amount of food and liquor that can be provided. A couple is authorized to buy "one skirt and Korean jacket for the bride, one new suit for the bridegroom, a set of bedclothes, four or five bottles of white distilled ginseng liquor, and three or four kilograms of sweets"—enough for no more than thirty guests. Normally, decorations are scarce, and guests simply wear their everyday clothes.

A special touch at weddings is the taking of pictures. This may well be the only occasion when ordinary North Koreans are photographed. The services of a photographer are available on such special occasions, at a substantial cost, which many families cannot afford.

Honeymoons are virtually out of the question. A newlywed couple typically takes three or four days off from work (on paid vacation). It is unlikely that the couple will be able to live together for several months, perhaps even for a year or more. They have to wait to be assigned housing by the man's place of work. Sometimes, but not often, they live together at one or the other's parents' home in the interim.

CHILDBIRTH

The stress of women's lives has been cited as a major factor contributing to North Korea's low birthrate which has been of major concern to the regime. In the late 1960s, some 10 to 15 percent of married women were reportedly "unable to become pregnant." The regime itself finally concluded that this was caused by excessive work and undernourishment. After the many casualties of the Korean War and the exodus of thousands of people who fled south at that time, North Korea's population was much lower than it had been in 1948. The Communists tended to view South Korea's much larger population as a military and economic advantage that North Korea had to match. Seeing itself in competition with South Korea in all areas, it adopted a policy of rapid population growth. For a combination of reasons, however, the birthrate continued low, lower than it had been in prewar days and lower than the birthrate in South Korea. As one North Korean official acknowledged later, "Stopping the declining birth rate became an important social problem." The regime's sensitivity to the subject was so great that in the mid-1960's it stopped publishing demographic data to conceal the declining birthrate.

For more than twenty years after the war the regime promoted larger families by means of a program that subsidized the cost of additional children beyond the second child. Other incentives included paid maternity leave and reduced work schedules for mothers of three or more children under the age of thirteen. The program had little effect, however, especially in the cities, where the number of children rarely exceeded two per family. Factors tending to limit the size of families, other than the general health of working mothers and the high incidence of sterility, were the high costs of rearing children, late marriages necessitated by the requirements of military service, the availability of birth control devices, and the government's relaxed attitude toward abortion.

Sometime around 1976, during a time of serious food shortages and other economic problems, the regime reversed its long-standing population policies. Contrary to previous instructions, women were now "advised" to have no more than two children. Failure to comply resulted in public criticism, the withholding of food rations, and censure of party members, which sometimes resulted in job demotion. To reinforce these policies, the government raised the legal age of marriage from twenty-six to twenty-seven for women and from twenty-nine to thirty for men.

In the face of minimum improvement in the diet, the regime has continued its population control policies. Until current austere living conditions improve, it is unlikely to switch back to its former policies favoring a faster population growth. Concern over the continuing high level of sterility of the population, presumably caused by overwork and poor nutrition, is not the concern that it once was. Current programs featuring the distribution of birth control devices, the availability of abortions free of charge (to women already having two children), and the popularization of surgical procedures to produce sterility are likely to be continued. The Women's League distributes literature on the subject of birth control, as well as free birth control devices. It is interesting that the reasons cited for birth control are the possible harm to the mother from multiple pregnancies and the loss of production due to pregnancy-related absences. There is no mention of the problems caused by population growth, suggesting that the regime does not want to admit the real reason for limiting the size of families or, possibly, that it does not want to foreclose the possibility of switching back to a policy favoring population growth at some later date.

The regime proudly proclaims the improvements in maternity care. After twelve weeks, a pregnant woman must register in her local clinic. A midwife verifies her pregnancy and advises her on the kind of food she should eat and what kind of work she should be excused from performing. Regular visits to the clinic are scheduled up to the time of delivery. Almost three-fourths of all childbirths now occur in hospitals; painkilling drugs are routinely used during childbirth. By law, new mothers are entitled to seventy-seven days of paid maternity leave after the birth of each child. After that, whether they like it or not, the child is sent to a nursery. Mothers are allowed to visit the nursery every three hours to feed their babies; except for these interruptions, they work a regular shift. Only if they have three children under the age of thirteen do they get a reduced work schedule of six hours per day. Otherwise, they work eight hours, go to two hours of political study each night, and pick up their babies at the nursery on their way home around 10:00–10:30 P.M.

<u>A PURITANICAL LIFE</u>

Defectors have reported many unhappy marriages in North Korea, but it is difficult to know how seriously to take these observations, considering the difficulties in making comparative judgments on these subjects and the problems in relying on personal observations of a limited number of individuals; however, there are some reasons for thinking that their observations are sound.

Basically, the problems in North Korean marriages seem to reflect the everyday stress and strain of life. Courtships are extremely limited due to the long working hours. In most cases, both spouses return home after 10:30 P.M., eat supper, and go to bed. They leave for work at 7:00 A.M. the following morning. Couples simply do not have much time together. One North Korean woman remarked, with some derision, that her husband "worked so hard that the only thing he was capable of doing upon returning home was loud snoring. I'm a mother to him, not a wife."

Affections between husband and wife are never displayed in public, in fact, not even in private in front of children. "If couples did, they would be criticized, even by their own children." Romance, as opposed to love, is simply not part of North Korean life, either before or after marriage.

Feelings of love, which are not a major consideration before marriage, are presumed to develop over the years. In many cases they do. However, where they do not and the marriage is unhappy, there is no prospect of divorce and almost no chance for extramarital romance.

Adulterous relationships are dangerous. If discovered, they result in job demotion and expulsion from the party. There are enough instances of this happening for there to be no doubt about the party's swift and inexorable punishment. Only the elite are thought to be immune from such extreme repercussions; however, even they must be careful. There were rumors that the minister of defense was having a relationship with his private nurse, but when it became known, he sent her away. In the words of one defector,

> not even the elite can risk public exposure of an adulterous relationship. For most people, opportunities are very limited. Adultery is almost impossible in a rural hamlet. Everyone works together and knows where everyone else should be. People are missed at once if they do not go home after work. Besides, the working hours are so long that there is not time or energy left over.

Apparently, most people do not consider the risks worth taking.

The regime has adopted a very puritanical attitude on matters of sex. An Armenian song-and-dance troop visiting Pyongyang in 1978 offended North Korean sensibilities by appearing in see-through costumes and performing some explicit songs and dances. The North Korean Workers Party canceled the group's tour outside Pyongyang and told the Soviet embassy that while such presentations might be acceptable to the Soviet people, they were not acceptable in North Korea.

However, foreigners who have visited North Korea have found that North Koreans are very interested in talking about sex. While they are outspoken, even crude, in discussing the subject, they seem to have little sex education and only limited sexual experience. "It is a little like talking to children with a seventh or eighth grade sex education."

There is no organized prostitution in North Korea today. It would be impossible to use hotels or inns because of the close police surveillance, and the police are difficult, if not impossible, to bribe. Foreign visitors report no offers made by women during their visits to North Korea. However, some prostitution is still discreetly practiced around railroad stations and restaurants. Most of the free-lance prostitutes are girls whose parents are away from home much of the time. Some foreign diplomats have apparently had affairs with North Korean women working as maids in their embassies.

With no nightclubs, bars, gambling places, prostitution, or nudity, and very few murders, thefts, and kidnappings, the regime feels very self-righteous about these issues and very disdainful of Western society and its "decadent" lifestyle. This should not be underestimated as an important element in North Korea's cognitive view of their society as vastly superior to that of South Korea and the United States.

With no opportunities for the kind of social evenings away from home that Korean husbands have traditionally enjoyed, North Korean husbands are at home every evening, as soon as they finish work and evening study sessions. In that sense, they are together with their wives more than traditional Korean husbands were. In spite of the lack of intimacy, a strong bond of trust and confidence is built up over the years. In a society in which it is dangerous to trust anyone, the bonds between husband and wife and parents and children can be much more important, and certainly much more supportive, than they are in other societies. Husbands and wives provide the only sounding board that most people have. The confidences that are exchanged about grievances and discontent form the basis of perhaps the only true and lasting closeness and trust that most North Koreans ever know.

Although it is dangerous to make broad generalizations on subjects like the relative happiness of men and women in a society like North Korea's, it does seem that women have definite cause to be more dissatisfied than men with the radical social changes of the past forty years.

For all its efforts to play up the femininity of women, the North Korean regime has effected social changes that make the lives of men and women much more similar than they were in pre-Communist days. Traditional female roles have been endangered from the many hours of work outside the home. This alone could cause considerable female dissatisfaction. On top of this, there is compelling evidence that women work harder and longer than men and have a greater natural aversion to particular features of the North Korean Communist system, such as its thorough politicization of society and its strict controls over family life.

Like other Communist countries, North Korea is quick to cite the improvements in women's lives in terms of education, careers, better maternity care, and relief from household chores. The general impression gleaned from its publications is that women have fared very well. While this is not altogether inaccurate, it is only half the story. The sacrifices that women have had to make for these material gains may well outweigh the improvements in many women's minds. As a group, women may well represent a potential dissident element in society. Sensing this, the regime has been at pains to promote just the opposite impression.

Under the banner of full equality between the sexes, the Communists have forced a totally new lifestyle on North Korean women who had absolutely no choice in the matter. They were forced, practically overnight, to go from one extreme to the other.

13

Working to Death:
An Exhausted Population

In North Korea, women continue to work after they marry as a matter of course; work is a lifetime career. Virtually all able-bodied women work until retirement age. Women assume the traditional responsibilities of home and children on top of their career responsibilities. Social equality with men has meant only a more difficult life for women—with many hours devoted to hard work on the job and additional hours devoted to political study and volunteer labor—leaving little time at home with the children. Despite the regime's efforts to lighten women's work, by establishing children's nurseries and rice-cooking factories, there has been no significant reduction in household chores. Furthermore, reduced child care responsibilities have been a source of dissatisfaction fully as much as a source of relief.

According to all available sources, major complaints are the lack of help at home, too little time with one's children, and too much time in political study. There are also feelings of job discrimination in the assignment of women to the most menial jobs, such as carrying dirt on construction projects. The regime has tried to inculcate respect for these menial jobs in emphasizing their contribution to the building of the state. As one official maintained,

> We used to look down upon the women who were assigned to manual jobs. Since the liberation of our country in 1945, however, the state has encouraged low-class workers to have pride and a sense of mission. Nowadays, we do not have even the remnants of conventional job prejudices that exist in other countries.

Other evidence flatly contradicts such official claims.

Women are not spared from heavy work, either. Almost half of the stevedores observed at Nampo Port appear to be women. Other women have worked as rock drillers, a physically demanding and dangerous job, without the benefit of protective gear, such as hard hats, protective glasses, and safety belts, which are worn by men. Female workers in fish-processing plants are reported to work in temperatures twenty degrees below zero without rubber gloves: "They warm their hands in warm water kept in barrels. Although exhorted to work harder, many girls linger as much as thirty minutes at the barrels."

Women, as well as men, are enormously overworked. For women, the day begins earlier and ends later than it does for men. In rural areas and urban areas without indoor plumbing, working wives and mothers arise at least half-an-hour earlier to fetch water from a centralized location. Men arise around 6:00 A.M. Usually, an hour (from 6:00 A.M. to 7:00 A.M.) is spent in washing, dressing for work, and eating breakfast. Apparently, this is a hectic time in most households. Mothers do not have the leisure of staying home a little longer to clean up the house; like everyone else, they must be at work by 8:00 A.M. Morning exercise music is blared over the radio loudspeakers during this hour. Participation in morning exercise drills is voluntary; however, there is pressure for people to take a few moments out to do exercises in the interests of appearing revolutionary. Residents of Pyongyang have been observed in the streets outside their apartments "doing exercises to the music."

It takes most North Koreans about an hour to get to work. Young children are dropped off at nurseries or kindergartens on the way. During the morning rush hour (from 7:00 A.M. to 8:00 A.M.) buses and subways operate at maximum capacity. Long lines of people can be seen patiently waiting at bus stops. Twice a day, during rush hours, from 7:00 A.M. to 8:00 A.M. and from 10:00 P.M. to 11:00 P.M., the city of Pyongyang comes alive. Workers can also be seen going to and from their homes or going about the city on errands during the rest period from 1:00 P.M. to 4:00 P.M. However, most workers are inside during these hours, either eating their lunch or taking a nap. During all other hours of the day, the streets of Pyongyang are virtually deserted. Foreign visitors have described it as a ghost town.

All across North Korea, from 8:00 A.M. to 9:00 A.M., workers are engaged in meetings. From 8:00 to 8:30, there is a political study session under the direction of a party guidance official. It is the time set aside for study of the day's editorial in the party newspaper *Nodong Sinmun*. New party and government policies and decisions are relayed to the populace. According to one source, people have become "indifferent" to these sessions; they simply accept them as part of their daily routine. Foreigners who have observed some of the morning propaganda sessions have noted that "there are usually a few serious listeners, a number of people sleeping, and others conversing, laughing, and joking. The 'group leader' usually ignores his audience and continues to read from his book or newspaper." From 8:30 to 9:30 office directors and plant managers lead a discussion of work plans for the day or week or, perhaps, entire month. Workers pledge their best efforts to exceed the planned goals.

Actual work starts at 9:00 A.M. and continues until 1:00 P.M. with a short break from 10:00 to 10:15 for exercises. The rest period lasts from 1:00 P.M. to 4:00 P.M. Many workers bring their lunch from home and eat at their desks or on the construction site; others eat at their organization cafeteria; others go home for lunch and a nap. Occasionally, workers might lunch at a nearby restaurant.

In any case, most take a nap after lunch. Conditioned as they are to a sixteen-hour day away from home, North Koreans need an afternoon nap. Guides assigned to escort foreign visitors around North Korea have insisted that foreigners take a two-hour rest in their hotel rooms from 2:00 P.M. to 4:00 P.M. The guides have been observed sleeping in rooms nearby. All hotel services, including mail, meals, and telephone service are unavailable between those hours. Office workers can sleep at their desks or go home, if they prefer. Otherwise, they spend the rest period reading, visiting with their coworkers, exercising, or doing errands. Once or twice a month, sports activities are organized during the lunch break; on these occasions, everyone is required to participate in the games. Although the activities are fun, they preempt the time normally available for a nap or errands.

Work continues from 4:00 P.M. to 8:00 P.M. after which evenings study sessions and self-criticism meetings are conducted from 8:00 P.M. to 10:00 P.M. Mothers with three or more children under the age of thirteen are excused early. They work a six-hour rather than an eight-hour workday, finishing work at 6:00 P.M. after which they attend a special study session until 7:00 P.M. They get home between 7:30 and 8:00 P.M. All other women get home between 10:30 and 11:00 P.M. On the way home, they pick up their children at the nurseries and then stop at the central kitchens to pick up their cooked rice. Older children are at home waiting, usually sleeping, but sometimes doing their homework or the housework.

There is an unchanging regularity about people's lives. Their schedule is the same six days a week, fifty-two weeks a year. Everyone conforms to basically the same schedule. All across North Korea people are doing exercises, eating breakfast, and getting ready for work during the same morning hour. Virtually everyone is studying the same party editorial during the same half-hour period. Almost everyone sleeps from 2:00 P.M. to 4:00 P.M., and most people study from 8:00 P.M. to 10:00 P.M. During the other hours of the day, people are working. They work the same eight hours and sleep during the same six hours (midnight to 6:00 A.M. There is no curfew that actually forces them to be home at a certain time each night; the controls are more subtle than that. Curfews have been imposed at times of national emergency, such as immediately after the capture of the *Pueblo* in 1968 and during the August 1976 Panmunjon crisis. Otherwise, there has been no regular curfew, as there was for years in South Korea. On the other hand, there is absolutely nothing to do after 10:00 P.M.; moreover, buses and other public transportation run only sporadically after 11:00 P.M., making it difficult, if not impossible, to get home. Furthermore, people are so tired that they only want to go home and sleep, anyway. Virtually no one is out after 11:00 P.M. except an occasional foreigner and the security personnel. Workers on the night shift are inside the factories.

Women generally do not go to bed as early as men. They have to stay up later to finish the household chores. On top of doing the cooking, laundry, and cleaning, they fetch all the water for the family and make all the charcoal briquettes used in cooking. By and large, North Korean men still expect to be treated in the traditional fashion and refuse to contribute to household chores. They expect their wives to do all the household work.

Very much aware of the problem, the regime has tried to lighten women's work. The introduction of rice-cooking establishments has afforded families the opportunity of purchasing carry-out food for the evening meal. Another new trend has been the substitution of bread for rice, for the same reason that it eliminates cooking. As one of the main goals of the six-year plan from 1970 to 1976, the regime sought to free women from housekeeping work by increasing the production of home appliances such as refrigerators, laundry machines, and other electrically operated equipment. However, the plan fell short of its goals, particularly in consumer-related fields, necessitating less expensive, more original solutions to the problem such as the establishment of carry-out food services.

It is interesting that the regime has not sought social change as an answer to the problem, for example by exhorting men to share the household work with women. The concept, which has gained increasing acceptance in Western societies in recent years, is alien to traditional Korean culture. Preferring to work within established social customs, Kim Il-song and his associates tried various economic solutions instead.

Another major complaint of women is the exorbitant amount of political study required. While perhaps accepting the need to work, women resent the intrusion of politics in their lives. Their objections stem not only from the competing demands of political study and the family on their time and energy but from the natural aversion of many women to politics. There is a lot to memorize: Kim's speeches, dates of his guerrilla exploits, details of the constitution, and policies of former party congresses. There are also written reports to be submitted on assigned topics. Many women find the assignments tough, as well as boring.

The new generation of North Korean women, practiced as they are in self-criticism and the constant study of Kim Il-songism almost from birth, may be somewhat more comfortable with the highly politicized life in North Korea today than the older generation was. On the whole, however, women are probably more dissatisfied than men with the highly politicized society that is North Korea today.

Studies of the former Soviet Union and contemporary Chinese society have highlighted the dissatisfactions of women in those societies. Available evidence suggests a not-too-dissimilar picture in North Korea. While it is true that women have enjoyed the rewards of increasingly successful professional lives in Communist societies, they have paid dearly in terms of enormously complicated personal lives.

PART THREE

The Dream versus Reality

14

Pyongyang: Kim's Dream City

So great is the difference between living in North Korea's capital city of Pyongyang and living elsewhere in the country that some feeling for Pyongyang is absolutely necessary to gain an appreciation of the privileged life in North Korea. For Americans, used to thinking of Washington, D.C., as the political capital, New York as the financial capital, Hollywood as the movie capital, and Detroit as the auto capital, it may be difficult to appreciate the importance of Pyongyang. It is the center for everything—the government, the arts, science, and technology. It epitomizes the narrowness of North Korean society at its apex. There may be greater equality of life in North Korea than in most other countries, but there is all the difference in the world in living in Pyongyang and not.

Kim Il-song built a showcase city in Pyongyang that is not only atypical of the rest of the country, but atypical of the Far East in general. In the natural beauty of its parks and rivers, the grandeur of its public buildings, and its wide, tree-lined avenues—all sparkling clean—and the careful control of the people living there, which creates a unique impression of a spacious, uncrowded Asian city, Pyongyang strikes many observers as one of the most beautiful cities they have ever seen. An Australian journalist who described it as a "ghost town, hushed, remote, withdrawn from the normal explosion of color and sound which characterize most other Asian cities," was nonetheless "struck by its beauty, especially at night." In winter, with snow on the ground, the city has an "eerie, frozen beauty." Its likeness to a Siberian city—with its Russian-style architecture relieved by a few modern buildings of Korean design—is even more pronounced than at other times of the year.

In the spring and summer, one's impression is of flowers, trees, and parkland. Pyongyang, which means "capital of willows," is described by the North Koreans as a city within a park. Moranbong and Potong-gang parks, together with the larger Taedong-san Park, which has a zoo, a botanical garden, and a Disneyland-type amusement park, account for more than one quarter of the total area of the city. The broad, six-lane avenues have median strips planted with flowers and sidewalks bordered by trees. Schools are responsible for the upkeep of the flowers and trees in the section of the city within their jurisdiction; schoolchildren can be seen planting flowers every spring. Along the banks of the Potonggang and Taedong rivers, which run through the city, long rows of willow trees add to the natural charm of the city.

Pyongyang is not only beautiful, it is extraordinarily clean. Everyone comments on Pyongyang's cleanliness, especially in comparison to Beijing and Tokyo. Foreign visitors report seeing old women outside sweeping the streets and sidewalks constantly. As one visitor noted, "There was not even a single cigarette butt on the pavement. Trash baskets and cigarette receptacles are provided in all public places." One shudders to think what the punishment is for littering!

Every neighborhood group of five families is responsible for keeping the streets and sidewalks in front of their apartments immaculately clean. It is a job that older women, who are not likely to be working full-time, can do. In winter, they are responsible for removing the snow on the streets and sidewalks in front of their apartments. Apparently, the city has no other provision for snow removal. The regime also has other procedures for keeping the city clean. There are "wash points" on all the main approaches to Pyongyang where buses and trucks are washed before entering the city. Because many of the roads outside Pyongyang are unpaved, buses and trucks get very dirty. In Pyongyang, most of the streets are paved. All the main thoroughfares were resurfaced with asphalt shortly before the International Ping-Pong Tournament held in May 1979. Water sprinkler trucks are reported to spray the streets all day long. The city is a far cry from dusty, dirty Peking.

Part of Kim's design in creating his dream city, as he called Pyongyang, was to limit the size of the city's population. According to defectors, everyone wants to live in Pyongyang. There would be a mass movement of people into the city, were it not for the tight controls exercised by the government. In other Asian countries, such as Thailand, Burma, Indonesia, Taiwan, and the Philippines, where the capital city affords opportunities and pleasures lacking elsewhere in the country, one sees the natural flow of people into the city reflected in the high population of these cities in relation to the population of the whole country. In South Korea, Seoul's population represents about one-eighth of the country's total population. In North Korea, on the other hand, Pyongyang's population of 1 million represents only about one-seventeenth of its total population.

North Koreans cannot move into or out of Pyongyang without official approval. In this regard, Kim Il-song adopted some of the controls the Soviets used in Moscow. At one point, the Soviets put a ceiling of 8 million on Moscow's population based on housing availability. The only way to move into the city without a resident's permit was to marry a Moscow resident. There were reports of bogus marriages undertaken by Soviets desperate to live in Moscow. Literally thousands of people resorted to marriages of convenience to live in Moscow, Leningrad, and Kiev.

We do not have personal accounts of North Koreans going to such lengths to slip through the rules governing residency in Pyongyang. There may be some instances of this, but North Korean controls are much tighter than the Soviet controls were. The relative lack of travel into and out of Pyongyang and the stricter controls on marriages and divorce would make it much more difficult for North Koreans to fake a marriage to obtain a resident's permit.

In order to maintain its orderly, uncluttered appearance, bicycles and trucks are forbidden in certain sections of Pyongyang. Visitors are always struck by the lack of vehicular traffic in the city. Since there are no privately owned automobiles, the only cars present are those owned by the government and used to transport high-level party and government officials, university professors, distinguished artists, sports figures, and entertainers. Other people travel by bus or trolley or on the Pyongyang subway, if they cannot walk to their destination. The relative lack of traffic, combined with the absence of industry within the city, has kept the city free of air pollution, a troubling problem in most other areas of North Korea. The privileged in Pyongyang breathe fresh, clean air; the less fortunate in most other areas of the country live amidst serious pollution problems. There is no effort to regulate industry in the interests of environmental control.

Unlike most cities, which grow in a helter-skelter fashion, Pyongyang was planned. Reduced to rubble during the Korean War, it was rebuilt according to design. The streets, laid out in a north-south, east-west direction, give it a well-ordered appearance. Its public buildings, built on a grand scale, make it a monumental city, not unlike Washington, D.C., which is precisely the impression that Kim was striving for. For instance, the Mansudae Art Theatre, built in the early 1970s as an "arts showplace," is described by American visitors as even more beautiful than the Kennedy Center. Its elegant decor includes marble floors and pillars, high sculptured ceilings, mosaic wall decorations, and plush red carpeting. The deep-cushioned theater seats are extra wide and extra comfortable; there are large permanent screens on either side of the stage for instant translation of the opera into English, French, Spanish, or Russian; the men's rooms are reported to have the latest in electric-eye activated hand dryers. One can imagine the thrill of Pyongyang residents in seeing the elaborately staged opera *Song of Paradise* in such a magnificent setting.

The Korean Revolutionary Museum, built in 1972 in honor of Kim's sixtieth birthday, is a mammoth building, with over 100 exhibition rooms on its four floors. Although of unimpressive Stalinist architecture, it is imposing in its size alone, and a towering statue of Kim dominates its entrance. The Pyongyang Gymnasium, with a seating capacity of 20,000, is impressive from an architectural point of view and also for its being the largest gym in the Far East. The huge People's Palace of Culture, standing alongside the Pyongyang Gym on Chollima Street, is a beautiful building with traditional Korean lines. It has a meeting hall with 3,000 seats and more than 500 smaller conference rooms, banquet halls, study rooms, a cinema, and exhibition halls. The walls inside are decorated with large mosaics, and the building is surrounded by lovely gardens and lawns that are lighted at night. The International Friendship Museum is no less impressive. While not particularly attractive from the outside, its grand entrance hall creates an unforgettable impression. Kim's lighted marble statue at the far end of the hall is set off by one of the world's largest, most striking Oriental rugs, of a vivid red. Other buildings, such as the Health and Recreation Center, have magnificent entrance halls with marble floors and pillars and elaborate fountains. Almost all of these buildings have reflection pools on the grounds outside, with fountains of water spraying forth from pools in the center. Many of the fountains are lighted at night.

The newer buildings, like the People's Palace of Culture and the Kim Il-song Library, are striking examples of a new contemporary Korean style of architecture. The huge National Institute of Korean Medicine, covering more than 50,000 square meters, has eleven Korean-style roofs of blue tiles, similar to the striking roof lines of the Kim Il-song Library. Kim Il-song is reported to have personally approved the architectural design of the institute and to have selected "a scenic site for the building in East Pyongyang." Kim Chong-il was in charge of the day-to-day supervision of the construction of the building. These newer buildings stand out from the typical Soviet-style construction of most of Pyongyang's buildings, which were designed by architects trained in the Soviet Union in the 1950s and 1960s. As relations with the Soviets deteriorated in the 1970s, younger architects trained in North Korea developed their own style of architecture, a blend of the contemporary and the traditional Korean styles. The two groups have designed buildings of sharply contrasting styles. Apparently, they never worked together, but were assigned to different buildings, which reflect their very different backgrounds and training. The Soviet-trained architects who are still alive, now in their late sixties and seventies, were established members of Pyongyang's elite during the Kim Il-song years. The buildings they designed are monumental buildings—each and every one a showplace of its kind.

The showcase quality of Pyongyang is perhaps best illustrated by the Pyongyang subway. The mere existence of a subway in Pyongyang seems unreal, given the state of transportation facilities in the rest of the country. It is hardly typical of a country where most people walk to and from work and only the lucky are bused to their factories. The grandeur of it all only adds to its surreal quality. Built deep underground to double as an air-raid shelter, the Pyongyang subway, opened in 1973 but expanded since then to a total length of from 30 to 40 kilometers, ranges in depth from 80 to 200 meters underground. It is deepest where it crosses under the Taedong River. It is connected to the street by a series of long escalators, longer than any in the United States. The system, consisting of two separate lines intersecting in something of an X formation, has some fifteen to twenty stations which are said to be large enough to shelter the 1 million residents of Pyongyang and are reported to be very well ventilated. The subway trains, consisting of from two to four cars with a passenger capacity of 200 people each, run three to five minutes apart during rush hours but on a very irregular basis at other times. At 10:00 A.M., for instance, the subway stations are virtually empty. The North Koreans claim that 300,000 people commute to work on the subway each day.

The subway stations have marble floors and sculptured ceilings, exquisite chandeliers, and beautiful mosaic decorations. Those who have seen the subways in Moscow and Pyongyang, the two most elaborate subways in the world, say that Pyongyang's is far more beautiful. One observer even compared it to the palace of Versailles! In a more conservative vein, it certainly looks much more like the foyer of an impressive government building than a functioning subway. Apparently, it has a very smooth ride; according to one person who has ridden the subways in Paris, Moscow, London, China, and the United States, it has the smoothest ride of them all. Like the French subway, the wheels have small rubber tires.

The unreal quality of the subway reflects its fairy tale history. Kim Il-song was importing elaborate, expensive crystal chandeliers for the subway long after North Korea had become the first Communist country to default on its foreign loans and was struggling to maintain its international standing, unable to meet the interest payments, much less the repayment schedules, on its loans. In building the monumental city of his dreams, Kim was absolutely lavish in his use of crystal chandeliers, mosaics, lighted fountains, and elaborate landscaping.

The point in stressing the elaborate, beautiful, indeed imposing features of Pyongyang's showcase buildings and subway system is not to suggest that they are unique or even as beautiful as many other buildings in other countries. It is simply to give some idea of the incredible difference of living in Pyongyang and elsewhere in North Korea. In simply no other country is there such a striking difference between living in one city and living any place else in the entire country.

In most of North Korea, men and women frequent a bathhouse of relatively primitive design on the average of two or three times a month. In Pyongyang, the privileged go to the new Health and Recreation Center, open seven days a week (open to foreigners on Saturday afternoons only). The center has a showcase gym, a huge indoor swimming pool, elaborate sauna facilities, and an entrance hall of fountains and marble pillars no less impressive than the Mellon Art Gallery's inner courtyards. The residents of Pyongyang also have an indoor ice-skating rink, the first in North Korea. They have the most modern hospital facilities, unheard of anywhere else in North Korea. The maternity hospital has an inside television system which allows visitors to talk with patients and see newborn babies in the nursery. Foreign visitors to Pyongyang are almost always taken to the Pyongyang Maternity Hospital.

Although all North Korean children go to nursery school from the age of three months, only the children of the privileged in Pyongyang attend the 18 September Nursery, a showcase facility that was built to impress foreigners and does just that. As one of Pyongyang's major tourist attractions, it is shown to virtually all foreign visitors, even those who try hard to escape the routine tours. This school, which caters to the sons and daughters of Foreign Ministry officials, has a heated swimming pool (with a "rainbow slide" in commemoration of Kim Il-song's legendary climbing of a locust tree to catch a rainbow), a fancy merry-go-round with jet planes that plays a song about "Astro fighters flying high in the sky," an electrified "Reunification train" that stops at one station called "South Korea," and a plethora of expensive-looking well-built tricycles. None of the other 60,000 child-care and kindergarten facilities in the country, which together accommodate some 3.5 million children from the age of three months to six years, have any such facilities.

Older children in Pyongyang may be even more spoiled, compared to their contemporaries living outside of Pyongyang. After school, they can pursue extracurricular activities at the one and only children's palace in Pyongyang. This huge complex of four buildings, containing over 500 rooms, plus an assembly hall with 1,200 spectator seats, offers courses in music, dance, embroidery, the martial arts, science, mechanics, tractor driving, gymnastics, and painting and sculpture, as well as an assortment of sports activities (swimming, boxing, soccer, basketball, volleyball, weight lifting, and Ping-Pong). The equipment in the physics, biology, and chemistry labs impresses most visitors, but the training in music is even more noteworthy. One Westerner observed that the three grand pianos in one room would have been "unavailable to a student in his country until he had a master's degree in pianoforte." Most foreign visitors are impressed with the technical proficiency of the students studying ballet and violin. In the evenings, these youngsters put on musical shows that foreign visitors are hard pressed to avoid if staying in Pyongyang for more than two or three days. American journalist John Wallach described his evening at the children's palace in a series of articles he wrote on North Korea.

> Pyongyang must be the only capital city in the world where it is virtually impossible to attend a Verdi opera, hear a Mozart concerto being performed publicly or buy a Shakespeare play or Hemingway novel; but it is not for lack of talent.
>
> The talent is definitely there. A variety show staged at Pyongyang's imposing Children's Palace for several dozen foreign guests included everything from an 8-year-old virtuoso violinist to a complete ballet staged by 10-year-old acrobatic dancers.

The English titles for the numbers flashed on a slide screen alongside the stage: "We Sow Flower Seeds of Loyalty," "The Irrigation Water Flows In" and a work for a 250–member chorus entitled "My Country." Its verses, to the accompaniment of a Mantovani-like arrangement, included: "Molten iron flows out of the gas furnace. My country is being led to victory by the great marshal."

A Soviet diplomat sat in a nearby box just shaking his head in wonder and disbelief.

As many as 10,000 children, ages eight to sixteen, are reported to use the children's palace daily. A permanent staff of 500 full-time teachers, plus another 1,000 part-time teachers, direct their activities. Each school class in Pyongyang is given a schedule of after-school activities. Some classes go to the children's palace often for various activities; others are not so lucky.

North Korea's concept of an after-school center for extracurricular activities seems modeled after the Swiss experience; however, visitors who have seen the Pyongyang children's palace credit the North Koreans with much originality. After the Guyanese Prime Minister visited Pyongyang in April 1978, he sent Guyanese architects to North Korea to observe the operation of the children's palace. Kim himself was especially proud of the children's palace. He used to visit it three or four times a year. He was there for the opening of the first elevator installed in a North Korean building.

Pyongyang today is a very different city from the Pyongyang of 1963, when the children's palace was inaugurated and the first elevator was installed. Dramatic improvements in the construction industry have altogether changed the appearance of the city. There has been a boom in the construction of civilian apartments, as well as public buildings. Old buildings in whole sections of the city have been torn down and replaced by high-rise apartments. In 1970 some twenty apartment buildings of six to eight stories lined Chollima Street; ten years later, many times that number of ten- to twenty-story buildings stretched from one end of the street to the other. One visitor who returned to Pyongyang in 1980, after a year's absence, was "absolutely amazed at the change in the city in one year, especially the growth in apartment buildings." After coming up from the subway in a familiar part of the city, he was unable to find his way. Other sources who were in Pyongyang around the mid-1970s were equally amazed with the striking change in the appearance of the city ten years later.

The boom in construction in Pyongyang in the mid-1970s involved around-the-clock work by an unskilled construction crew of thousands of volunteer laborers (working through the night after a full day's work on their regular job) under the supervision of North Korean army engineers. One foreign visitor to the city reported seeing twenty-five construction cranes from his hotel window alone. The effort can be measured in terms of the speed with which some buildings were constructed, as well as the number and size of the buildings involved. The Pyongyang Gymnasium, the largest in the Orient, was constructed over a ten-month period in 1975. The Changgwangsan Hotel, the newest and most modern of Pyongyang's five major hotels, comprising twin eighteen-story buildings, was built that same year. The thirteen-story Pyongyang Maternity Hospital, a huge building with the most modern equipment, was completed in less than nine months, as part of the race to finish the construction of a number of prestigious projects before the start of the Sixth Party Congress in October 1980. The Kim Il-song Library, designed to accommodate 10 million books and to serve as North Korea's Library of Congress, was constructed in a matter of a few months.

Over the years, the quality of construction has improved from very poor to quite good. The Potonggang Hotel, built in 1972 to accommodate the South Korean delegations to the North-South talks, represented the ultimate in North Korean construction at the time. Its large plate-glass windows were of very poor quality; they made everything look out of focus. The glass in the new Sports Complex, completed in 1980, has no such distortion. Also, the elevator in the nine-story Potonggang Hotel was—and still is—very slow and works in a novel way, in that it stops at different floors in the order in which the elevator button is pushed. Thus, a person getting on the elevator last and wanting to get out on the fourth floor may ride up to the sixth floor, down to the second, and up to the eighth, before finally getting to the third floor. The heating in the Potonggang Hotel also reflects the limitations of North Korean technology, vintage 1972. Some rooms are reported to be unbearably hot while others are cold. Here again, the North Koreans have made significant improvements. New heating systems use hot water pumped in from the nearby Pyongyang Thermal Power Plant rather than hot water heated over a coal stove in individual apartment units. The toilets in the Potonggang Hotel were often out of order, and the water pressure was uneven. Moreover, electric lights were dim and flickering. New apartment buildings have corrected many of these problems. Some of the higher-story buildings have elevators now. Apparently, the older ones were built with a space for an elevator to be installed later, but the occupants had to use outside stairways. Newer apartment buildings have elevators, as well as outside stairways.

The North Koreans have instituted a novel system for ensuring that the privileged always enjoy the most modern conveniences. People are constantly moved in and out of apartments, as newer ones are built. Since apartment buildings are occupied by people working in the same office, government ministry, or factory, they can be moved as a group. There is no disruption of social ties, as one's neighbors move on together into a new, higher-standard apartment building.

Despite the significant improvement in the quality of construction and the improvement in living standards in general, it would be wrong to leave the impression that North Korean apartments, even the newer ones, are of superior construction. According to one Third World diplomat, "None of the walls are free from cracks. Most electric switches and outlets are defective. The wooden floors are not properly laid. Rain soaks through many of the roofs; the doors are narrow; and there are no screens on the windows."

For North Koreans, however, the improvements have been dramatic. For those who have seen Pyongyang rebuilt from the ashes of the Korean War, there is genuine pride in the glory of the city. This pride is reflected in the questions they often ask foreigners: "Do you like our city? Is it pleasing? Tell us how to make it even better."

Kim Il-song took great personal pride in Pyongyang. He considered it his "own creation," his "personal child." He loved the city and said he "would never risk its destruction." He once told some Japanese visitors:

> There is no city like Pyongyang in the world. Some Swedish people have asked me why we don't publicize Pyongyang more, since it is a city in a garden. I asked them to promote Pyongyang. We do not know how to publicize Pyongyang. We have accomplished many things, but we don't publicize them. We don't know how to promote anything.

As many Western observers have noted, North Koreans have "an obsession with economic progress and national identity and a disdain for backwardness." Kim is reported to have designed Pyongyang "to en-

hance the ego and morale of the whole nation, not just his own ego."
He was well aware of the importance of morale in accomplishing his
purposes. Once, when asked why "he claimed to have achieved the
goals of the six-year plan one year in advance when, in fact, the plan
had failed," Kim answered: "Why tell people that they have failed mis-
erably and thereby drop their morale into their boots?" Pyongyang is
one thing of which the North Korean people can be proud. If they derive sufficient satisfaction in the way of national pride to justify all their
hard work, then Pyongyang is a major accomplishment—politically as
well as materially.

Thus, Pyongyang seems to represent the paradox of the North Korean people—their pride in what they have accomplished—idealized in
Pyongyang—and their gnawing sense of being far, far behind and their
compulsion to make things seem better than they are.

The towering bronze statue of Kim Il-song on Mansu Hill overlooking the capital city of Pyongyang, which Kim built.

One of the many elaborate fountains in Pyongyang with the mammoth Korean Revolutionary Museum exemplifying the Stalinist architecture of the 1970s in the background.

Kim Il-song inspecting the produce of a food-processing plant.

Post-war construction of residential apartments showing the uniformity of design.

The construction of the People's Palace of Culture, one of Pyongyang's newer public buildings, illustrative of the return to a more traditional Korean architecture in the 1980s.

Wall paintings in the Pyongyang subway.

Kim Il-song giving on-the-spot instruction to an agricultural cooperative.

Kim Il-song visiting students at a middle school.

Young Pioneers wearing their standard blue uniforms with red scarves.

Kim Il-song receiving foreign visitors to North Korea.

15

The Privileged Life

For the privileged, most of whom live in Pyongyang, there is the opportunity for higher education, the challenge of responsible jobs, the prospect of promotion, the recognition of accomplishment, and the reward of a higher standard of living. Although by no means as luxurious as the life of a wealthy South Korean, the elite in North Korea lead a life so vastly different from that of the ordinary North Korean that their privileged status seems much greater than the relative privileged position of the rich or powerful in South Korea compared to the average South Korean citizen.

In their effort to create the impression of a classless society, the North Koreans like to cite statistics on income to support their contention of great equality in the DPRK. However, money is not a good yardstick of privilege in North Korea. Nor is the rationing system nor, for that matter, are any of the established rules and regulations. For the truth is that the system of privilege operates outside the established system—outside wages and rations and the normal distribution of goods and services.

Salary levels are a particularly deceptive measure of privilege. Outside of Kim Il-song, who was reported to have earned more than 300 won per month, the highest paid North Koreans are cabinet ministers who earn from 225 to 250 won per month. The highest paid professors at Kim Il-song University, provincial party secretaries, and top artists and musicians earn about 200 won. Vice ministers are paid 180 won. At the highest, these wages are only three to four times the wage of the average North Korean worker, who earns from 60 to 90 won per month. They are, at the very most, six times the wage of the lowest paid unskilled female worker, who earns from 35 to 40 won per month. If the wife of a cabinet minister does not work, as she usually does not, the family income is only about twice that of the average household income of from 120 to 150 won per month where both parents work. It is actually less than the family income of a professional couple who are likely to be earning 200 won per month together. Judging from salaries alone, the cabinet minister's family would be less well off than the family of a professional couple; but this is not so. Other perquisites make the cabinet minister's real income far higher, though incalculably so.

Cabinet ministers and other high-ranking officials receive many extra benefits free of charge. In addition to their salaries, they are entitled to the free issue of high-quality cigarettes, wool clothes, and leather shoes. Even if an ordinary citizen had the money, he could not buy any of these items; he would not have access to the special stores that carry them.

Access to these special stores is a major perk of the elite. Only party officials at the level of bureau chief and up are allowed to shop at these stores. Apparently, there are different shops for different levels of the hierarchy. One shop, used by Kim's relatives and the vice presidents and their families, offers imported items and North Korean products of the quality normally reserved for export. Another shop is for party secretaries and vice premiers; a third, known as Number 10, offers mostly food and clothing and is reserved for ministers, vice ministers, and chiefs of party departments; a fourth, known as Number 9, is for senior military officials, deputy ministers, lower-ranking officials of party departments and members of revolutionary families.

Not only are prices lower at these stores, but goods not otherwise available are for sale: leather shoes, wool suits, beef, pork, wine, liquor, candy, eggs, and anchovies. Except for some shoes imported from Japan, no foreign-made clothes are available in regular shops open to ordinary North Koreans. Beef and pork are almost never available; nor is fresh fish. Wine and liquor are available only on holidays, and beer is difficult to obtain outside of Pyongyang. The elite have ready access to all these goods, at discount prices, all year long. They do not have to stand in long lines to buy cigarettes or beer or other items in chronically short supply. The special stores insulate them from the normal inconvenience of shopping: chronic shortages and endless waiting in line.

According to one source, high-level officials are given special allowances for lunch (10 won) and other purposes. They are also given special gifts on important national occasions. On Kim Il-song's sixty-fifth birthday, for instance, all ambassadors, party secretaries, and factory managers received Sony color televisions, expensive stereo turntables, and wristwatches with Kim's picture, signature, and birthdate on the face. All of the party representatives to the Fifth Party Congress are reported to have been given a television, some of them a color television. Delegates to national agricultural and industrial meetings and winners of national sports events are usually given fountain pens or wristwatches.

North Korean embassies abroad are known to have been instructed to procure blackmarket items, including pornographic movies, for private showing to high-level North Korean officials. As it was in the former Soviet Union, there is probably no more striking double standard between the lifestyles of the elite and the ordinary North Korean than the established access of the elite to Western magazines, books, movies, and travel, which are banned for ordinary North Koreans. In the former Soviet Union, access to closed screenings of Western movies was a highly prized status symbol. The excitement of sharing something taboo was as great as the enjoyment of the movie itself. Presumably, it is the same in North Korea.

Cabinet ministers' families live in an exclusive complex of apartments in Pyongyang, known as the Executive Apartments. The complex, which is surrounded by a concrete wall and guarded by security guards armed with assault rifles, consists of four apartment buildings of twenty housing units each. The buildings are two- or three-story buildings, a luxury in North Korea since most high-rise apartments do not have elevators, only long walk-up stairways on the outside of the buildings. Individual apartments, occupying approximately 200 square meters, have three or four bedrooms, a living room, a separate dining room, a kitchen, a bathroom, and a storage room. The apartments are furnished with a color television, refrigerator, sewing machine, electric fan, and, in some cases, air conditioning—all beyond the hope of the average North Korean. The latter would have access to a black-and-white television and sewing machine in his apartment building or in the collective farm office, much as a college student in the United States has access to a television or laundry facilities in his dormitory.

The elite are driven to work in chauffeured limousines, provided by the government. One observer noticed a number of Mercedes-Benz sedans parked in front of the Executive Apartments. One can see such cars in front of government office buildings and a few other institutions such as Kim Il-song University but nowhere else. Kim Il-song himself used one of three luxury cars, either a white Mercedes-Benz 600, which seems to have been his favorite, or a Soviet-made "Jiru" open car which he used for official occasions, or a bullet-proof Soviet JIS-110 weighing

4.5 tons. A number of paintings of Kim suggest the elaborate interior of his cars which are suggestive of the famed plush interiors of the official limousines of top Soviet leaders. Kim also had a special train and plane at his disposal; apparently, he preferred to travel by train, using a plane only on rare occasions.

The elite have other special services at their disposal, including prestigious medical facilities. In the early days of his rule, Kim and other top government officials went to the Pyongyang Medical Hospital for their medical care. However, in the late 1960s a modern hospital was built to provide medical treatment exclusively to high-ranking Party and government officials. The hospital, which opened in February 1971, is officially named the Government Hospital but it is better known as the Ponghwa Clinic, after the name of the village where it is located, near the Executive Apartments where government ministers live.

The clinic provides its patients with expensive and rare medicines, many of them purchased from Japan. Such medicines are not available at regular dispensaries. The director of the clinic, a graduate of a Japanese medical school and later the Dean of Ch'ongjin Medical College, was Kim's long-time chief personal physician. In addition to the clinic, he operated a special medical service providing twenty-four-hour medical care for Kim on a house-call basis.

Most North Koreans are not aware of the existence of the Ponghwa Clinic, just as most Soviet citizens did not know about the Kremlin Clinic in Moscow. Both leaderships kept such prestigious facilities very quiet. If one walked past the Kremlin Clinic in Moscow, however, one would notice the large number of limousines parked out front and the chauffeurs idly whiling away their time as they waited for the leaders receiving special medical care at the clinic. One imagines very much the same scene at the Ponghwa Clinic, on a smaller scale.

There are special clubs for the elite that include bowling alleys and tennis courts. It is possible that some of the villas in the hills outside Pyongyang, including the villa where Kim met U.S. reporter John Wallach, may be country clubs of the elite. For longer periods of rest and recreation and a change in scenery, there are special resorts on the beach of Wonsan and in the mountains along the east coast. These facilities are sometimes used by visiting foreign dignitaries but, otherwise, they are reserved for top party and government leaders.

Members of the Political Committee are provided with other perks, including a private secretary, medical corpsman, cook, and bodyguard. Provincial party secretaries and others of equivalent or higher rank are entitled to a cook. There are conflicting reports about the services of maids. According to some reports, the elite can have domestic help; however, according to other reports, Kim abolished the use of maids as inconsistent with Communist teaching of a classless society. Kim may have been troubled by manifestations of privilege other than the use of maids. In the early 1970s he is reported to have abolished the network of special stores on ideological grounds; however, shortly thereafter, the stores reopened.

One can only speculate as to whether this suggests a difference between Kim and others of the top leadership on the proper limits of privilege. It may be that Kim was somewhat less interested in the materialistic things in life than others, including his own son. He seems to have had something of the ascetic in him, reminiscent of Ho Chi Minh. Despite all the trappings of wealth, power, and privilege in his later years, he spent the first-half of his life as a guerrilla fighter in deplorable conditions and he may have developed a taste for the simpler life.

His son Kim Chong-il, typical of the younger generation raised amidst privilege, seems to be a very different kind of person, with his reported love of fast cars and tennis. One gets the impression that this second-generation leadership, which has been exposed to the best education, finest clothes, good food, vacations at the beach with swimming and tennis, and access to cars, is hopelessly spoiled by the standards of the average North Korean. In a system which promotes the sons and daughters of the elite, by virtue of their having the best *songbun*, the people who get ahead are necessarily those who have grown up amidst relative privilege. They are likely to be somewhat out of touch with the great mass of people who lead very different lives. There is no leveling effect, common in other countries, of other social groups entering the leadership, be it the political, military, economic, or cultural leadership. The North Korean system promotes an elitism that is the very antithesis of the Communist notion of egalitarianism. It makes it harder, rather than easier, for the leadership to stay in touch with the people, as Kim, like Mao, constantly exhorted the party cadre to do.

Kim Chong-il and his friends have been known to enjoy driving cars at fast speeds on deserted roads late at night, hardly something most North Koreans do. Only the sons of the very privileged have access to cars. The mere opportunity of driving a car would be an exciting experience in North Korea. One can imagine the exhilaration of these relatively spoiled young people driving fast down a deserted highway at night—with no fear of getting caught for speeding. From all reports, the North Koreans habitually drive fast, much too fast for the comfort of many Westerners who worry about the poor lighting conditions, the bad condition of the roads, and the questionable condition of the cars. There is evidence of many car accidents, including one involving serious injury to the son of a very high official who was reported to have been driving at high speeds late at night.

The children of the elite are spoiled in other ways. They are guaranteed a college education, without regard for their ability or performance. They attend the finest middle schools and high schools, graduating at the top of their class, regardless of their grades. They are exempt from military service and spend their vacations at resort homes rather than on collective farms doing volunteer labor. After graduation from college, they receive the best jobs and, most likely, an opportunity to travel abroad. They join the party, marry someone of social prominence, and rise quickly through the ranks.

In his youth, Kim Chong-il was reported to have a tight circle of friends, fellow children of the elite, who had known one another for years, attended the same schools, vacationed together, worked together, and quickly risen to the top together. Some of the leading young professors at Kim Il-song University are reported to have been classmates of his at college. Song Chong-su, the deputy director of the new Pyongyang Maternity Hospital, was a classmate both in high school and at Kim Il-song University. Song Chong-su went on to medical school while Kim Chong-il remained at Kim Il-song University to become leader of the Three-Revolution Movement. Some of Kim's other friends and classmates probably have equivalent jobs in the Foreign Ministry, party apparatus, economic management structure, and cultural affairs departments. Their success is due not only to the fact that the are friends and classmates of Kim Chong-il but to the fact that they are the sons and daughters of cabinet ministers, party leaders, top economic managers, leading professors, or, possibly, North Korea's most famous musicians, artists, or generals. Theirs is a small, closed society.

Everyone in the group knows everyone else and what they are doing, but no one on the outside knows. Within the group, there was general knowledge of the details of Kim's family life that were kept secret from the public. Members of the group would be personally familiar with Kim Chong-il, his wife, and young children. They would also know Kim Chong-il's sister and her family. They would know that she studied physics at Kim Il-song University and that her husband, only thirty years old at the time, was the person who first suggested the idea of smuggling operations as a way of financing North Korean embassies abroad. Older, more experienced diplomats who might have questioned the wisdom of the smuggling operations, which exposed the North Koreans to foreign ridicule and censure, would never have dared to criticize Kim's son-in-law. Western observers have wondered about the fate of officials responsible for such egregious errors in judgment that have seemed to mark North Korean foreign policy. Few would have guessed that they could be traced to Kim's relatives who are, of course, immune to political attack.

Few people on the outside of this inner circle would know even the most basic facts about Kim Chong-il's private life today. Outsiders knew absolutely nothing about Kim Il-song's new family by his second wife, although, once again, the people on the inside were apparently very much aware of the comings and goings of his three younger children. While they keep in close touch with others in the elite inner circle, they are careful to keep personal matters secret from those on the outside.

This privilege of the elite to secure the best for their children could never be translated into monetary terms or measured against the lives of ordinary North Koreans. It is an incalculable advantage of the elite, more meaningful than any monetary measure of their privilege. In the former Soviet Union it was called *blat*, meaning influence or access: access to special stores, access to the best schools and vacation spots, access to government cars or the opportunity to travel abroad. If anything, *blat* is more pronounced in the DPRK because it involves fewer people.

Presumably, there would be a great deal of resentment and envy in the society at large if the perks of the elite were well known, but they are not. There is no flaunting of wealth or special privilege; on the contrary, it is hidden from public view, never discussed, and officially denied. Kim Il-song's many government homes, spread around the county, all had one feature in common. They were accessible only by long, twisting, unpaved roads through wooded areas that hid the homes from public view. The lack of private cars in North Korea rules out the possibility of unauthorized visitors even approaching these hideaways. The foreign visitors who met Kim at some of these homes were utterly amazed at the luxury and extravagance of the homes. One Middle East government official who claimed to have seen many "palaces" in his day said that none of them compared with "the palace I visited in North Korea."

He said he used the word guardedly but no other word would describe it properly.

Apparently, Kim had a home in each of the eleven provinces or administrative areas for his use whenever he visited that province. John Wallach, who was taken to a villa outside Pyongyang when he met Kim in May 1979, described it as "enormous, by far the most lavish villa that [he] had ever seen in the Communist world." It was surrounded by acres and acres of terraced planting, a swimming pool, and tennis courts. U.S. Congressman Stephen Solarz met Kim in another home, outside Hamhung, in July 1980. A much more modest home with reception rooms on the first floor and Kim's living quarters on the second, it was tucked away on a forested hillside far from public view. A separate guest house nearby seemed to be for the use of top government officials, and, possibly, visiting foreign dignitaries.

Even more impressive was the house in which Congressman Solarz stayed, the home built just outside Pyongyang for exiled Cambodian leader Sihanouk, who used to spend about one-third of the year in Pyongyang and the other two-thirds in China. This house could rightfully be called a palace. Built on a hillside about fifteen minutes from downtown Pyongyang, it has a man-made lake with a dock and several rowboats. The house itself, of traditional Korean design, opens onto a large courtyard, surrounded by three wings of the building that house office rooms and extra guest rooms. The house is fronted by a wide veranda that opens into a large entrance hall with a grand stairway that looks very much like the stairway in the Grand Hotel in Taipei. On the left is a huge ballroom or reception room, with a large mural at one end of the room, crystal chandeliers, and wood paneling. Beyond that is a large, formal dining room with more crystal chandeliers and another large mural. Upstairs, on either side of the hallway, where there is a grand piano which Sihanouk used to play, there are a number of guest rooms, each with a private bath. Both the rooms and bathrooms have striking fourteen-foot ceilings. According to Sihanouk, army troops built the home in 1974, and a company of troops provided special security for him. It is unclear whether the North Koreans used this house when Sihanouk was out of the country, but presumably they did. Kim Il-song was reported to have a house near Sihanouk's home in the hills northeast of Pyongyang. Presumably, he built the house for Sihanouk on the scale of his own house.

Kim had another hilltop villa north of the city of Kaesong near the DMZ. The villa, hidden in the woods, is accessible only by a twisting, unpaved road which suddenly becomes paved near Kim's house. The home, built in the traditional Korean style with cement plaster walls and cement tile roof, is near a stream in the middle of a peach orchard. There are several adjoining buildings, including two smaller homes for ministerial-level government officials, a central dining room, and living quarters for the security company of approximately 120 men who guard the complex. It is thought that the North Koreans used these government-owned villas, normally set aside for Kim's use, for other purposes when Kim was not in residence.

In 1979 the government was reported to be building two new mansions for Kim—one on the beach on the east coast near Hamhung and one on the beach on the west coast near the Chinese border at Sinuiju. The two "annexes," as they were referred to, took two years to be constructed. The DPRK imported 1 billion (Japanese) yen worth of interior construction materials for the projects, plus the services of Japanese construction engineers to oversee the projects. The cost of the homes suggest interiors of expensive crystal chandeliers, mosaic wall decorations, plush carpeting, and wood paneling—the hallmarks of North Korea's finest buildings. The Sinuiju annex was reported to consist of one main building, four smaller attached buildings, a swimming pool, and a man-made lake. The Hamhung State Guest House is a ten-story building with living quarters and office space for Kim and his cabinet and guest facilities for visiting foreign dignitaries. Special North Korean military checkpoints are located on the roads leading to both "annexes"; unauthorized people are not allowed near either area. According to a reliable source, the facilities were intended to provide Kim with "vacation retreats and also a safe residence during national crises."

Kim's official residence used to be in the Potonggang District of Pyongyang, not far from the Potonggang River and Moranbong Park. The Mansudae Opera House and Soviet embassy were nearby. In late 1977, he moved from this residence to a much larger presidential mansion that had been under construction for months. The house itself is reported to be a huge three-story building with a five-story Presidential Hall and another three-story Conference and Museum Building nearby. The complex is surrounded by a moat on two sides (for security) and formal gardens and lawns on the other sides, protected by several guard posts. Former residents of Pyongyang tell of seeing Kim drive from this home to his government office in the mornings. Apparently, no effort was made to conceal his movements around the city. However, his home, set back from the street and cordoned off from normal traffic, was not visible to public view. No foreigners were ever taken there.

All these homes (and presumably Sihanouk's home, as well) belonged to the North Korean state, of course, not to Kim Il-song personally. This is in keeping with the Soviet practice of giving Soviet leaders special homes for use during their tenure in office. The homes go with the job. It may be that others beside Kim used them when he was not in residence. Kim Yong-nam, for one, seemed to be staying at the villa where he and Kim met John Wallach late one night in May 1979. At these homes, Kim and the top leaders had all the amenities imaginable, including elaborate banquets, day or night (John Wallach and Kim Yong-nam dined at one o'clock in the morning), color television, tennis, and swimming. The presence of tennis courts suggests the influence of Kim Chong-il, who is reported to love tennis. There are no reports, certainly, of Kim ever playing tennis.

North Koreans had no idea how Kim and his coterie lived. They had an image of Kim as a man of the people who toured the provinces in relative simplicity, with a three-car escort perhaps, but otherwise with little fanfare. He used to walk around the factories and cooperative farms, eat in their dining halls, and talk with the people. He was engaged on these inspection tours of the country as many as 120 days out of the year. They believed him when he said, "I am just an ordinary person, born on a farm." They knew nothing about his lavish homes all around the country, just as they knew nothing about the special stores in Pyongyang or the country clubs and exclusive restaurants of the elite. Their experience with officials in authority was at the local level, with party secretaries at the township level or the manager of their factory or cooperative. These people do not live all that differently from the average person. Villagers can reconcile their lifestyle with the notion of things being fairly equal for all people in North Korea, even though they might be vaguely aware of the privileges of living in Pyongyang from pictures they have seen. The rarified lifestyle and hidden wealth of the privileged few in Pyongyang are not well known. For that reason, it is not a political issue.

The only people, other then the elite themselves, who may have some idea of the full extent of privilege in the DPRK are people on the fringe of the elite who may know enough to resent the extremely privileged life of the top leadership but who also have a vested interest in the system, being members of the privileged class themselves. They would be afraid to discuss their feelings with anyone, even in private and certainly not in public.

This brings us to the one area in which the elite have no special privilege: political freedom. In North Korea, as one rises through the ranks to the top leadership, more, rather than less, is expected in terms of political obeisance to the cult of Kim. As one has more to lose in a fall from power, one is naturally less inclined to jeopardize one's career in a less than fulsome show of fidelity. Thus, one finds the most exaggerated worship of the cult at the upper levels of the government. From all reports, the ambassador in an embassy is the most fanatical observer of the cult. He got where he is that way; as ambassador, he can hardly afford to be less enthusiastic in his praise of Kim than anyone else in the embassy. It may not be a measure of his true feelings, but it is the price of survival. Since there is no way to fake certain objective measures of one's loyalty to Kim, such as the amount of time spent in Kim study or self-criticism sessions, the ambassador is likely to set the example in terms of long hours of study of Kim's teachings and wholehearted participation in criticism sessions.

Apparently no one is ever above suspicion, especially intellectuals and creative people. Party officials have been particularly zealous in monitoring the activities of North Korea's top artists and musicians. Six government people sat in on one foreign reporter's interview with North Korea's leading actors, more than for any other group he interviewed. Kim had singled out artists, actors, and athletes as needing special and constant indoctrination. Whereas most people were supposed to attend mutual criticism sessions once a week, artists and actors were ordered to attend such sessions every other day, since "they are more prone to infidelity, jealousy, vanity, lack of discipline and in-fighting." It was felt that "these elements might become disenchanted with Communist ideology, that they were particularly susceptible because of their travel to foreign countries, where they could observe and do things they could not do in North Korea." Foreign Ministry personnel are routinely brought home for a month's political reindoctrination every two years. Their privileged status brings them no respite from constant political surveillance; quite the contrary, in some cases, they are actually earmarked as potential troublemakers, who are constantly to be watched and constantly in need of political reindoctrination. In this, they are not privileged, although in every other respect, they lead a life of special privilege beyond the wildest dreams of the ordinary North Korean.

It is difficult to estimate the size of the North Korean elite, but its numbers probably do not go down very far past the level of cabinet minister, vice minister, party central committee member, brigadier general, senior economic manager, top scientist, artist, musician, actor, sports entertainer, or scholar. These are the true elite—the group of party and government officials who run the country, the senior economic officials who direct the economy and manage the major industrial facilities, and the leaders in science, culture, and the military. For outstanding service to the state, a leading scientist, famous musician, or champion athlete can earn a privileged status in the North Korean elite—status, but not power. That is the essential difference that marks the political elite from other members of the elite.

16

Real Life

Excluding the privileged top 10 percent of the population, how do others in North Korea live? With no access to special stores selling premium goods at discount prices, they have no means of acquiring high-quality cigarettes, imported foodstuffs, wine, or liquor (except on national holidays). Whatever their income, they cannot buy leather shoes or woolen clothing. They could never afford a color television or refrigerator or sewing machine, provided only to the homes of the elite. Only the privileged would have such items, although most people would have access to them in their factories and cooperative farm offices. The lucky, roughly one out of five, would have a wristwatch; fewer still, a bicycle. No matter what their income, they could not buy more than their allotment of rationed goods—rice, corn, sugar—although with extra income, they could buy more nonrationed goods, such as meat. The privileged might eat pork or chicken three or four times a week and beef several times a month; most people eat meat only once a month.

Typical housing for the ordinary North Korean family consists of a living-dining room, one bedroom, kitchen, and shared toilet facilities, regardless of the size of the family. Education and medical care are free, but, there is a world of difference between the medical and educational services provided for the privileged and the nonprivileged. Access to chauffeured cars and luxurious vacation retreats or the possibility of being exempted from volunteer labor is out of the question.

This gives some idea of the different world of the nonprivileged and the privileged, but it is still very important to differentiate between the average and poorer social classes in North Korea. Great differences exist, some of which are not easily measured in monetary terms. For instance, the difference between getting one's allotment of food grains in rice versus a mixture of rice and other grains is more significant to North Koreans, who prefer rice to any other food grain, than the difference in cost. Similarly, the opportunity for higher education with its guarantee of a better job could never be measured in monetary terms.

In North Korea the intangibles in life are not a matter of free choice. An unskilled worker who must subsist on a lower standard of living has no choice as to where he wants to live, what unskilled job he wants to do, or what he might be willing to give up to send his son to college or to take his family on a vacation. His disadvantage in life in terms of his material standard of living is underscored by his deprivation of the intrinsic joys in life.

In contrast, as we have seen, the privileged derive psychic income from important nonmonetary benefits far greater than their monetary advantages. They get preferred food rations, receive superior education and medical care, have the challenge and satisfaction of more stimulating jobs, and are given better housing in more desirable locales (usually in the bigger cities, possibly even Pyongyang). Moreover, they have the satisfaction of knowing that their children will be similarly treated. The poorer classes live with the realization that their children, unless unexpectedly lucky, will remain at the lower levels of the social stratum just as they have. In terms of psychic income as well as real income, they are at the bottom end of the receiving line.

WAGES: WORKING FOR PEANUTS

To judge from wages alone, there would seem to be considerable equality in North Korea. The privileged would appear to live roughly twice as well as ordinary North Korean working people and about three times as well as the lowest-paid unskilled workers. The government likes to cite statistics on wages precisely because of the impression of equality that is conveyed. It is not that the government claims are wrong; but the statistics are misleading because money is a poor measure of living standards in North Korea.

Table 16.1, compiled from the wealth of material available on wages, shows the range in salaries from 150 to 250 won per month for the elite, 0.1 percent of the population; 100 to 150 won per month for the privileged 10 percent of the population; 60 to 90 won per month for the average citizen; and less than 50 won per month for the lowest 15 percent of the civilian labor force and noncommissioned officers in the military. The equality in the system derives from the fact that from 75 to 80 percent of the civilian workforce earns an average salary of from 60 to 90 won per month; the privileged and the underprivileged together account for less than one-fourth of the total work force.

As can be seen in Table 16.1, there is a range of salaries for each category of wage earners in North Korea. For instance, wages of industrial workers vary depending on the type of production involved, the size and location of the factory, and the worker's job classification and seniority. Miners, defense-plant workers, blast-furnace operators, and skilled laborers in key industries constitute the "elite"—measured against the "average" workers. In addition to drawing higher wages, they get extra food rations (including meat, oil, and liquor), woolen fatigues, and more time for recreation after work. Unskilled workers in light industry, especially young girls who work in textile factories, are at the opposite end of the spectrum.

The location of a factory is an important determinant of wages. Workers in factories located in provincial capitals enjoy higher salaries and better working conditions; those in rural, small-scale factories earn significantly less. Job classification and seniority also enter into the picture. Workers in a given factory are ranked on a scale of from 1 to 8, depending on the nature of their jobs. There is normally a five-won differential between grades. A work-team rating system, introduced in 1963, further adjusts wages on the basis of performance. Each factory has a wage assessment board, composed of members selected from among the employees, which determines job classification and judges employee performance. Each worker's performance is rated daily and weekly; salaries are computed on these ratings. The change to more frequent ratings was made to ease the dissatisfaction of workers who produced more but received the same income. The revision resulted from visits to work sites of Three Great Revolution teams under the guidance of Kim Chong-il. Workers can be rewarded or penalized for such things as the care they take of equipment, the quality of their work, their initiative in solving production problems, and their safety record. As a reward for meeting production quotas, wages can also be augmented by different kinds of bonuses amounting to from 15 to 20 percent of base wages.

One finds a similar spread in the wages of engineers, doctors, professors, and government officials—a spread that was approximately the same as in the Soviet Union and China. The North Korean wage and remuneration system actually came from the Soviet Union, with a few

Table 16.1
Salary Ranges of the North Korean Workforce
(in won per month)

Kim Il-song	300
Cabinet ministers	225–250
Provincial party secretaries	200
Highest-paid university professors	180–200
Vice ministers	180
Senior military (rank of general)	160–180
Senior engineers (grades 5 and 6)	150–180
Actors, artists, musicians	150–180
Senior journalists	150–180
Colonel, lieutenant colonel in NKPA	130–150
Plant managers of first-class enterprises	120–150
Middle-level engineers (grades 3 and 4)	120–150
College professors	120–150
Foreign Ministry officials (section or bureau chiefs)	110–135
County party secretaries	100–120
Skilled workers, heavy duty laborers, miners	90–120
Engineers (grades 1 and 2)	90–120
2d Lieutenant and captain in NKPA	90–120
Assistant college professors	90–110
Doctors	80–130
Teachers in high school, middle school, or elementary school	80–120
College graduates	80
Newspaper reporters (grade 1 to 3)	70–120
Lower-level Foreign Ministry officials (below section chief)	70–90
Average worker	60–90
Unskilled laborers	40–45
Unskilled female clerks, workers	25–40
Noncommissioned officers	5–45

modifications. Although the wage spread was nowhere near as large as in Western countries, it was typical of the wage range in other Communist countries.

While wages have increased over the years, prices have remained essentially stable, suggesting an improvement in living standards. However, an increase in purchasing power is meaningful only in terms of the goods that can be purchased on the open market. It has no bearing on personal consumption of rice and other staples that have always been rationed or other important consumer items, such as housing, education, and medical care, which are provided essentially free of charge. About all that can be said is that there probably has been an increase in consumption of nonrationed consumer items with the increase apparently spread rather equally throughout the population. Consumer items affected would include clothing, nonrationed foods, cosmetics, entertainment (movies, dinners out) and travel.

However, it should be noted that wage increases are more indicative of the very low level of wages in the 1950s than of any spectacular rise in living standards. It is noteworthy that the wage increases have come in major increments rather than in steady increases, an example of the spasmodic quality of a command economy. A pattern has developed with major wage increases being announced at the beginning of a decade.

One should look at wages in North Korea as something of a cross between wages, as we know them, and children's allowances, which are given for extra expenditures above and beyond the housing, food, clothing, education, and medical care provided by parents, which, in North Korea, except for some food and clothing, are provided by the state—not equally to all people—but essentially free of charge. Wages cover extra expenditures for food, clothing, cigarettes, entertainment, haircuts, cosmetics, books, and dues to various organizations.

Thus, a higher wage can mean the difference between a more varied diet and the standard North Korean diet, one or two extra suits or dresses in addition to the clothes issued by one's factory, office, or school, occasional dinners at a restaurant or other entertainment (movies), travel to visit one's relatives on special occasions, or the purchase of a major item such as a wristwatch or bicycle. It can also mean additional savings.

The limited role of money in the economy is reflected in the distortion between wages and prices. Prices, especially prices of nonessential goods, are disproportionately high relative to wages because the open market plays such a relatively minor role in the distribution of goods and services. Since most goods, including the basics, are distributed on a non-monetary basis, avoiding the use of money and limiting consumer choice, a nylon sweater and two pairs of nylon stockings, considered nonessential luxury items, are priced as high as the average North Korean's monthly salary, effectively limiting a person's purchase of such items to one a month.

If one considers wages alone in relation to prices, North Korean workers are literally "working for peanuts." The average daily wage of 2-1/2 won does not even cover the cost of one kilogram of peanuts (peanuts sell for 5 won per kilogram). It is far less than the cost of one meter of nylon cloth, much less silk or wool; it is about one-third the cost of a pair of nylon socks and less than a fifth of the cost of a pair of ladies' nylon stockings. It could buy one meter of cotton cloth, or one toothbrush and toothpaste, or one private bath in a bathhouse and a cake of soap, or one set of Ping-Pong racquets and balls, or a haircut and styling. The average worker must work four days to buy a short-sleeved cotton shirt, one month to buy cotton overalls or a good nylon sweater, and two months to buy a blanket or the poorest quality overcoat. This assumes that he has no other expenditures for food, clothing, or other necessities. There is no way he could ever hope to save enough money to buy a refrigerator (the smallest ones sell for 300–400 won), or a black-and-white television, which sells for from 300 to 700 won (depending on whether it is of North Korean or foreign manufacture). Imported color televisions and Swiss and Japanese wristwatches cost more than he earns in an entire year.

PRICES

All one has to do is to look at a list of North Korean prices, keeping the wage structure in mind, to appreciate how little the average worker can buy with his earnings. The list of prices of selected goods in Table 16.2 has been compiled from the wealth of data on prices collected from a wide variety of sources reporting over a long period of time. We can be reasonably confident of the accuracy of these prices, certainly of the range of prices given for each item.

One of the distinguishing features of the North Korean economy is the uniformity of prices of goods sold to North Koreans throughout the country, the similarity of goods and services available in rural and urban areas, and the provision of similar shopping facilities in different areas. Although the relatively small size of the country makes this

Table 16.2
Prices of Selected Goods in North Korea

Goods	Cost (in Won)
Rice (kg.)	0.08
Soy sauce (1 liter)	0.2
Sugar (kg.)	1.5–3.5
Cucumber	0.15
Salt (kg.)	0.10
Squash	0.08
Egg (each)	0.15–0.25
Candy (kg.)	0.2
Pears (kg.)	0.5–1
Apples (kg.)	0.5–1
Peaches (kg.)	0.5–1
Chinese cabbage	0.5–0.10
Tomatoes	0.3–0.6
Hot peppers (kg.)	4
Soybean oil (liter)	4
Fish (fresh, frozen or salted)	0.5–2.5
Cooked fish	0.3
Chicken (kg.)	2–4
Whole chicken	5–30
Pork (kg.)	6–8
Beef (kg.)	7–9
Dogmeat (kg.)	3–4
Whole dog	10–150
Rabbit	1.5–10
Cigarettes	
pack of 20 (filters)	0.25–0.70
(nonfilters)	0.5–1
Lighters	3
Flint	0.25
Regular rice meal with 200-gram food ticket (rice, fish, vegetables)	0.5–1.5
Regular noodle meal with 200-gram food ticket	1–2
Dogmeat and rice soup with 200-kg. food ticket	1–1.5
Rice cake soup (with 200-gram food ticket)	0.7
Cooked rice (bowl)	0.5–1
Beer (bottle)	0.5–2
Wine (liter)	3–4

possible, it was Kim's overriding concern to establish a basic equality in the system—with allowances for the people at the top, of course, but with enforced uniformity for all others—that dictated it. With obvious pride, and apparently with no distortion of the truth, Kim used to boast that "any item sold in a North Korean 'daily necessity' store can be bought in the most remote area at the same price as in any other place." Fixed state prices for certain items such as fresh fruits and fresh fish vary throughout the year, depending on their availability at different seasons; however, at any given time, there is one standard price throughout the country.

Another noteworthy feature about the price structure is the relatively low price of basic necessities—such as rice, fruit, and other basic foods (excluding meats), haircuts, public baths, subway fare, school supplies, and fuels—and the disproportionately high price of luxury items, including wool, finished clothing, and electrical appliances. The government subsidizes the low price of rice, sugar, and other food necessities, as well as student uniforms and work clothes, thereby controlling the quantity of the goods that can be bought through a rationing system, but charges high prices for luxury goods, especially imported ones, such as Japanese and Swiss wristwatches and Soviet and Japanese televisions. Consumption of these goods can be curtailed by their high price alone. The government buys rice from collective farmers at a higher price than the subsidized price of 8 chon (or .08 won) per kilogram. In the case of imported luxury goods, on the other hand, it buys color televisions, foreign-made wristwatches, and high-quality woolens for much less than it charges its own citizens. Thus, the price system, together with the rationing system, is geared to the even distribution of basic necessities at a low price which everyone can afford and the selective distribution of scarce, nonrationed, nonessential goods to the privileged few who can afford their artificially fixed high prices.

The regime has actually made an effort to reduce the price of basic necessities over the years by covering the cost of increased government subsidies of the price of these goods by raising the price of luxury goods. In 1972 it lowered the price of sugar and work clothing and raised the price of cosmetics. In 1978 it raised the price of black-and-white televisions from 500 to 700 won and watches from 300 to 500 won. These price changes have reinforced the discrepancy between subsidized low prices of basic necessities and artificially high prices of luxury goods.

In other words, prices reflect what the regime thinks is important and not important to the people's welfare. Consumer goods that are deemed essential are subsidized by the state; those considered nonessential are priced at artificially high prices, with little regard to their cost. The state makes a profit on the latter, which compensates for the loss it incurs in subsidizing the former. The disregard for cost as the prime determinant of price distorts the price structure compared to free-market economies. Thus, the won/dollar ratio that might be computed on the basis of basic food/clothing requirements in North Korea is far different—very much lower—than the won/dollar ratio based on a comparison of North Korean and U.S. prices of such consumer durables as televisions, sewing machines, refrigerators, wristwatches, and bicycles. The disparity makes any computation of the won/dollar ratio for all consumer goods significantly less meaningful.

It is clear that the regime makes no effort to convert won prices into U.S. prices at a fair rate of exchange when pricing goods for sale to foreigners in North Korea. At the official rate of exchange of 1.85 won to $1, one won equals $0.54, but foreigners exchanging U.S. dollars for won in North Korea have reported different exchange rates of 1.57, 1.69, 1.71, 1.80, and 1.94 to $1 depending on where they exchanged their money. At the official rate of 1.85 won to $1, overnight lodging in Pyongyang, which would cost a North Korean up to 3.8 won (not including meals) should cost an American about $2. However, hotel costs are far higher than that for foreigners. An average meal at a hotel, which costs a North Korean 2 or 3 won costs a foreigner from 10 to 12 won (about $6). Some foreign visitors have reported paying as much as from $15 to 20 for a meal worth only about a third of that in the United States or Japan.

Dollar prices at the foreigners' store in Pyongyang are similarly inflated. Tomatoes, which sell for 0.3–0.6 won per kilogram to North Koreans, sell for 5 or 6 won at the Foreigners' Store in Pyongyang; cotton and nylon cloth, which cost North Koreans from 2 to 4 and from 7 to 12 won, respectively, cost foreigners from 10 to 20 and from 20 to 40 won per meter; an ordinary shirt, which costs a North Korean from 14 to 16 won, costs a foreigner at least 25 won. Similarly inflated prices have been noted at the Foreign Seamen's Club in Haeju and other stores selling goods to foreigners. At the Seamen's Club, apples and pears, which cost North Koreans from 0.6 to 1 won per kilogram, were selling for from 3.4 to 3.6 won per kilogram. Foreigners have often made the mistake of quoting prices at these foreigners' stores as representative of the prices North Koreans pay for goods, without realizing that there is no relationship between the two. One needs to be very careful to exclude prices from the foreigners' stores in sorting through available price information on the internal price structure. Since few foreigners are taken to North Korean stores, one has to rely basically on defector information in this regard.

In short, the regime charges foreigners even higher—much higher—prices than it charges the privileged few in North Korea who can afford to buy luxury goods. Moreover, it often suddenly increases the price of goods sold to foreigners or changes the exchange rate for foreign currencies to make an even greater profit. The same room in the Potonggang Hotel that cost 60 won in 1975 cost 66 won a night in 1977.

Prices in North Korea are now higher than prices in China and about three times as high as prices in the United States or Japan. Obviously, the regime has found a good way of acquiring desperately needed foreign exchange to repay its overdue loans from Western creditors. Foreigners' shops accept only Japanese yen, U.S. dollars and British pounds.

FAMILY FINANCES

The reality of high prices and low wages has wrought a social revolution of unprecedented proportions—all the more revolutionary considering North Korea's Asian context. In the short span of thirty years the Communists transformed a society in which women traditionally stayed in the home into the most modern of societies in the sense of women working outside the home. In North Korea, virtually every able-bodied woman works from the time of leaving school until retirement age; the only exception are wives of the elite. The country may well rank first among the countries of the world in this respect. Although the regime has released no statistics on the percentage of the female population of working age in the labor force, all available information supports the conclusion that it must be close to 100 percent, which is higher than it is in other Communist countries and much higher than it is in most non-Communist countries and other Asian countries.

Their new role in life has been forced on North Korean women by economic necessity; it has clearly not been a question of equal rights, or women's lib. Older women especially resent the need to work. The younger generation, imbued with Communist ideals, may be somewhat less resistant. Typical of the case studies is the story of the mother of five children, who was forced to work as an elevator operator simply to make ends meet, despite her social position as the wife of a high-level military official in the privileged circle in Pyongyang. Her monthly salary of 70 won (on top of her husband's salary of 150 won per month) was essential to support a family of seven. With that many children, the family enjoyed few luxuries, except an occasional dinner at a restaurant. Only the privileged would think of having five children; indeed, that choice might be considered one of the real privileges of the elite.

If a husband makes less than 100 won per month, a wife has no choice but to work, especially if there are children. The average working-class family needs two working members of the family to gain a minimum degree of comfort. As it is, two average incomes, totaling from 120 to 180 won per month, barely cover expenses for food and clothing, depending on the number of children.

The number of children in a family is clearly the crucial factor in the equation. A highly paid Kim Il-song University professor, who earns 200 won per month, and his wife, who earns another 170 won per month, who had no children were reported to be able to save about 50 percent (or 185 won) of their income. Another professor at the same university and his wife, who had four children and whose combined income was something less than 370 won per month, could save only about 10 percent (or 35 won) of their income. A third couple with a combined income of 200 won and three children was able to save about 10 percent of their income (or 20 won). Depending on the size of his family and whether or not his wife works, a cabinet minister may or may not be accumulating savings; if his wife does not work, as most cabinet ministers' wives do not, he may actually have less disposable income and smaller savings than the university couple mentioned above. Of course, he will still have a higher standard of living by dint of all the perks of his office.

The simple fact is that most people (except for the elite) cannot afford to have more than two children, even with both parents working. It is not surprising that the average number of children per family is 2.2, low for an Asian country. The pure economics of the situation has forced most parents to limit the size of their families, against their own wishes for more children and contrary to traditional Asian mores.

All one has to do is to look at a typical family's budget to appreciate the economic forces at work. Monthly expenditures for basic necessities for a family of five (depending on the age of the children), membership in different organizations, personal habits (smoking), and the season of the year (heating), run between 75 to 100, about two-thirds of the average family income (see Table 16.3). At the higher end, family expenditures of 100 won, which would be above the national average wage and would imply a second income, would still cover only the basic necessities: rice and vegetables and fish occasionally (no meat), standard issue of work clothes and student uniforms (no dress clothes), necessary haircuts and public baths (no hair styling including permanents and no private baths), travel to and from work (no trips outside the city), and possibly a movie or two but not the theater or a dinner in a restaurant.

Even with the addition of a second income, resulting in a combined family income of from 150 to 160 won per month (the national average), a five-member family cannot afford much more than the basic necessities. With shoes selling for from 5 to 10 won, a dress cotton shirt from 14 to 16 won, a winter cap for from 10 to 15 won, and a ready-made winter suit (synthetic fiber) for from 40 to 60 won, an extra 50 or 60 won per month does not buy much in the way of extra clothing for five people. It virtually rules out the major purchase of a watch or bicycle, unless the family is willing to skimp on food and clothing and every-

Table 16.3
Monthly Expenditures for Basic Necessities for a Family of Five

Basic Necessity	Cost (won)
Rice	6–7
Side dishes (vegetable and fish only)	20–25
Heating and cooking fuels	4–7
Water and electricity	3
Clothes	15–20
Haircut (twice a month)	3
Bathing	2
Transportation	2
Party fees	2
Factory and other dues	2–5
School supplies	5–10
Sweets for children	5
Cigarettes	0–5
Recreation	5–10
TOTAL	74–106

thing else for several months. It does allow more in the way of recreation—more trips to the zoo or to a children's recreation park, an occasional dinner out, or possibly a trip to visit relatives. And it does afford a better diet, meaning a more varied diet, including chicken and pork once or twice a week and beef maybe once a month.

It seems fairly clear that only the privileged (with a combined family income of over 200 won per month) can afford to have two or three children in relative comfort—meaning the enjoyment of a more varied diet, some recreation together and extra clothing, and warmer clothing or perhaps more stylish suits and dresses. It is not a luxurious life by any means.

This is substantiated by firsthand accounts of children of privileged families, who, although earning well over 200 won per month, felt lucky to be given a few extra won on special occasions to take their school friends out to dinner. A professional couple without children can do fairly well, but not if they have children. Defectors say that, "it takes ten years of constant saving for parents to prepare for the wedding of their children." Costs involved include the costs of the wedding ceremony and reception and money spent in setting the couple up in housekeeping. The more money a family can provide, the better the chances of getting a good husband or wife for their son or daughter. Even the privileged would never think of splurging on a television or refrigerator so long as they had unmarried children at home to provide for.

If one is not of high enough rank to get a television or refrigerator with one's apartment or as a special gift from the government, there is practically no chance of ever acquiring one. If one thing is clear from the statistics on family income, it is the improbability of most people ever saving enough money to buy anything of greater value than a clock, a rice cooker, a blanket chest, or a quilt. Indeed a cotton padded quilt is likely to be one of a North Korean's most treasured possessions, probably a gift from his parents on his wedding. He is not likely to make an equally expensive purchase until he buys the same thing for his children, after years of saving.

SHOPPING

The sense of uniformity reflected in a standard price for goods and services throughout North Korea is reinforced in the way Kim organized commercial activities throughout the country. From the beginning, he embraced the idea of self-sufficient neighborhoods featuring living and shopping facilities together. As the chief engineer of the city planning department in Pyongyang explained it:

> The inhabitants' life is taken into account in city planning. One block of living quarters comprises 5,000–6,000 inhabitants, which is administered as a unit (called "*dong*"). Shops supplying rice, vegetables, fish and other foodstuffs are located within a range of 500 meters of all residents. In every *dong* there is a barbershop, beauty parlor, tailoring shop, public bathhouse, shoe repair shop, noodle factory, fuel supply depot, a branch post office, a clinic, a children's nursery school, and a children's library.

All the shops and other facilities within one *dong* are administered by the government administrative committee for that *dong*. In rural areas, where there are fewer inhabitants, the same group of stores is provided for each county, whose population probably is also about from 5,000 to 6,000 people. The organizational structure, which is very simple and direct, is illustrated in Chart 16.1

In Pyongyang many of the newer multistory apartment buildings, which house thousands of residents, have this same cluster of stores on the first floor of the apartments—a major convenience to the privileged residents of these modern facilities. Wherever one travels in North Korea, one sees the same grouping of stores that Kim considered essential to everyday living. The facilities may vary in terms of physical appearance and attractiveness, but they are stocked with essentially the same food, and clothing, and household wares. Only the stores in Pyongyang and other large cities would stock televisions, sewing machines, and refrigerators, but most stores would probably carry wristwatches and bicycles.

The residents of each apartment building and each neighborhood are expected to shop in their own neighborhood stores; indeed, they are registered to shop only at their own neighborhood stores. They cannot redeem their rice rations elsewhere. From the viewpoint of most people shopping is easy because all of the stores essential to everyday living are within easy walking distance. From the regime's standpoint, there is a greater control over consumption. Each store can track the purchases of its registered customers; the store can simply subtract the amount of rice bought each day from a family's combined monthly rice ration. There is no need for coupons. If a family is going out to dinner at a restaurant, it can authorize the purchase of so many grams of rice by

Chart 16.1
Organizational Structure of Commercial Enterprises
within a *Dong*

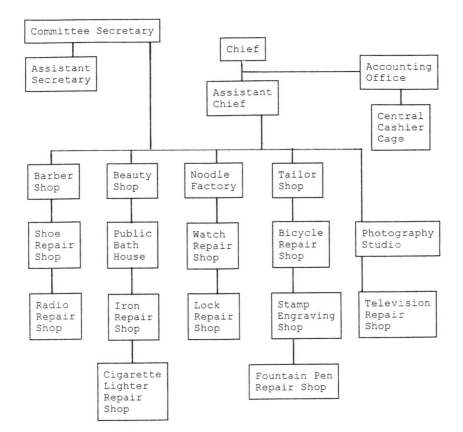

issuing coupons for that amount and simultaneously deducting the amount from the family's running account. Similar records can be kept on a family's purchases of sugar and other rationed goods. It is much easier to enforce the rationing system this way than by giving coupons for every purchase of a rationed commodity at whatever store the individual chooses.

The carefully planned availability of essentially the same kinds of stores to all people, wherever they live, contributes to the sense of homogeneity that is so striking about North Korea. Just as one travels around the country and sees the same prefabricated dining halls at different factories and schools and military installations, one sees the same group of stores, often in the same layout, at every cooperative farm, every major military installation, and every neighborhood in the cities. The people are all exposed to essentially the same shopping experience and environment. In the larger cities, there are also bookstores, photo studios, pet stores, flower shops, music stores, optical shops, and sports equipment stores scattered around the city, but most shopping is done in the neighborhood stores.

The mode of shopping is the same everywhere too, which also contributes to the sense of uniformity. There is a central cashier for each cluster of stores. An individual must first tell a sales clerk what he wants to buy; the clerk then enters the item and the price on a form, which the customer takes to the cashier; after paying for the item, the customer takes the receipt to the sales clerk or to the barber or the post office official or to the public bathhouse. This procedure, which is standard everywhere, is modeled after the Soviet practice.

In North Korea, unlike the Soviet Union of former days, one does not hear so many complaints about poor service or the rude behavior of the clerks in the stores. The regime's control over the people is too tight to allow such infractions of the rules. People do not wait in lines the way they did in the former Soviet Union, either, because of the controlled number of shoppers in most stores.

In organizing North Korean society on the self-sufficient neighborhood concept, Kim avoided some of the other problems encountered by Soviet consumers who complained of "having to walk long distances to get a pair of shoes repaired or find some similarly trivial but necessary service." In the Soviet Union, residents of many housing subdivisions were forced to shop downtown or at long distances from home by the lack of forethought in planning or the delay in constructing commercial areas near residential areas. This is not true in the DPRK, where living and shopping facilities have been constructed together as a unit. North Korean cities have no real downtown, in a shopping sense. In comparison with the former Soviet Union, shoppers do not have to carry packages long distances on the bus or subway. Whatever they might buy in Pyongyang's specialty stores they would have to carry home on the bus or subway, but this would not be their everyday shopping. Foreign visitors have noted "long lines of people carrying large bundles, waiting in line for the bus and subway." These people probably had been shopping at one of Pyongyang's several big department stores. In 1977 there were two such department stores, known as Department Store 1 and and Department Store 2, but since then other stores have been opened. These larger department stores, typically five-stories high, are open seven days a week from 9:00 A.M. to 9:00 P.M. They are usually quite crowded. They are hardly typical of most North Korean stores, however.

Finally, there is no sense of competition with other consumers, which was a major irritant to Soviet shoppers. With much less money to spend, North Korean consumers buy many fewer items. Most household furnishings are provided with housing. Major purchases of household linens and blankets and kitchen pots and pans are made when a couple gets married. Apparently, parents spend most of their savings to buy these things for their children. They make few major purchases after that except clothing. There is no need to shop for everyday clothes since they are provided by one's work unit or factory. Since only the privileged few can afford extra clothing, there is not the keen competition for clothes, especially good-quality clothes, that there was in the Soviet Union. Most purchases are made for food, school supplies, personal hygiene items, and entertainment.

The hassle associated with shopping in North Korea, then, is occasioned by the fact that everyone shops at the same time: on the way to work, on the way home, or during the midday break. There is no other time to shop because virtually everyone is at work or attending school. On the way to work, people stop by the stores to place their orders for the evening meal; on the way home, they pick up their food; during the break, they do errands, which might include a trip to the barber shop or beauty parlor, or they shop for school and office supplies. Visitors to North Korea all attest to the emptiness of stores during the day except during these rush hours.

North Koreans must also shop everyday. Without refrigeration, most people have no means of keeping food fresh, especially in summer.

Although Kim's planning avoided many of the problems encountered by Soviet consumers, North Koreans still have not solved the tedious problem of having to shop every day.

17

Consumer Goods and Services

Having gotten a sense of the way in which the regime controls the distribution of food and other consumer goods through both monetary and nonmonetary means, including a system of rationing and special stores, one must then investigate the less obvious controls placed on the quality of goods distributed through various government networks to appreciate the different living standards of the elite and privileged, ordinary and underprivileged. Important differences are hidden beneath the surface.

FOOD

The North Koreans have had little to cheer about food, the most politically charged consumer issue, for years. Having achieved the goals of earlier economic plans in ensuring a minimum subsistence for everyone, the Communists failed to meet the goals of the six-year plan from 1970 to 1976, the seven-year plan from 1978 to 1984, and subsequent plans in raising food consumption much beyond that level. Due to a series of natural calamities, including prolonged droughts and severe cold fronts, which have resulted in poor harvests and difficulties in meeting export quotas of nonagricultural products which, in turn, required the lowering of food imports (meats and canned fish) and the diversion of agricultural products (rice and fruits) from domestic consumption to export, the regime has not been able to raise daily rice rations or introduce greater variety into the diet. After enjoying a steady improvement in their diet in the late 1950s and 1960s, North Korean consumers must be very disappointed with the lack of progress since then. Although any dissatisfaction may have been somewhat alleviated by improvements in other areas, such as housing and clothing, it has been held in check primarily by tight political controls.

Food grains—the staple of the North Korean diet—have been rationed since 1957, and there has been no significant increase in these rations during the past thirty years. Information on this subject is probably more voluminous and more consistent than information on any other aspect of North Korean life. Thus, we can be fairly confident of the accuracy of the statistics on grain consumption cited in Table 17.1.

Rations are allocated on the basis of the kind of work one does—heavy versus light work—rather than on the basis of rank. A general serving with the ground forces gets 700 grams, whereas a noncommissioned officer on sea duty gets 800 grams; both get less than an ocean fisherman or a coal miner. A military officer can have his rations cut with a change of assignment from the Joint Security Area

Table 17.1
Per Capita Consumption of Grain

Worker	Daily Consumption (in grams)
Miners, blast-furnace operators, iron casters and certain other heavy industrial workers, defense industrial workers, deep-sea navy divers, ocean fishermen	900
Military personnel serving with the Military Armistice Commission	850
Air force pilots, naval personnel on sea duty, agents of the Special Liaison Department, and other specialized military officers	800
All other military officers, all other heavy industrial workers, all light industrial workers, clerical workers, technicians, engineers, government officials, teachers and professors, party officials, college students	700
High school students, disabled persons retired from work on medical disability, females over age 55 and males over age 61	400
Preschool children (depending on age)	200–300

to Pyongyang, even while being promoted in rank. Despite their rank, cabinet members and vice premiers get 700 grams per day, the average ration. There is an interesting equality about grain rations, in other words, based on the energy involved in one's job, rather than on the status of the job. If a person takes a day off from his job, he does not receive his full food ration for that day. For this reason, workers stay on the job unless they are seriously ill.

Rations for children are considered generous compared to rations for adults. A family consisting of adults only is generally less well off, in terms of rationed food, than a family with children. It is not at all uncommon for childless households to be short one or two days' supply of grain each month. These households are forced to subsist on gruel or noodles after their supply of grains run out. Of course, they can compensate for their disadvantage in rationed foods by buying more nonrationed foods since, without children, they have relatively more disposable income than families with children. They might also be able to buy rice and other food grains on the black market. Families with young children are sometimes willing to sell extra rice at black market prices. However, at black market prices of 2 or 3 won per kilogram, which is between twenty-five and thirty-five times the regular price of rice, only small amounts of rice are sold secretly.

It should be mentioned that North Korean families never receive grain rations for anyone other than members of the immediate family. When they have visiting guests or relatives, or a wedding or funeral, they must ask their guests to bring their own rice rations.

Ironically, farmers are more likely to suffer grain shortages than people living in cities. The rations for those living in the cities, plus the extra supplies that the government requisitions for export or for the military or other purposes, are taken from cooperative farms, and then the rest of the harvest is divided among the farmers on the basis of the work performed and the size of the harvest. In years of poor harvests, the farmers are more likely to suffer shortfalls in consumption than the urban population, although it too has experienced cuts in grain rations in bad times.

The grain ration has officially remained the same since 1957, but there have been temporary (unofficial) reductions in rations at times of crisis. It is difficult to be absolutely sure of the precise duration of these reductions, but we have corroborating evidence as to the general timing of some. In either 1968 or 1969, not long after the *Pueblo* incident, the government reduced rations by three kilograms per person per

month (equal to a four-days ration). Housewives were expressing dissatisfaction in carefully guarded private conversations. It was rumored
that the policy was part of the government's effort to stockpile food in
the event of hostilities. The heightened tension after the capture of the
Pueblo made the story plausible, but it is more likely that the shortfall in
rice production necessitated cutbacks in consumption. The regime has
repeatedly claimed to be stockpiling food in preparation for hostilities,
and the population has tended to believe the government. However,
there is good reason for thinking that no such stockpiles exist.

Rations returned to normal about 1972. However, in early 1976,
they were cut again, this time by from 20 to 30 percent. Again, the official line was the need to stockpile food in the event of war; but again,
two years of drought in 1975 and 1976 made economic causes the
more likely explanation for ration cuts. Not only were workers given
only 25 or 26 days' supply of grain each month, but the percent of rice
in their total grain ration was also cut. Apparently, these cuts continued
for years, not so much because of poor harvests but because of
stepped-up rice exports to meet balance-of-trade deficits. The disas-
trous weather conditions of the past several years, resulting in unprece-
dentedly poor harvests, are certain to have brought drastic cuts in
rations, bordering on widespread famine, according to some reports.
One wonders if the regime deliberately creates periods of heightened
tensions with South Korea and the United States at times of agricultural
crisis to create a plausible explanation for the food cuts. Recurring periods of aggressive foreign policy, abruptly abandoned before there is any
real chance of war, could well be explained by domestic economic crises
that force the regime to justify continued sacrifice in the absence of any
hope for immediate improvement in food consumption. The regime
calculates that it can contain international tensions, short of war, until
the food situation improves.

Despite their dissatisfaction, the people have accepted the reductions
stoically. Most North Koreans believe the government's claim to be
stockpiling rice for distribution to the starving South Korean masses on
the happy day of reunification. They would probably be shocked to
learn the truth that no such large stockpiles exist and that rice exports
have paid for North Korea's overdue debt repayments and imports of
nuclear plants.

As important as one's total allotment of grain is, the percentage of
rice in the grain ration is equally important. North Koreans vastly prefer
rice over all other food grains. Only the elite, laborers assigned to very

hazardous jobs, some military officers on special assignment, and sick patients in hospitals receive their full grain allotment in rice. Typically, the privileged (the 1 million residents of Pyongyang plus another 600,000 North Koreans) receive 90 percent of their grain rations in rice and 10 percent in corn; the rest of the population receives 70 percent in rice and the rest in corn.

The decline in rice consumption in recent years has been a major source of dissatisfaction. The substitution of other food grains has been of meager compensation. North Koreans have not developed a taste for corn, barley, or wheat. Foreigners have described the grains served in lieu of rice as "a dirty-looking millet and barley mixture" which they generally find to be "unedible." Although North Koreans may not have as sophisticated food tastes as these foreigners, they have a definite preference for rice over other food grains and a clear disenchantment with the regime's practice of substituting other grains for rice.

Only the very few who receive their full allotment of grain in rice can eat rice three times a day. Seven hundred grams of uncooked rice will provide approximately three medium-size bowls of steamed rice. A North Korean, who receive 50 percent of his grain ration in rice (about 350 grams), is eating about 1-1/2 bowls of rice a day, supplemented by another 350 grams of wheat flour or corn meal. He is likely to eat rice twice a day and corn at the third meal.

The kind of rice a North Korean is allotted, polished or unpolished, is also important. Only a very limited number of high government and party officials enjoy polished rice. A cabinet minister who receives 700 grams of grain a day but receives his entire grain allotment in polished rice is more favored than a blast-furnace operator who receives 900 grams of grain per day, 50 percent in unpolished rice, 40 percent in corn, and 10 percent in wheat flour. The North Koreans have found a way to ensure an adequate diet for those who do heavy work and need more food to eat while still preserving the privilege of the elite who get the finest, if not the most, rice—not to mention all the extras in the way of meats, fresh fruits, and imported delicacies. Thus, there is an element of fairness (in the amount of rice) but a cross-current of social class distinction (in the quality of the rice) in the rice rationing system.

Other than grain, the only foodstuffs that are rationed are cooking oils, meats, soy sauce, soybean paste, bean curd, and kimchi (Korea's native dish). These foods, like grains, must be purchased with ration cards; they are not distributed free, though their prices are considerably lower than nonrationed food of the same type. Cooking oils are in chronic short supply; the ration of one liter per family per month is apparently far from adequate. Each family gets two or three kilograms of soybean paste and two kilograms of soy sauce a month, also inadequate. Meat is even more scarce. One or two kilograms of meat is rationed to every household (about 500 grams or 1.1 pounds for each family member) at subsidized low prices on North Korea's five national holidays: New Year's day, Kim Il-song's birthday (15 April), May Day, Liberation Day (15 August), and National Founding Day (9 September) and on special occasions like weddings and funerals. The great majority of North Koreans eat meat only on these special days. This may not be as much of a deprivation to North Koreans, however, as it seems to Americans. Most families in Korea in prewar days "could afford meat only once a month, sometimes only once every six months." The average North Korean today probably eats about the same amount of meat as fifty years ago.

Meat is available for sale on an unrestricted basis (no ration coupons required) but at very high prices which only the privileged can afford. Residents of Pyongyang eat pork or chicken once or twice a week and beef once or twice a month, but this is hardly typical of the majority of the population. Dishes using pork and beef are also available at high-class restaurants in major cities. Ordinary people are more likely to eat meat at these state-operated restaurants than to buy it for home cooking.

One of the advantages of serving in the military is the privilege of eating meat three or four times a week, possibly more often. The authorized amount of meat is 75 grams per day. Although this amount is usually issued, the men may not eat it every day. When meat is supplied to military units, it is usually in the form of live pigs. During the hot season, military units have to consume all of the available fresh meat since there are no refrigeration facilities. Thus, there may be temporary shortages several days of the week. If they do not eat meat for three days in a row, a four-day amount of meat will be given on the fourth day.

Meat supplies consist almost exclusively of pork; only 300 grams of beef are issued two or three times a winter. Some military units raise their own pigs, but others are supplied with live pigs once or twice a week. Most have their own farm on which they also grow vegetables, fruits, and spices. Each company is given a food production quota, in accordance with annual food production plans issued by the Ministry of National Defense. These food supplies are supplemented by other food, particularly rice, which is procured from cooperative farms. Each man is issued 750 grams of vegetables and another 750 grams of rice daily. These military food rations are far superior to those of the average civilian. Even so, many young NKPA servicemen are reported to be unsatisfied; others in the military think they are well fed (see Table 17.2).

Young men discharged from the military must adjust to a drop in food consumption, especially meat and polished rice. As civilians, they will probably eat meat five or six times a year, after having had it regularly as part of their military rations. This is one of many examples of favoritism to the military, another is warm woolen clothing which most North Koreans would dearly love to have.

The quality of meat, especially beef, is very poor. Foreigners find it tough and stringy. Only old or sick cattle are slaughtered for food; healthy cattle are kept for work or milking. The North Koreans are reported to be breeding milking cows by crossing an ox or water buffalo with a female cow to get a hybrid second-generation cow. Most people prefer pork to beef, believing that pork is more sanitary. Other meats in the North Korean diet include rabbit, duck, and dogmeat. Dogs are raised for food, not pets. Kim Il-song reportedly had a distinct preference for dogmeat. Not surprisingly, there are several well-known dogmeat restaurants in Pyongyang.

There is some confusion about whether fish is rationed. It is hard to reconcile the conflicting information on the subject except to say that fish is in short supply, whether it is available on a first-come, first-served basis or a rationing system. The principal marine products in the diet

Table 17.2
Daily Food Rations for Enlisted Men and Officers
up to the Rank of Lieutenant Colonel

Food	Quantity (in grams)	Food	Quantity (in grams)
Rice	750	Pork	75
Wheat flour	50	Fish	50
Edible oil	20	Red peppers (dried)	2
Soy sauce	30	Fruits	unknown
Soybean paste	100	Vinegar—daily (from May to Sept.)	
Salt	20	Potatoes—daily (from Nov. to March)	
Vegetables	750		

are pollack, yellow corvina, squid, tuna, shrimp, lobster, sea slugs, octopus, crab, whale, oysters, and herring. Because of the lack of refrigeration, fresh fish cannot be provided to most cities (except Pyongyang); people eat mostly salted fish.

The Communists have not changed the age-old Korean custom of each family preparing its own supply of kimchi. In early November of each year, each family is issued from ten to fifteen kilograms of cabbage and from twenty to thirty kilograms of radishes, plus other seasonings, to make roughly twenty kilograms of kimchi. By the end of November, most families have completed the pickling of these ingredients. Kimchi is stored in large earthenware containers buried in the ground. The contents stay fresh during the winter except, apparently, the kimchi of some apartment residents who complain that they have no ground in which to bury their pickle jars; their kimchi goes sour within a few months.

Vegetables, which are apparently relatively abundant are not rationed. There may seem to be little variety in the vegetables, from an American point of view, but it is the same variety as in South Korea or in Korea traditionally: cabbage, bean sprouts, turnips, green peppers, spinach, onions, pumpkins, red beans, and soybeans. The average person eats about 300 kilograms of vegetables a year, or about 90 grams a day; military personnel consume more. Although to Americans an unrelieved diet of rice and vegetables probably seems dreadfully unvaried, particularly with so little variety in the vegetables themselves, this is the traditional Korean diet.

The major fruits are apples, peaches, and pears, but it is not easy for North Koreans to buy fresh fruit, even in season, because most of the fresh fruit crop, especially the better fruit, is exported. The fresh fruits available to North Koreans are definitely of inferior quality compared to exported items. Foreigners have commented on the "dry, unsavoriness" of North Korean apples and peaches, a striking contrast to South Korea's delicious fruit, which is one of South Korea's great agricultural triumphs. It must be remembered, of course, that the traditional fruit-growing area in Korea—the so-called fruit bowl—is in the south. Most of North Korea's fruit that is not exportable is canned for domestic consumption. Canned apples and pears are described as "very irregular in shape and size, not fit for marketing in other countries, and far inferior to South Korean canned fruit."

Sweets are popular, and there is little concern for the dangers of sugar in the diet. Ice cream, made from soybeans, is a favorite treat in summer. Expenditures for candies account for a surprisingly large percentage of family expenditures. Special stores sell cakes and candies; when a new shipment of candy arrives, there are long lines at the counters for two or three days until the supplies are exhausted and the people have to wait several days for another shipment. Confectioneries are particularly scarce in rural areas, and farmers have to travel to nearby towns or cities to buy them.

In short, the basic diet for most North Koreans is rice and vegetables, three times a day, with fruit occasionally (when in season), meat five or six times a year, and chicken two or three times a month. The monotony of the diet is vividly illustrated in the following description of one defector's diet over a period of years:

	Breakfast	Lunch	Supper	Snacks
Main food	Miscellaneous grains (rice, corn, barley)	Same	Noodles	None
Side dishes	Kimchi, hot sauce, fish, vegetable soup, wild greens	Same	Same	None

Another defector described his diet as follows:

	Breakfast	Lunch	Supper	Snacks
Main food	Rice and misc. grains	Same	Noodles	
Side dishes	Kimchi, pork, fish, vegetable soup, wild greens, mushrooms	Same	Same	Fruits (in season), canned apples, cider

Foreign seamen and technicians who have observed the lunches brought by North Korean workers to work corroborate defector reports. Port workers at the ports of Hungnam, Ch'ongjin, Nampo, and Haeju have been observed eating box lunches consisting simply of semipolished rice or a mixture of rice and other grains and bits of pickled vegetables.

The only other firsthand accounts of typical North Korean meals come from foreigners hospitalized in North Korean hospitals. An injured sailor who spent three weeks in a North Korean hospital in Chongjin was given the exact same meal three times a day for three weeks: a bowl of brown, unpolished rice and a side dish of pollack and kelp. He grew sick of the same menu and asked for something different, whereupon he was given bread instead of rice once a day. Another seaman in another North Korean hospital got a bowl of unpolished rice, soybean paste soup, two fried eggs, and a small piece of pork for every meal for eight days. North Korean patients in the same room said they had never eaten eggs or pork before.

Another seaman hospitalized in yet another hospital saw North Korean nurses collecting and eating rice left over from patients' meals. On one occasion, the doctors and nurses caught and killed a stray dog in the hospital compound to make soup for the seaman.

Thus, whatever its caloric value, the diet is not a balanced or varied one. Heavy on carbohydrates, it is low in fats, proteins, vitamins, and minerals. Whether he or she lives in the city or countryside, the average North Korean eats almost no meat, limited amounts of fish and poultry, very little fruit, and few fats. The diet revolves around cereals, in carefully regulated amounts, and available vegetables, fresh and pickled.

The effect of the diet on health is difficult to determine. Judging from pictures of North Koreans, from both official and foreign sources, the people look robust and healthy. Foreign technicians who have lived in North Korea for months report having seen no Koreans who seemed to be suffering from undernourishment or any kind of nutritional deficiency. On the other hand, other visitors to the country have thought that many workers looked undernourished, pale, and thin, lacking in motivation or incentive. Foreign businessmen have noted low morale of North Korean trade officials who complain about the shortage of rice, sugar, meats, and milk. Others have found North Koreans listless, lazy, and unenergetic. It is difficult to determine the cause for such behavior and appearance. No doubt, people are tired and exhausted from overwork, constant political indoctrination, lack of sleep, and boredom. Thus, the problem may not be a problem of food, basically, but of other things, perhaps in combination with deficiencies in diet. Much more information is needed to make any kind of definitive judgment.

SMOKING AND DRINKING

Expenditures for cigarettes account for a surprisingly large percentage of family expenditures. Kim Il-song, like many of the top leaders, was a chain smoker. It was no secret that he smoked constantly, drank a lot of coffee and tea, but generally refrained from alcoholic drinks. Many foreigners have observed that their North Korean guides were chain smokers. Perhaps, fortunately for them, most North Korean cigarettes are very mild.

Apparently, periodic campaigns have been mounted to reduce cigarette smoking, although the regime is in a hypocritical position in this regard. On Kim's personal instructions, military personnel were not allowed to smoke. After discharge from the army, there are not the same strictures against smoking, although the government discourages young people from smoking. College students are not supposed to smoke, but, according to a reliable source, as many as 70 or 80 percent had been smoking from the age of fifteen or sixteen, not openly, but secretly in the dormitories, behind closed doors, with the windows open. Most North Koreans smoke inexpensive, nonfiltered, North Korean–made cigarettes; it is considered prestigious to smoke the more expensive, imported filtered cigarettes. In the countryside, farmers make their own cigarettes out of tobacco leaves wrapped in pieces of newspaper.

In their on-again, off-again efforts to reduce smoking, the authorities have used the arguments that smoking is "harmful to human health, a waste of national resources, and a feudalistic and bourgeois custom." However, they have not stressed the health risk to the extent that the United States has. As it is, smoking is becoming more popular, rather than less, especially among young people, who have few ways to rebel. Smoking provides one way to rebel. The only real constraint to the spread of cigarette smoking seems to be the limited supply of cigarettes and the aggravation of standing in lines to buy one pack at a time. The shortage of cigarettes, combined with the growing demand for them, led the regime to begin rationing cigarettes in the fall of 1980. At that time each person was allowed to buy seven packs (20 cigarettes to a pack) per month. North Koreans, who had previously asked for food and drink from foreign seamen who visited North Korean ports, started to ask for cigarettes. North Korean stevedores were seen taking cigarette butts from their pockets and rerolling them into a single cigarette.

There is not the same ambivalence on the part of the regime when it comes to drinking. Alcohol is not rationed so much as it is priced out of the market. On national holidays, it is sold at subsidized low prices, just like meat. Otherwise, beer and liquor are available at exorbitant prices which only the privileged can afford. The Communists have all but wiped out the traditional Korean custom of men getting together after work on weekdays and on weekends for a social gathering of drink and song, a custom that still flourishes in South Korea. There are no bars in North Korea (where only drinks are sold). Beer and liquor can be purchased at some of the more expensive restaurants and hotels, but since the great majority of North Koreans cannot afford to go there, they are likely to enjoy a drink only on national holidays and at weddings and funerals.

Naturally, some young men, who can afford the price, drink a lot, although they usually confine their drinking to home. Instances of public drunkenness are rare. Drinking can adversely affect one's career. This is particularly true of the Foreign Ministry where officials, serving abroad, have much greater access to liquor. The subject of a person's drinking habits is likely to be discussed at the weekly self-criticism sessions at every embassy abroad. Apparently these sessions have had beneficial results in the reformation of problem drinkers, North Korea's answer to Alcoholics Anonymous.

It is interesting to consider the effect of the virtual abolition of social drinking on a society in which there are so few escapes from the constant tension of hard work, incessant political indoctrination, and total lack of personal freedom. Of all the changes in custom, the loss of any opportunity for men to get together socially for an evening of singing and drinking may be one of the Communists' most basic sociological changes, considering its long-standing tradition. It is another of the escape valves that the regime has systematically closed.

Overview

The picture that emerges from all of this is of a society provided with the basics, as far as nutrition, with little variety in the diet, few luxury foods, virtually no social drinking, but a tolerance for smoking. Compared to pre-World War II days, things have improved. People who lived through the Japanese occupation and the Korean War know how much better they eat now than during the hungry years before and after the war. They can appreciate the accomplishment of having wiped out starvation and widespread malnutrition. A Korean American who returned to North Korea for a visit after thirty years in the United States expressed these feelings: "My impression of the country, especially compared with my childhood, is that it is prosperous. When I was growing up (my family were and still are typical farmers), we could afford meat only once a month (sometimes six months). Frequently even rice could not be obtained, and we had to live on barley and corn." The older people may think the Communists have done well to provide a diet to every North Korean that provides more than an adequate caloric intake even for the intense activity that is demanded of the population. There is no question that the people have plenty to eat, in terms of total calories. Moreover, allowance is made for those who do heavier work and need to eat more. In short, many probably feel that Kim Il-song went a long way toward solving the food problem that has plagued the North Koreans for decades. Others, especially younger people, may not be so happy. In terms of the recent past, things have not improved and, in some respect, have actually deteriorated.

Disappointment over the food situation has probably been intensified over the years by the raising of false expectations. Dramatic improvements in food supplies in the late 1970s and 1980s engendered high hopes for continued progress during the 1990s. No such dramatic improvement in food consumption has occurred. Instead, North Korean hopes have been dashed by an actual decline in rice consumption, if not in grain consumption, by continued shortages of fresh fruits, meats (except poultry), fish, kimchi, cooking oils, cigarettes, and liquor. The one conspicuous exception has been the improvement—a dramatic improvement—in the availability of poultry and poultry products. The average North Korean now eats two or three eggs a week (as scrambled eggs, raw eggs on noodles, or boiled eggs in soups).

Thus, the food situation looms as the most serious consumer problem for the regime, all other consumer areas have registered much more significant gains during the past twenty years. The people want more rice, meat, fish, oils, fruits, and candies; in short, more variety of foods. They also want better-quality food—more polished rice, better meat, and tastier fresh fruits.

Whatever their complaints, North Koreans appear to have accepted food shortages stoically. Because they have been told about food crises all over the world, most people believe that things are no worse in North Korea than in most other countries and much better than in South Korea, where they have been led to believe the people are starving. They probably think the regime has done the best that could be expected, under the circumstances. They are impressed with the country's gains in irrigation techniques, which have helped combat the effects of droughts; and they are also impressed with the gains in mechanization, chemical fertilizers, and improved food strains. What they do not realize is how much food, especially rice and fruits, is exported. Instead, they believe that the government is stockpiling food to feed the hungry masses in South Korea as soon as reunification is achieved—a worthy goal, in their view, considering the regime's success in making reunification the all-important goal of all North Koreans. Another reason for the people's stoic acceptance of food shortages may be their satisfaction with gains in other consumer areas.

Considering all the controls in the society, the North Korean consumer can be expected to continue to be as docile and long-suffering as he has always been, even in an area that so vitally affects his well-being as food. Barring another year or two of the natural calamities that seriously affected agricultural production in 1996 and 1997, the regime should be able to handle consumer dissatisfaction much as it always has, with no lessening of its controls and continued rationalizing of its difficulties with excuses that the people accept as legitimate.

CLOTHING

Most visitors to North Korea describe the people as well dressed and healthy in appearance. It should be remembered that most visitors go only to Pyongyang. Increasing numbers, but still very few, visit Wonsan, on the east coast, and Nampo, on the west coast, the two cities on either end of North Korea's only turnpike which traverses the width of the country and connects Pyongyang with both seacoasts. A very few Westerners, primarily technicians directing the construction and initial production of North Korea's newest and largest industrial plants, have lived for short periods of time in cities other than Pyongyang, Wonsan, or Nampo. Visitors have also been allowed to enter or exit North Korea by train through China, giving them a view of North Korea from Pyongyang to Sinuiju, on the Chinese border, but only what they can see from the train. Finally, foreign seamen have caught a glimpse of North Koreans working in the port cities. With these exceptions, the vast expanse of North Korea has been hidden from foreign view. Thus, foreigners' impressions are just that, impressions rather than valid information about clothing situation.

To be sure, the impression of the people being well dressed is born out in photographs from official sources. More significantly, it is confirmed by defectors, but with certain caveats, which stress the overall impression rather than the truth behind the surface impression.

There is no question that the people are well dressed in the sense of their being adequately and appropriately attired for the work they do and their clothes being well-fitted and clean. As far as cleanliness and neatness are concerned, the regime insists on certain standards, and everyone complies. Sunday is inevitably taken up with doing the week's washing and ironing. By Monday morning, the week's supply of clothes has been mended, washed, and ironed, and it is ready for another week's wearing. The same clothes are readied in the same way each week for roughly one year, after which the people are issued the next year's supply of work clothes. If the old clothes are still in good enough condition, they can be worn along with the new clothes, which results in a larger wardrobe. Most often, they are completely worn out and are used only for work on volunteer labor projects.

Clothes are distributed through one's school, factory, office, or cooperative farm at a nominal charge, subsidized by the state. Military uniforms are distributed free of charge. The price of these state-supplied clothes has no relation to the high price of ready-made clothes and clothing material available on the open market; the latter are for sale to those who can afford extra clothing not deemed essential by the state. One set of work clothes, distributed by the state, costs about 20 won, whereas a Western-style suit, sold on the open market, costs 127 won. Most of the cuts in the price of clothing during the past ten years have been in the price of state-supplied goods for daily wear. Luxury goods sold on the open market have actually become more expensive.

No formal rationing system exists, but only certain clothes are distributed, depending on one's place of work or school. Those in more privileged jobs or schools may be issued the same quantity of clothes but clothes of superior quality. If the regime deems it wise to give ocean fishermen, who are exposed to cold conditions on the open seas, warmer clothing than office workers in Pyongyang, it can do so directly, leaving no chance that others more privileged in other respects can buy woolen clothing at the expense of fishermen.

All preschool children and students, from kindergarten to college, are issued school clothes (including underwear and shoes) once a year, on Kim Il-song's birthday, which contributes to the festive celebration of the day. Since North Koreans do not celebrate their own birthdays with presents, Kim's birthday is a much more exciting day. Usually the children receive other gifts besides clothing—candies and toys.

There is a basic uniform, in other words, for every job and every school, with some provision for variety within proscribed limits. For instance, schoolgirls, who wear navy blue polyester jumpers with their red Young Pioneer scarves around their necks, appear to have some choice in wearing either a jersey or blouse and either a red or white one. It may be that they are issued both and simply wear one or the other on different days. Schoolboys wear dark blue polyester pants with varying knit shirts, either long or short-sleeved, depending on the season. Girls are issued both summer and winter blouses. Some schools, especially the prestigious schools in Pyongyang, insist on the exact same uniform all year long. Students at the Foreign Language School always wear blue pants, white shirt, and tie. All of the men and women at a particular plant will be issued essentially the same clothes, with some variation in color but not style. This is also true of farmers at any one cooperative farm, miners at one particular mine, port workers at any one port, office clerks in the same ministry or department, and teachers in the same school or city.

It appears that both children and adults receive two sets of clothes each year, one for summer and one for winter. Younger schoolgirls receive two jumpers (and presumably two blouses) and boys receive two pairs of pants and two shirts. Older girls wear two-piece blue suits instead of jumpers. All girls, regardless of their age, wear low-heeled vinyl shoes or tennis shoes; boys wear Oxford-type vinyl shoes or tennis shoes. Adult males working in offices wear dark blue or black Mao-type uniforms. Only a few high-level government and party officials wear Western suits and neckties; interestingly, Kim never did, as Mao never did. Depending on their work, women wear black or navy-blue suits or pants outfits, usually with a white blouse. Farmers and laborers are issued appropriate clothing. Many farmers still wear the traditional Korean white shirt or blouse and black trousers or skirt, but more and more are wearing brightly colored shirts and jackets. Port workers and other laborers are issued khaki fatigues.

In both style and fabric, then, there is a standardization in clothes that makes them easier and cheaper to produce, but more monotonous and boring to wear. To imagine the clothing situation in North Korea, one needs only imagine a lifelong extension of wearing a school uniform. The overall impression created is one of social uniformity, without class distinction, and an appearance of neatness and equality. Other than the time and money that might be "wasted" on buying individualistic clothes and, in some cases, the sense of pride in being associated with a certain institution, the enforced uniformity in everyday work clothes is more likely to produce a negative reaction, especially among individualistic people, who object to the enforced monotony of always wearing the same clothes as everyone else. Over time, the uniformity is likely to wear thin. One may wear only three or four or five basic uniforms in an entire lifetime, depending on how many schools one attends and how often one changes jobs. Saturday afternoons and Sundays offer the only opportunity for wearing something different.

Thus, while people are adequately clothed in generally attractive and colorful, if not highly stylish, clothes, there is no depth in their wardrobe. Having little in the way of extra clothing, they are exceedingly careful to keep their clothes in good condition. They are used to ironing and mending their clothes from an early age. Appreciating the care that must be taken to keep their clothes in presentable condition for a year of constant wear, children do not engage in rough play in their school clothes. Even so, by the end of the year, most boys' pants are full of holes, mended as well as possible, but nonetheless badly worn. Children are especially careful of their shoes. Even with the best of care, tennis shoes are apt to wear out long before students are entitled to new ones. According to reliable sources, many tennis shoes wear out after one month's wearing.

Since most clothes, especially children's clothes, are distributed on the same day—Kim Il-song's birthday—it is interesting to consider the difference in appearance of clothes shortly after Kim's birthday and later in the year. A few visitors to North Korea have commented on the worn-out condition of people's clothes; however, the great majority stress the good condition of North Korean clothes. It would seem that the explanation for the disparity might be the timing of the visit. Visitors would certainly get a very different impression depending on whether they visited shortly after or long after the issuance of new clothing.

A good example of the misleading impression that can be created is the impression that women convey of being better dressed than they are. At a glance or in a picture, it might not be noticed that most women do not wear stockings, a very expensive item in North Korea. Foreign diplomats stationed in Pyongyang and in a position to observe ladies' dress over a long period of time have been struck by the nearly complete absence of stockings, even in winter.

Presumably ladies' feet suffer without stockings, since virtually all North Korean shoes are vinyl and apt to be very uncomfortable without stockings. It is interesting that most pictures of North Koreans taken outside are taken in the summer, when the absence of warm overcoats, gloves, and hats would not be apparent. Indeed, in remembering the pictures in North Korea's pictorial *Korea* over time, one remembers no pictures of North Koreans strolling along the streets of Pyongyang in winter, but many, many pictures of happy groups of North Koreans in the warm sunshine of the summer months. The pictures of women in brightly colored dresses, without stockings, seem appropriate then. The shortage of underwear, like the shortage of stockings is a major complaint of North Koreans.

According to defectors, it is the lack of warm clothing in winter that is by far the most common complaint. It would be interesting to know more about the prevalence of colds and other illnesses that might be traced to inadequately warm clothing, as well as cold housing.

Although some clothes are made of cotton, most are made of rayon or some other chemical fiber like nylon or vinylon. Woolen clothing is scarce. Only military and elite civilians are issued wool clothes, and only the elite can afford to buy them; a wool suit costs more than six months' pay for the average worker. Leather, like wool, is prohibitively expensive; only the elite wear leather shoes.

A few large textile plants in North Korea—the February 8 Vinylon Plant at Hamhung and the Sariwin Synthetic Textile Mill—make the bulk of the country's clothing materials. Until 1975 rayon and vinylon, made from wood, limestone, and coal, were the principal fibers produced. Since the mid-1970s, the regime, to improve the quality of clothing, has developed the capacity to manufacture other synthetic fibers including nylon, acrylon, and tetron. These materials are made into clothes at many small knitwear and clothing factories scattered around the country; the Manyondae Knitwear Factory, the Kangso Knitted Goods Mill, and the Kanggye Spinning and Weaving Plant are good examples. These factories make ready-made clothing for specific schools, offices, cooperative farms, and factories within their jurisdiction. For instance, the Sadong Children's Knitwear Factory in Pyongyang makes clothing for the preschool children in Pyongyang. It is reported to have the capacity for making three pieces of knit goods for every preschool-age child in Pyongyang. Other knitwear factories provide similar clothing for preschool children in other areas. Clothing factories need only produce limited styles of clothes required by the particular schools and factories in their immediate vicinity. Each year they produce the new year's allotment for the same students at the same schools and the same workers at the same factories. They are familiar with the style of clothing since it does not change much, if at all.

Although hardly stylish, North Korean clothing has improved significantly in recent years in terms of both color and variety. The monotonous uniformity of black Korean-style skirts and white Korean-style jackets has long since disappeared, especially in the cities, if not in all areas of the countryside. Children now dress in bright reds, whites, and blues, plus shirts of other colors. Women's clothes come in a variety of colors and patterns. The impression that North Korean clothes give now, in striking contrast to their drab appearance in the 1960s, is one of bright color. Visitors are struck by the great difference between North Korea and China in this regard.

The change in North Korean clothes dates from the early 1970s. In July 1972, the Central Committee of the North Korean Women's League published a propaganda booklet in color on the "Dressing Style of Korea." It and other publications reveal a sense of pride in women's fashion. There has clearly been a far greater concern for and attention paid to clothes in North Korea than in China (at least under Mao). Whether this reflected Kim's personal preferences for stylish, colorful dress or his recognition of its importance as a morale booster is difficult to judge. It may be another of the ways in which he tried to impress foreigners. Whatever the motivation, it has clearly accomplished both purposes. The improvement in dress is one of North Korea's most significant advances, from the consumer point of view. Foreigners cite it as one of the most striking impressions about North Korea.

Visitors are struck as well by the increased use of hats, handbags, and cosmetics. In Pyongyang, even teenage girls wear lipstick and other cosmetics and experiment with new hair styles. Young girls adorn their hair with large bows of colored netting that seem somewhat out of place with their more tailored clothes but are nonetheless very feminine and colorful. As one Western observer remarked, "Women and girls appear to take great care with their appearance." In this, they are clearly different from their Chinese counterparts, who only recently broke away from Mao's strictures on Western dress and the use of makeup.

Since the early 1970s, Western dress has rapidly replaced traditional dress in the larger cities, especially Pyongyang. Very few of the women in Pyongyang wear the traditional Korean skirt and blouse today. However, the regime can easily create just the opposite impression when it wants to. At the time of the International Ping-Pong Meet in Pyongyang in April 1979, about three-fourths of the women spectators at the games appeared in traditional dress. Obviously, the authorities had ordered everyone to wear their Sunday best to impress the foreign visitors. Presumably, those who wore Western clothes were the elite who could afford to buy the relatively expensive Western clothes. The regime is known to have gone to great lengths to impress foreign visitors

on other occasions, such as the visit of U.S. Congressman Stephen Solarz in July 1980.

It is amazing how easy it is to change major aspects of the city—the
dress of the people, the sudden absence of military units in the city, the
flow of traffic, and crowds in the streets. It is merely one demonstration
of the chameleon-like quality of the world's most controlled society.

Men are conspicuously less well dressed than women. Perhaps they
are simply trying to emulate Kim Il-song, whose trousers were often
much too long, while his son and new leader Kim Chong-il's pants are
typically short and baggy.

In sum, North Korea's clothing distribution system has ensured a
basic equality in dress that most North Koreans probably find politically appealing. Just as everyone receives adequate food, at least in
caloric intake, so all North Koreans have appropriate clothing, in
quantity and quality, but nothing extra. "Clothes are very practical,
and suited to one's work; they are not ostentatious." There is little display of extravagance even with the elite. Differences are subtle between
a wool and vinylon suit, for instance, or between leather and vinyl
shoes, or, a synthetic overcoat and fabric cap and a woolen overcoat
and fur cap.

Most qualified observers are of the opinion that North Koreans are,
by and large, better dressed than their Chinese counterparts and certainly much better clothed than they were in prewar days. According to
defectors, the people are well aware of the improvements over earlier
days. However, despite the regime's efforts to improve the quality of
clothing, it still remains a major problem. "Shoes are still poorly made,
of inferior materials, with no heels." "Stockings are very baggy, thick,
and unattractive." As in other Communist societies, the emphasis is
always on quantity rather than quality. Compared to South Korea, the
quality of clothes is mediocre at best, but the North Koreans know little
about South Korea.

For the ordinary person, clothing is still the most expensive item in
the family budget. The average family might spend one-third to one-
half of its combined family income on clothing, yet is still able to afford
only one man's nylon sweater with one month's surplus income. At 100
won per meter, it could not afford one meter of wool material from the
family income for any one month.

In short, the clothing situation is something of a paradox. Despite
some improvement in the quality of clothing and striking changes in
the general attractiveness of clothes, which creates a definite impression

of progress, the North Korean consumer is still far from satisfied with both the quality and quantity of his or her clothes. Although the overall impression that a visitor may get is one of the general attractiveness and color of North Korean clothes, the reality for North Koreans is a very limited wardrobe in terms of style and color, and, most important of all, the inability to choose one's own clothes. Whereas foreign observers may be impressed with the improvements in style and color, or the favorable comparison of North Korean clothing with that of China, North Koreans tend to focus on the continuing poor quality and limited supply of clothes, in general, and the chronic shortages of particular items, such as underwear, socks, and warm clothing. Foreign observers are not likely to sense their frustration along these lines.

OTHER CONSUMER GOODS AND SERVICES

It is no surprise that foreigners might get a misleading impression of the general availability of consumer goods in North Korea, given Kim's mania for dressing up reality at all costs. The same thinking that would create a dream city like Pyongyang, not at all typical of the rest of the country, would want to impress foreign visitors to the city with a display of luxury goods in foreigners' stores that not only are not typical of North Korean stores across the country, but actually do not even exist outside Pyongyang. The foreigners' stores and the goods they sell are reserved exclusively for foreign visitors.

Few countries would go to the lengths that the DPRK does to impress foreigners. For U.S. Congressman Solarz's visit in July 1980 and for important international gatherings like the International Ping-Pong Meet in Pyongyang in April 1979, the regime stocked Pyongyang stores visible to these visitors with a wide variety of consumer goods not normally sold at these stores. John Wallach of the Hearst papers, in Pyongyang at the time of the International Ping-Pong Meet in April 1979, was impressed with the display of goods in "the well stocked stores along Chollima Street." As the days went by, he was increasingly struck by the lack of customers in the stores. After two weeks in Pyongyang, he was convinced that practically nothing was being sold. At the conclusion of the Ping-Pong games, the authorities removed the items that were never intended to be sold and were there just for show.

A North Korean citizen cannot walk into a store and buy a watch or television, radio or lamp or iron, or any such major purchase, even if he has the money, without an authorization card or coupon from one's factory or office for each such purchase. These coupons are given out for different reasons; in some cases, they are procured through obvious favoritism, in some cases, distributed on a rotating basis. Very often, an individual who gets authorization to buy something does not have the money. In that case, he may buy it for a friend with the friend's money, expecting his friend to reciprocate the favor at a later date. According to defectors, he is not likely to sell the authorization card because of the possibility of its being reported to the authorities. One can afford to trust only one's closest friends in any such joint effort.

Through the combined use of authorization cards and an artificially skewed price system, which subsidizes the costs of necessary goods and services, such as haircuts, public baths, laundry soap, and school supplies, and puts a premium on the price of watches, sewing machines, refrigerators, and other luxury goods, the regime controls the distribution of all consumer goods much as it controls the distribution of food and clothing. The people are assured of a fairly equal distribution of the basic necessities but given little leeway to indulge their taste for other goods. In the words of one defector,

> Consumers are satisfied with lower-priced consumer goods but are not satisfied with high-quality items, especially silk, woolen clothing, and luxury items such as watches, radios, sewing machines, electric irons, and leather shoes. High-quality clothing is simply not available; luxury items, though available, are much too expensive, priced way out of the range of ordinary citizens . . . (who) are not really expected to buy luxury goods.
>
> Basic necessities can be purchased but not quality goods. The latter include radios, tape recorders, stockings, high-quality toothpaste, automobiles, bicycles, and name-brand medicines.
>
> One can buy clothing, school supplies, and other basic daily needs in the stores, but no luxury items. Medicines and radios are very expensive.
>
> The people (in Pyongyang) want watches, better clothes, a refrigerator, television and bicycle, in that order. They are not as interested in radios. In the countryside, people are more interested in bicycles. They need them to get around. Many people ride bikes, including school children. In Pyongyang, there is no place to keep a bicycle, since people live in apartments and there are no elevators. Moreover, there is good bus and subway service.

Although it is difficult to generalize about such things, it would seem that most families have a flat iron; one out of five probably own a bike; one out of ten, a watch; fewer still, a sewing machine or television (although all have access to television in their apartment building, cooperative farm, or office); and one out of a hundred families, a refrigerator.

Japanese- and Swiss-made watches and foreign medicines are the three most sought-after items in North Korea. Korean residents in Japan who send goods to their repatriated relatives in North Korea are advised "to send watches, medicines, and currency." The Japanese repatriates sell them on the black market for exorbitant prices.

Recognizing the demand for watches, the regime invested in a modern new watch plant imported from Switzerland in 1978 and 1979. Production includes several types of manually wound wristwatches, priced for the ordinary citizen at from 110 to 140 won. Initial production was 400,000 watches per year, with a target of from 600,000 to 800,000 watches. The plant has met a major consumer demand; however, even at production of 700,000 watches per year, it provides a watch for only one out of twenty-five North Koreans each year. Coupons to purchase a watch are issued once a year. People in each place of employment who do not have a watch are given consideration, but those with high production quotas or special enthusiasm in party activities are given preference. In actual practice, even those people with coupons and with the money to buy a watch often are not able to do so because of the lack of watches.

Everyday items that can be purchased without coupons include towels, toothbrushes, toothpaste, plastic combs, knives, stationery items, and children's toys. Basic community services that are not rationed and are provided at subsidized low prices include haircuts, hairstyling, and public baths. The regime has put a premium on cleanliness and the clean-shaven look. Only old men and farmers wear beards—a significant departure from the past. There is at least one barbershop and beauty parlor in every village and every ward or *dong* in the larger cities, and roving barbers service the more isolated areas. They travel from factory to factory on a continuous basis. Even with the increase in the number of barbershops, they are apparently always crowded; people usually have to wait in line and sometimes have to come back the next day. A haircut and shave cost 50 and 20 chon, respectively (0.5 and 0.2 won). Children's haircuts cost 30 chon (0.3 won). Customers typically wash their own hair and the barber cuts it. In the larger cities, men pay 2 or 3 won for a hair cut, hair washing, drying, and styling at the fancier barbershops.

Women can pay up to 3 or 4 won for a permanent wave, the most expensive service provided. Although it has always been a major expenditure in most family budgets, expenditures for hair styling seem to be growing as family incomes grow. It is amazing how rapidly Western hair styles have grown in popularity. Most men, both old and young, wear their hair in Western cuts; women seem to prefer a short cut and permanent wave. Hair styling has definitely contributed to the impression that North Koreans give of being well-groomed and well-dressed in a relatively modern Western style.

Each village and *dong* in the larger cities has a public bathhouse, as well as a barbershop and beauty parlor, which are generally open from 5:00 A.M. to 10:00 P.M. Adults pay 30 chon and children 10 chon for a communal bath and 40 or 50 chon for a private bath or shower. Most people in the villages take baths in their homes after heating water in a bucket. They probably visit a public bathhouse no more than two or three times a month. People in the cities, especially the larger cities, frequent bathhouses more often, partly because the facilities are so much superior to those in the countryside. The elite in Pyongyang bathe in the luxurious new Health and Recreation Center, which features the ultimate in saunas, hot whirlpool baths, and gym equipment. Thus, the range in quality in bathhouses is striking. Whatever their facilities, the services are provided at subsidized low prices.

Visitors to North Korea who might be taken in by the display of consumer goods in stores that most North Koreans could never afford are not so easily fooled by the poor quality of many goods for sale. Visitors have noted the inferior quality of household utensils, handbags, and stationery supplies, in particular. Vinyl handbags are very heavy and their fittings are not good. The postage stamps that a Swiss visitor bought in his hotel gift shop had no glue on the back. Ballpoint pens, although attractive in appearance, are reported to smudge a lot; the tips of fountain pens rust easily. Ink, reported to be of roughly the same quality as ink in South Korea, is poorly bottled in bottles that leak. Although stationery paper is reportedly good, comparable to the highest quality in South Korea, other paper products such as toilet paper are notoriously bad, as "rough as sandpaper" in one Westerner's words. Cosmetic cream, produced at the Pyongyang Cosmetic Factory, is reported to be "similar in quality to that produced in South Korea in the early 1950's, in other words, not fit for export." Perfumes produced at the same factory are made of "water, alcohol and cheap perfumes." "Eyebrow pencils are of inferior quality and unpleasant to apply." "The dye in most towels comes off in water, and the towels do not have much pile." "Handkerchiefs are also inferior in terms of bleaching and workmanship." "Silk scarves, produced at the Sinam Textile Factory, are inferior in both dying and workmanship, about ten to fifteen years behind South Korea's textile industry." "Carpets are much inferior in quality to South Korean products." "Nail clippers are strong enough, but not well designed." "Knives are generally crude in their workmanship, inferior to most South Korean knives." "The same [is true] for can openers." "Electric cords, an insulated single wire, are also of inferior quality." "Electrical appliances are even cruder." By U.S. standards, all North Korean washing machines are obsolete; there are no automatic controls or spin dry, each operation must be hand started, and every machine has a capacity of only three or four pounds of clothes. North Korean refrigerators are equally behind contemporary U.S. models with only about one-third the capacity and no ice-making capability.

On the positive side, observers have noted that "safety matches are of good quality, superior to those made in South Korea and definitely of export quality. The heads contain a large quantity of combustibles that ignite well and are moisture resistant." "Scissors, produced at the Knaggye Ironware Factory, are well-tempered and of good workmanship."

According to many reports, North Koreans, at least the more sophisticated ones who live in Pyongyang and other big cities, are not satisfied with the quality of goods and are increasingly prone to a new materialism that threatens to pressure the regime with demands for televisions, more clothes, and more watches. According to a salesgirl in one of Pyongyang's larger department stores, "The general North Korean consumer has now begun to demand products of better quality." Western visitors who have taken copies of catalogues from U.S. stores such as Sears have reported the "fascination" of North Koreans with products pictured therein, especially electrical appliances, televisions, tape recorders, calculators, electronic games, and hand tools. Apparently, most people do not believe that such products are available to the average U.S. citizen. Other visitors to the DPRK tell of the people's "curiosity" about fountain pens and cigarette lighters which "they ask to hold, examining them closely and turning them over and over in their hands."

As hard as the regime may try to insulate its people from foreign advances in consumer goods, it seems they are becoming more and more aware of others' progress. Knowledge of their true situation in relation to other countries is likely to be the most dangerous problem for the regime in the future.

18

Personal Savings

With controls on consumption, effected through low monetary wages, a skewed price structure favoring basic commodities over luxury goods, rationing of essential commodities, and strict control over other purchases through an authorization card system, most North Koreans are able or, more accurately, forced to save money. People do not save with the thought of buying expensive consumer goods, such as televisions or refrigerators, because of the uncertainty of ever being issued an authorization coupon and the need to save money to set their children up in housekeeping. When they finally spend their life savings, it is likely to be on basic necessities for their children, not luxury goods.

In April 1979 all residents of North Korea were required to exchange their cash holdings for an equivalent amount of money in newly printed paper currency. There was speculation at the time that the move was an initiative by the regime to confiscate the people's savings above a certain amount. This was not the case, however. The government returned the money collected on a one-to-one basis. The purpose of the move seems to have been the desire of the regime to switch to a North Korean–printed currency. Up to 1977, the DPRK had used currency printed in the Soviet Union, which involved a continuing dependency on the Soviet Union for new supplies of money and gave the Soviets inside information on the amount of money in circulation. In keeping with his *chu'che* philosophy of national self-reliance and independence, Kim wanted his own currency, printed in the DPRK. According to one source, the government originally planned to issue the currency in September 1978 to commemorate the thirtieth anniversary of the founding of North Korea on 9 September 1948. However, it was unable to produce sufficient quantities of the notes in time, and consequently the issuance of the currency was deferred until April 1979. It was planned that everyone would have their new currency by 15 April, on Kim's sixty-seventh birthday. The timing of the move, just one month before the International Ping-Pong Meet in Pyongyang in May 1979, suggested a desire to have the new money in circulation by the time the foreign visitors arrived. As Kim might have hoped, most visitors were impressed with North Korea's crisp new paper bills featuring color engravings of Kim Il-song and pastoral scenes of North Korea that emphasized North Korean nationalism rather than the international Communist solidarity themes of the old currency.

According to the NKPA, 1,500 won was the largest amount of cash exchanged by any military officer. Officers averaged from 700 to 800 won; highly trained noncommissioned officers of long service, 500 won; and enlisted men, from 10 to 15 won. At least in the case of military officers, this suggests average family savings equal to about six months' salary or about four months' combined salary of husband and wife. The top savings of 1,500 won would equal about ten months of a full colonel's salary or about sixteen months of a second lieutenant's salary. Assuming a combined family income of about 160 won per month (the national average income per family and a reasonable monthly income for a lower-level officer and his wife), a first lieutenant in the army and his wife who save 5 percent of their combined income could save 800 won in about nine years. By saving 10 percent of their income, the upper likely limit, they could save that amount in just over four years.

It is difficult to say how typical this is. It must be remembered that military officers are at the upper end of the pay scale and can be presumed to save more than most North Koreans. It does appear that North Koreans save more today than they did in prewar days, when a large percentage of the population in both Koreas had substantial debts.

In effect, the Communists have accomplished a kind of forced savings through a less direct method than compulsory savings. Their system of rationing and strictly controlled wages and prices has proved effective in limiting consumption below current income levels. In so doing, they have removed the personal financial insecurity of many Koreans in prewar days. This should not be overlooked as a major accomplishment, say defectors, who cite the sense of financial security as one of the most comforting aspects of life in Communist Korea, in contrast to life in the United States where, they are told, there is financial insecurity. It is interesting that defectors mention this as one of the improvements in life in North Korea.

19

Housing

A major factor contributing to the sense of material security that North Koreans seem to feel is the government's provision of housing, essentially free of charge. Early on, Kim committed the regime to a significant degree of responsibility in the housing area, unusual even for a Communist regime. Of all consumer wants, housing consistently received top priority. For many years, state investment in housing construction was second only to investment in heavy industry, surpassing state investment in major fields such as transport, agriculture, and light industry. Although the share of state capital allocated to housing has gradually declined, the total amount of state investment in housing has grown steadily. Private and cooperative investment, which used to account for almost three-fourths of the total investment in housing in the early years after the Korean War but declined to 30 percent in 1958, virtually disappeared in the 1960s. Since then, the national government has assumed full responsibility for the housing of all citizens, in rural as well as urban areas.

Housing construction increased with each successive development plan. Some 600,000 housing units were built from 1954 to 1960, 800,000 units from 1961 to 1969, and over 1,000,000 in the 1970s. By 1976 North Korea had constructed new housing for almost three-fourths of its urban and rural households—a notable accomplishment.

The dramatic change can be seen in many cities. In 1967 there were an estimated 20,000 homeless families, out of a total 200,000 families, in Pyongyang. These people were homeless in the sense of not having a home of their own, not in the sense of living out on the streets. Most of these families lived with other families, but about a third were split up and living in dormitories of their respective workshops. From 1965 to

1967, ten new apartment buildings were constructed in Pyonyang an-
nually, with a total capacity of 1,000 families. At that rate it would have
taken twenty years to build new housing for the 20,000 homeless families, assuming no growth in the population. Since, from all appearances,
housing construction in Pyongyang in the 1970s greatly surpassed that
of the late 1960's, it seems safe to conclude that there are now probably
few, if any, homeless families in Pyongyang.

In Sinuiju, a city of 100,000 people (approximately 20,000 families)
situated along the border with China, roughly 15 percent of the city's
population was homeless in 1967. As in Pyongyang, the city authorities put as many as possible of the 3,000 homeless families into extra
space in the houses and apartments of the other 17,000 families; the
rest had to live in dormitories in their workshops. The people reportedly were pleased with the progress in housing construction in the 1970s
and 1980s.

The figure of 10 or 15 percent of the population being homeless in
1967 and 1968 may be quite representative of the country as a whole.
Hungnyong had a population of 10,000, consisting of 2,000 families,
240 of which were homeless. Sixty percent of the 240 homeless families
were living in workers' residences with other families and 40 percent
were split up in dormitories in their respective workshops.

From all accounts there are few, if any, homeless families in North
Korea today. The regime can properly boast that it has basically solved
the housing problem, in providing a housing unit to every family,
though it may still have a long way to go in meeting its goal of a two
room (plus kitchen) apartment for every family of five or more.

It is interesting to consider why Kim, among Communist leaders,
has given such high priority to housing. After the Korean War, there
was a desperate need for new housing since an estimated 28 million
square meters of housing, or about 35 percent of all housing in the
country, was destroyed in the war. The damage to the cities was much
greater than the damage in the rural areas; Pyongyang was devastated.
As Kim was fond of telling foreign visitors, only two buildings in Pyongyang were left intact. North Korea faced a more acute housing shortage
than any other Communist regime, including the East European Communist regimes after World War II.

Before the war, the DPRK was considered to have better housing
than any other Asian Communist country. The average floor space per
capita of six or seven square meters was considerably above that of
China, North Vietnam, and Mongolia. Kim may have been particularly

concerned to repair the damage in this area in which the DPRK had always had an edge.

Long after the war damage had been repaired, however, and the increase in population was addressed with commensurate advances in housing, Kim continued to give high priority to housing construction, above other consumer wants. By 1960 he had established a very favorable competitive position with South Korea, which had also suffered devastating war damage, as well as a huge influx of refugees from the north that made the housing situation that much more acute. South Korea has been slower to address the housing problem, constructing only about 2.5 million square meters of urban housing, compared to 8.7 million square meters in North Korea. Kim had an edge in the race with South Korea that Seoul was hard pressed to overcome, even during the economic boom of the 1970s.

Long-time observers of the Korean scene stress the importance of the competition between North and South Korea as a key motivating force in the decision making of both Koreas. The impact of North Korea's dramatic improvements in housing certainly was not lost on South Korea. Just as Kim's building of a subway system in Pyongyang influenced Seoul to begin construction of a subway of its own in the early 1960s and the building of increasingly impressive government buildings of monumental size in Pyongyang inspired the building of South Korea's new government complex on Yoido Island, so Kim's lead in housing seems to have spurred South Korea to devote more resources to public housing projects. Kim's model for building workers' homes near the factories where they work may also have been the inspiration for similar housing projects in South Korea, such as that undertaken by the Hyundae Shipbuilding Company. The two Koreas have clearly had a direct influence on one another in such areas. One certainly cannot discount the impact of the inbred competition between the two countries on Kim's zeal in the housing area, an area that lent itself to his purposes in a number of ways.

First of all, housing dramatized the regime's commitment to consumer welfare better than most other things. Foreigners could see the gains in housing more easily than they could see improvement in food, clothing, or education. The cement tile roofs of North Korea's rural homes were visible evidence of a higher living standard as compared to the thatched roofs of most rural homes in China. A foreigner traveling on the train from Peking to Pyongyang could not help but notice the difference. An impression of progress was dramatically evident in the huge new housing projects in Pyongyang.

North Koreans also may have been inclined to overlook deficiencies in other consumer areas when they saw the improvements in housing. From all reports, the people mention housing, first and foremost, when they talk about how the Communists have improved their lives. The psychic income from a dollar spent on housing was unquestionably greater than the psychic income, to North Koreans personally and to North Korea as a state, of a dollar spent on food or clothing. That was clearly of great importance to Kim Il-song, who, by his own admission, saw as one of the main advantages in building a dream city like Pyongyang the psychic boost that it gave the whole country.

The paradox is that while North Koreans generally acknowledge the advances in housing and give the regime credit in this area, they nonetheless cite cramped housing as one of their major complaints. Crowded housing conditions usually head any list of common grievances, including the shortage of meat and lack of variety in the diet, the cost of warm clothes and the poor quality of other clothes, the scarcity of medicines, and the limited opportunities for higher education. While they appreciate their one-bedroom apartment as an improvement over the past, North Koreans look forward to the regime's promise of a two-bedroom apartment for every family of five or more.

The problem for the regime, then, is one of rising expectations. Housing construction, whatever its impressive record, has still not kept pace with demand. No other consumer area seems to have presented the same challenge. Although demand obviously does not play the role in North Korea's command economy that it does in a free market economy, the planners must be influenced by their reading of consumer wants in deciding consumer allocations. The promise of a two-bedroom apartment suggests tacit recognition by the regime of the priority of housing in consumer wants. The government has made no comparable promise with respect to food or clothing, apparently feeling less pressed in these areas.

With this impetus on the demand side, housing construction is also boosted by a certain momentum on the supply side. Having devoted an inordinate amount of resources to housing in the early years, the regime created a supply situation that tended to perpetuate the priority of housing construction. As one of the most advanced industries in North Korea, the housing industry has become a kind of model industry that Kim Il-song could promote as competitive with other industries in

South Korea and Asia as a whole. For all these reasons, then, housing construction has a momentum that is likely to ensure its position as one of the top industries in North Korea, much to consumers' delight.

URBAN HOUSING

Whereas in prewar Korea individual family dwellings were the traditional housing in both rural and urban areas, Kim's answer to the postwar urban housing crisis lay in building multistoried apartment complexes of prefabricated construction. Besides offering a more rapid way of building housing, prefabricated construction was less costly, saving on the use of both labor and materials. For both reasons, it was a sensible solution to North Korea's housing problems, except for certain problems that may, in the long run, prove more costly.

Certain disadvantages inherent in the process are the need for a large pool of cranes and other transportation facilities to move the precast concrete panels, the danger of damage in transit, and the monotonous and unattractive appearance of standardized construction, especially on so large a scale. The more recent trend away from precast "Stalinist-type" government buildings toward a neo-Korean style of architecture constructed on the site suggests some awareness of the aesthetic costs that the DPRK paid in choosing the least expensive, most rapid solution to the housing problem in early days.

A more serious problem may be the problem of quality. Much of the prefabricated construction of the 1960's and early 1970's was of poor quality, compared to the better quality of traditional methods of brick construction done on the site. Many of the early prefabricated apartments, built at the time when the North Korean housing industry was still at a relatively low level of technical proficiency, have received major repairs and, in the long run, are likely to need to be replaced sooner than normal. North Korean construction of the 1960s is famous for its ill-fitting windows, cracked walls and ceilings, uneven floors, leaking roofs, and warped plate glass. Some of the early multistory apartment buildings are reported to have settled at a noticeable angle. All of the high-rise apartments built before the late 1970s still are without elevators, central heating, or running water, despite the original plans to add these features later. Although high-rise apartments were built with a space left for elevators to be installed later, the North Koreans have found it impossible to install elevators in these buildings because the intervals between floors are not uniform, so that elevators cannot be adjusted to stop level with each floor. Furthermore, the shafts are neither aligned nor uniform in size. It is doubtful that the elevators would ever work properly.

According to one West European engineer,

> The typical apartment building in Pyongyang resembled apartments we had seen in Moscow. At first glance, the quality seemed not too bad, but on closer inspection I had the same feeling that I had when I inspected factories—that no good semi-technicians existed in the housing industry as in other industries. The technical details and workmanship of the prefabricated concrete panels were in many cases so poor that the building without a doubt would have been rejected in most countries. The lack of finish was very apparent, at least to a construction engineer, as soon as you crossed the border between North Korea and China. In China the bond in the brickwork fits, the glass in the windows is plane so it is possible to look through it without distorting the view totally. The apartments are constructed in a monotonous style and lack modern conveniences. The rooms are separated by concrete block walls that are simply wallpapered.

In recent years, North Korean technology in housing construction has improved dramatically. Many of the newer apartment buildings are over twenty stories high, compared to the typical five- or six-story apartment houses of the 1960s and the ten- to twelve-story buildings of the 1970s. The visual impact of rows and rows of these high-rise, prefabricated apartments is striking. The monotony of the architecture, combined with their size, produces a kind of numbing effect, which anyone familiar with the huge housing developments on the outskirts of Moscow knows well. The inside of the buildings are, if anything, more drab than the exteriors, although most foreigners now find the exteriors equally depressing because the concrete slabs are showing unattractive stains with aging.

The newer apartments are an improvement in their more modern conveniences, such as central heating, running water, flush toilets, and elevators that work. Pyongyang is way ahead of the rest of the country in this respect, as might be expected. It was the first city to have multistory, prefabricated apartment buildings in late 1950s and the first city to introduce central heating in the early 1970s. Pyongyang's system of central heating was inspired by the traditional Korean *ondol* heating system, in which the floors of Korean homes are heated by hot water conducted through pipes laid directly under the floor. The water is heated by a coal-burning stove in the kitchen of each home. The new central heating system in Pyongyang uses hot water piped from a single thermoelectric power plant located directly behind the Potonggang Hotel, near the Potonggang River. Domestically mined coal is used as fuel. A temperature of 80°C is maintained in supplying hot water piped over relatively long distances in pipes measuring eighty centimeters in diameter. The hot water is piped into Pyongyang's apartment buildings through pipes under the floors of the apartments. Some offices in Pyongyang are heated by radiators similar to Western-style radiators by using hot water piped from the same Pyongyang Thermal Plant.

Although it comprises only about 15 percent of the total urban population, Pyongyang has received more than 30 percent of total urban housing construction funds for many years. During the 1970s, residential construction in the city was even more impressive. In recent years, construction of multistory apartments in Wonsan, Hamhung, Kaesong, Ch'ongjin, Sunchon, and other large cities has been almost as impressive, in terms of housing units completed. We have little information about to the details of construction; presumably, these apartments do not have the modern features of Pyongyang's newest apartments.

The standardization of North Korea's prefabricated housing is such that one can talk about the average or typical urban apartment with a reasonable degree of confidence. There are three or four basic designs for individual apartments that are used over and over again. Apartments have from one to three rooms (3 meters by 4.5 meters or about 9 feet by 14 feet) plus a kitchen (2.5 meters by 3 meters), a bathroom, and a storage area. The occupants of older buildings usually share a communal bathroom at the end of each corridor, as in barracks or dormitories. Generally, these older buildings do not have running water or flush toilets. In the apartments that do have running water, it is often available only on the first floor, because of poor water pressure. In Pyongyang, residents get their water from the Taedong River, but well water is still used in the suburbs. Most foreigners consider the water in Pyongyang not potable and rely on bottled drinking water that is available at all hotels. They report getting "a milky solution smelling of bleaching powder" when they first turned on the faucet, but the water cleared after it ran for a while. The disadvantage of living on the upper floors of a high-rise apartment building, with no elevator, is brought home by the thought of carrying water, groceries, and other household items up ten or more flights—on an outside stairway.

North Korea's goal has been to provide a two-room-plus-kitchen housing unit to every household of five or more persons and a three-room-plus-kitchen apartment to every household of nine or more. The country still has a long way to go to accomplish that goal. The typical apartment still consists of one room plus kitchen, which houses all size families. Government claims notwithstanding, it is clear that the size of one's apartment is determined by one's socioeconomic position rather than the size of one's family. Apartment buildings are built to house people who work together, either at the same factory or in the same government ministry. Apartment buildings in Pyongyang designated for officials of the Ministry of Defense generally have two- and three-room apartments, regardless of the size of the families, whereas apartment buildings housing the workers at the nearby Pyongyang Thermal Power Plant have one-room apartments, without regard to the size of the families. These differences are readily apparent from firsthand accounts of the living arrangements of a wide assortment of North Koreans.

According to a reliable source within the North Korean army,

A major in the DPRK army had a comfortable apartment (two bedrooms, living/dining room and kitchen) in "Area 3," within walking distance of the Pyongyang Hotel. "Areas 4 and 5" had even better quarters for higher-ranking officials. As one's rank goes up, one can live in these other areas and enjoy additional privileges. For instance, a high-government official can live in a fine single family house (5th class) and receive larger food rations and use government villas and rest homes.

"Type-3" residences are homes for the vice-chairmen of Party provincial committees and chairmen of government administrative committees at the ward level. They consist of three rooms and a kitchen. "Type-4" residences are for vice-ministers and assistant deputy chiefs of the Central Committee. These residences have three rooms, one reception room, and kitchen. "Type-5" residences are for cabinet ministers and deputy chiefs of the Central Committee. They have five rooms, one reception room, and kitchen.

Privileged families assigned to important government ministries are likely to be moved out of older apartments as newer ones with more conveniences become available. When ambassadors and other senior diplomats return from overseas, either for periodic briefing and de-briefings or for permanent reassignment, they are reunited with their families in these new apartments.

Whether one lives in Pyongyang or elsewhere, North Korean hous-ing is segregated on the basis of the work people do and their seniority on the job. Since jobs reflect education which, in turn, reflects *songbun*, it is essentially segregated housing on the basis of *songbun* or socioeco-nomic class distinctions. One has no opportunity to spend more money on better housing, at the sacrifice of other consumer wants, even if one has the money. One is assigned to one's apartment in a building pro-vided to one's enterprise or government ministry or factory, just as one is given the same clothes or assigned the same doctor or taken to the same vacation spot as all one's coworkers. In short, one's life is alto-gether determined by one's job, the central point of reference in North Korea's Communist society. One lives, eats, works, studies, shops, and vacations with the same group.

Some believe that Kim was primarily motivated by political consid-erations—namely, the promotion of group identity over family or indi-vidual identities—in his commitment to housing based on workplace. Group identity is constantly reinforced when one does everything to-gether with the same people, people who do the same kind of work, rather than people one might seek out as friends. It makes it easier to control the population by differentiating people into groups on the ba-sis of the job they do. People can be grouped together for medical care, education, housing, political indoctrination, militia training, distribu-tion of consumer goods, and vacations. From the regime's point of view, society is neatly organized according to the Communist view of man as an economic being, a unit of production. One's value in life lies in one's contribution to state production. Housing, like everything else, is apportioned accordingly.

UTILITIES

Unlike other Communist regimes, the DPRK provides housing es-sentially free of charge, with a "fee" of only 1 or 2 percent (3 to 5 per-cent for privileged families) of total family income to cover the cost of utilities and furnishings. The North Koreans refer to this as a "fee" rather than rent, which is a capitalist term implying value earned from the private possession of property. The fee for an apartment varies ac-cording to people's monthly income, rather than the size of the apartment or the cost of utilities consumed. Some effort has been made in recent years to assess people for the amount of water, heat, and electricity consumed, with the introduction of individual meters that record consumption in some of the newer apartments in Pyongyang. Kim Il-song acknowledged that the people's wasteful use of utilities prompted this change. Generally, however, there is a standard charge, based on income. The charge is slightly higher during winter months than during the summer due to increased heating charges.

In all Communist countries, housing costs are subsidized by the government. In North Korea, however, the housing fee is low even for a Communist country. Compared to the United States, where consumers pay roughly one-fourth to one-third of their income for housing, North Koreans spend less than 1 percent of their monthly income as a housing fee, which essentially covers the cost of utilities. And what do they get in the way of utilities?

Electricity

All North Korean apartments have electricity; one of the regime's proudest accomplishments is that it had brought electricity to all North Korean homes by 1968. The voltage is very irregular, however, and the lights are dim and flickering. Because of the shortage of timber, electric power poles are made of cement. Standing about six meters tall and averaging between fifteen and twenty cubic meters in size, they present a rather formidable appearance. The electric wires look far too thin for the voltage they carry. The electric supply in North Korea is 220 volts, 60 cycles AC. However, the voltage supply is highly unstable, showing variations from 165 to 180 volts on 220-volt lines. Because of this fluctuation, 100-watt bulbs reportedly give out a brightness of only about 50 watts. Moreover, electric clocks are usually inaccurate because of power fluctuations and stoppages.

Electric switches become defective often, and the bulbs blow out after short use. Electric power meters are also unreliable. They always record high consumption of electricity. When foreigners have complained, the authorities have insisted upon their accuracy.

Electric outlet sockets, unique in design, feature three connections (live, neutral, earth). The earth connection in the socket is not through a hole but through a copper pin that protrudes out. Consequently, the matching electric plug has two copper pins (live and neutral) and one hole (Earth). All the appliances bought from other countries have to be changed before they can be used in North Korean sockets. Moreover, the kitchens in some apartments have a four-connection socket, and a four-pin plug has to be used even though only two pins of the four-pin configuration are connected (live and neutral). Since these sockets have no earth connection, many common electrical appliances from other countries cannot be used in kitchens.

Ordinary citizens are allowed to use only one 40-watt bulb per room, ruling out reading at night. Moreover, they are required to turn off all lights by midnight, although party cadres are not bound by these regulations. One foreigner's impression of North Korean homes was that

> the rooms are very spartan, illuminated by a single electric bulb hanging without a shade in the middle of the room. Floor and table lamps are rare. Fluorescent lights are used in places like corridors of apartment buildings, first floors of department stores, and as outside lights, but incandescent bulbs are used in homes and most other places.

People's eyesight is reported to suffer as a result of the poor lighting.

With so much of the electric power supplied by hydroelectric sources, the country suffers from periodic power shortages during periods of drought. The regime's solution to the problem has been strict curtailment of civilian consumption, as well as reduction of industrial use. According to one resident of Pyongyang,

> Electric power, which had always been low and fluctuating, deteriorated noticeably during 1976-78. The power supply to the diplomatic community in Pyongyang was better than in the city at large, where consumption of electricity was severely restricted and the power supply to private residences cut off during the day. The areas of the city inhabited by foreigners was generally lighted at night to give the false impression of adequate electricity supply. Even so, in April 1978, electricity in the diplomatic areas was discontinued for two to three hours every day.

The situation in 1979 seems to have been no better. Foreign guests at the International Ping-Pong Meet held in Pyongyang in May 1979 were asked to conserve electricity and water. Many of the lights in the hotel hallways and in stores and along the streets were turned off and those that were on were dim and flickering. It was noted that the lights around Kim Il-song Square were not lighted every night.

During the 1978 drought, electricity was turned off in each province for one day, on a weekly basis. It was turned off every Saturday in Hamgyong Namdo and all shops were closed. As part of the nation-wide drive to conserve electricity, the Kaesong area was reported to have been without electric power every Monday for several years, and Ch'ongjin was without power during the daylight hours every Friday. In other areas, electricity was turned off for periods as many as forty-eight to seventy-two hours every week. In connection with the worsening electricity situation, the North Koreans designated different days of rest for each province, city, county, and district when the electricity was suspended to the area: Sundays for South Hwanghae Province, Mondays for Kaesong, and Tuesdays for South Pyongan Province.

A favorite subject for criticism at party criticism sessions is an individual's excessive use of electricity. Peer pressure has been sufficient to cause most people to limit their use of electricity; however, the regime has apparently still been unhappy about the wasteful use of electricity by "some elements" in the society, prompting party officials to take a very stern line against offenders. In a determined effort to reduce personal consumption of electricity, the regime finally resorted to putting meters in the newer apartments in Pyongyang to record the amount of electricity used. Up to then, there had been a flat charge for electricity based on family income.

Water

As with electricity, water has been rationed during periods of drought. This explains the inconsistent reports from some sources who stoutly maintain that water was not rationed and other sources who claim that it was. In the late 1970s the situation became critical enough that army engineers were being moved to water points to oversee the proper use of water supplies. In Sinp'o city, water was supplied only two hours a day, from 5:00 A.M. to 7:00 A.M. "During the hours when there was no piped water, people had to get water from wells, and many workers were late in getting to work every day." Water at the Ch'ongjin Hotel in Ch'ongjin on the East coast was turned on only from 8:00 P.M. to 11:00 P.M. At all other times there was no water in the hotel. The hotel, which had only twenty rooms, was the only Western-style hotel in Ch'ongjin at the time.

There are difficulties with the plumbing in even the more modern apartments in Pyongyang. According to one resident,

> The apartments are heated and provided with hot water from 7:00 A.M. to 10:00 P.M. and cold running water at night. The water supply system, though adequate, has one serious defect—the water taps often make roaring sounds. The vibrations in one tap travel to all the taps in the whole apartment building, so the roaring sound can be heard all over the building. It is very irritating, waking people up from their sleep. It poses a particularly serious problem to families with infants or small children.

Heating

All North Korean homes, whether apartments or separate housing units, are heated in the traditional Korean *ondol* method of heating the floors by conducting hot water through pipes laid under the floors. The water is heated by a coal- or wood-burning stove in the kitchen of each home. The same fire that is used to cook food can be used for heating. Individual apartments in large apartment buildings can be heated independently of one another in this way except for the newer apartments in Pyongyang that are tied into Pyongyang's central heating system. Believed to have been conceived and designed by Kim Il-song himself, the new system has been touted in North Korean propaganda as one of the wonders of Pyongyang. However, there is some question about the efficiency of the system. There is the obvious problem in maintaining a constant temperature as the water is piped relatively long distances from the Pyongyang Power Plant to different apartment buildings. It is almost unthinkable that North Korean engineers would not have foreseen this problem. However, it is quite likely that they would not have mentioned the defects in Kim's thinking and planning in an area in which he had no technical expertise.

Because of the cold North Korean winters, heating requires a major allocation of scarce energy resources. Absolutely no use of oil is authorized for private home heating; North Korea is completely dependent on imports for oil and prefers to use scarce supplies for gasoline and other purposes. Coal (or wood) is used as heating fuel. In the late 1970s the Pyongyang Thermoelectric Power Plant was reliably reported to be shut down from 11:00 P.M. until 3:00 A.M. every night because scarce supplies of coal were being diverted to other uses, including former gas-consuming vehicles that had been converted to charcoal-burning vehicles.

Individual family fuel rations appear to have been cut in recent years. Each household is now being allocated around 200 kilograms of coal per month for cooking and heating. Fuel rations are collected from nearby coal supply points. Normally, each housewife produces round coal briquettes from the coal with a tool that is sold at local stores for about 10 or 15 won. Some housewives mix dry dirt or clay in the coal to stretch their fuel allotments, though briquettes made in this fashion do not burn as long as regular briquettes. People are usually able to save some fuel in summer, happily so, since 200 kilograms is not considered sufficient for the winter months. To supplement their fuel supplies in winter, people gather firewood from designated areas for use in both cooking and heating. Those living in rural areas are fairly lucky in this regard; people living in the city are pretty much limited to collecting dead branches and grass. To conserve coal, other households use kerosene stoves for cooking during the spring, summer, and fall when they do not need to make a fire for heating. Hot plates are also used, and rice is often cooked in a special rice-cooker that uses electricity.

Families can compensate for the shortage of fuel by consuming only one hot meal a day. All food is prepared in the morning and eaten cold later in the day. This is impossible when the weather is extreme, of course; with the lack of refrigeration, food spoils in exceptionally hot weather and freezes in winter.

In the larger cities, people can have their dinners cooked at the rice-cooking establishments that prepare carry-out food for workers who bring in uncooked rice in the morning and pick up cooked dinners on the way home from work. These carry-out restaurants enjoy a booming business in offering a way to economize on fuel and an opportunity to reduce cooking chores after a long day at work. The food is still hot when people get it home, since rice-cooking establishments are located on the first floor of each of the multistoried apartment buildings.

Another way to save heating costs is to substitute bread for rice. The willingness of North Koreans to eat bread rather than rice, which they very much prefer, suggests the seriousness of fuel shortages and the pressure of cooking chores on an already exhausted workforce.

Telephone Service

With rare exceptions, telephone service is not available in private homes. Telephones are installed only in the homes of high-ranking officials of vice-minister level and above and a few other people who need a telephone for official purposes, for instance, drivers of high-ranking officials. Otherwise, phones are authorized only for state-operated enterprises or cooperative agencies, such as communications departments or post offices.

Every village has at least one public phone, usually located in the post office, for use by its citizens. In Pyongyang and other major cities, public phones are available at the post office, Central Telephone Exchange, Communications Departments, and major department stores. Most are coin-operated, automatic, dial phones and are not attended. Outside Pyongyang, public telephones are generally semiautomatic or crank-type phones and are attended by an attendant who places the call. The telephone charge is 10 chon per call, three minutes per call. As suggested by the limited number of phones, North Koreans are not accustomed to making personal calls. Essential information, including notice of a death in the family or travel plans, is normally communicated through official channels.

RURAL HOUSING

Although apartment houses are rapidly replacing single-story dwellings in the cities and at industrial sites, rural housing still consists primarily of single-story dwellings, each having one bedroom, a living room, a kitchen, and a storage area, which house, on the average, two families. Although many are relatively primitive, built with local materials such as stones, mud, sorghum stalks, and rice straw, with lime-coated walls and cement-tiled roofs, rural dwellings built since the war are considered modern by Asian standards. Usually, two of the rooms in these homes have hot-floor rooms; all are electrified; but few have inside plumbing. Several families normally share an outside latrine. The people use well water or install pumps to get water.

Virtually all of the rural homes that are visible to foreigners on the train ride from China to Pyongyang or on prescribed car trips from Kaesong to Pyongyang or from Pyongyang to Nampo and Wonsan appear to have cement-tile roofs: the status symbol of rural housing in Asia. These homes are known to have been given priority in postwar housing reconstruction in a calculated effort to impress foreigners who are allowed to see only a narrow view of North Korea from the train or highway. The regime has been quite successful in this regard. Most objective observers who enter North Korea from China by train, having seen both the Chinese and North Korean countryside on the long ride from Beijing to Pyongyang, are impressed with North Korean rural homes as being "much cleaner and prettier than the rural dwellings in China." Those familiar with the prewar Korean landscape are impressed with the modern improvements, especially the number of homes with cement-tile roofs.

We have no way of knowing exactly how many homes in the more remote provinces, out of sight from the main thoroughfares, have such tiled roofs. The few foreign visitors who have visited the more remote areas report seeing straw-thatched farmhouses in these areas. These more isolated villages have obviously had to wait their turn so that thatched-roofed dwellings in villages closer to the major highway and railroad lines could be replaced with modern homes ahead of them. Although they are no match for the white-washed adobe homes with cement-tile roofs built since the war, these straw-thatched farmhomes are a vast improvement over the old cave-type houses that were frequently observed during the war.

In the years immediately after the war, rural homes were constructed almost exclusively with cooperative and private capital (on the model of the Soviet Union and China) and with primitive construction materials that were procured locally. Beginning in the 1960s, however, they were built with state funds and modern construction materials allocated by the central government. Rear-line military units were used in building both single-story homes and apartment buildings. In addition, students, housewives, and office workers were mobilized in a competitive effort to build some 100,000 modern rural housing units per year.

Modern rural dwellings, built with state funds, are owned by the state, just as urban apartments are. Only the old straw-roofed homes and a very few single-story houses in a few cities are still owned by individual North Koreans. The regime tolerates this semblance of private ownership knowing that these houses are all slated for demolition as soon as new homes can be built. Just as old homes in whole sections of Pyongyang were demolished after the war, with no compensation to private owners, and a whole new skyline of high-rise apartments were constructed, thatched-roof houses in rural areas have been replaced by state-owned tile-roofed homes. The owners have no say when the state decides to renovate a whole village and build a new housing complex.

Not surprisingly, North Koreans are reported to have a strong preference for individual housing over apartment living. Whether this is simply a traditional preference or whether it is because they dislike carrying trash, water, coal, groceries, and other items up and down stairs of high-rise apartments that have no elevators, it is, from all reports, a clear-cut preference. People living in detached homes in the countryside also have the advantage of being able to grow their own vegetables and raise a few chickens or hogs as a way of supplementing their income.

In contrast to most other countries, rural housing in North Korea tends to be more crowded than urban housing. Most often, people in rural areas share a home with one or two other families. Whereas most countries, unable to stop the natural flow of people to the cities, have their worst housing problems in urban areas, North Korea has eased the housing crunch in its cities by strict controls over the migration of people to the city, but it has not succeeded in alleviating the over-crowdedness of rural housing to anywhere near the same degree.

HOME FURNISHINGS

In probably no other country have so few foreigners ever seen the in-side of people's homes as in North Korea. Many a request to visit a home or apartment has been turned down with the response, "I'm sure you are aware that well-mannered Orientals dislike strangers peeking into their homes."

Korean Americans who have gone to North Korea to visit relatives have never been allowed in their homes. In the week-long and much-publicized reunion in May 1979 of the Korean interpreter of the U.S. Ping-Pong team with his mother and sisters, whom he had not seen for thirty years, the interpreter always met his relatives in his hotel or in other public places. A Korean American professor, whose brother-in-law is one of North Korea's foremost architects and a well-established member of the elite, has visited his brother-in-law in Pyongyang on sev-eral occasions but has never been allowed in his brother-in-law's apart-ment, despite the fact that the apartment must reflect the perks of his brother-in-law's privileged position. The architect always comes to the professor's hotel.

The few apartments that North Koreans have taken foreign visitors to see have clearly been set up as display homes for that very purpose. The visitors themselves may not be aware of the pretense involved since their North Korean guides go to elaborate lengths to make the stop at a home seem quite spontaneous. Without discussing it with others, the foreigners could hardly know that most other foreigners just "happened" to visit the very same house. That conclusion can be drawn from interviews with a good many visitors to North Korea. Interestingly, almost every American who visited North Korea in the 1970s was taken to the apartment in Pyongyang of a lady who sells tickets at a local movie theater. Because of her job, she is at home during the day. Her apartment, complete with a television and small refrigerator, is hardly typical of the average worker's apartment. Fewer than one in ten apartments have a television and fewer still a refrigerator. Her apartment bespeaks an upper-class home. Either the woman is misrepresenting her job (or her husband's job) or her apartment has been specially furnished for the propaganda role it plays.

The disingenuousness of North Korean guides in professing to pick an apartment or restaurant at random is illustrated in the story of a Korean American who visited Pyongyang in 1980. Having repeatedly asked his guide to take him to an ordinary restaurant, not one reserved for foreigners, he was finally taken for lunch to a restaurant that the guide pretended to spot while they were driving around Pyongyang. Inside the restaurant, the visitor happened to overhear someone in the kitchen say: "The important visitor we have been expecting is here." Shortly afterward, after having been dissuaded from ordering anything on his own, he was served an elegant lunch that had obviously been prepared in advance.

So it is with official tours to people's homes and with official photographs of people's homes. Pictures in North Korean magazines such as *Korea* are obviously staged. There are just too many televisions, refrigerators, radios, and sewing machines to make them "typical." If they are typical of anything, it is a privileged home, certainly not the average one. The pictures do give some idea of the state of technology of North Korean home furnishings and home appliances, however. For instance, pictures of modern hotel rooms suggest a general level of technology reminiscent of the Soviet technology of the late 1950s, both in furniture and home appliances.

Contrary to what the regime might like others to believe, home furnishings typically consist only of a low folding, wooden table for eating (people sit on the floor to eat), one or two tall wooden wardrobes, one wooden pantry cabinet (for kitchenware), one wooden desk, one or two blanket chests, necessary cooking utensils and dining wares, a stove, and an electric iron. Blanket chests are used to store the blankets and quilts that North Koreans wrap themselves up in while sleeping on the floor. There are no beds, of course. Koreans accustomed to sleeping on a heated floor rolled up in a blanket or quilt tend to regard Western-style beds as very cold. Due to the limited amount of floor space, families do not usually purchase additional furniture even though it is plentiful in local markets.

One of the striking things about North Korean homes is their orderliness. "Living quarters are small, neatly arranged, and so orderly that they look like military barracks." Most impartial observers agree that "they are much tidier than homes in South Korea."

What the furnishings alone do not convey is the crowdedness of North Korean homes when all five or six members of the family are at home or are sleeping. Housing is inadequate primarily in the sense of its being cramped and crowded. Wooden chests are lined up against every available wall, leaving little room for sitting or sleeping. Wardrobe chests are crowded with the clothes of five or six people in one, possibly, two chests.

Typically, each person has his or her own corner of the room where he or she sleeps. If it is a two-bedroom apartment, family sleeping arrangements may change over time, lessening the tension created by everyone in the family, whatever their ages, sleeping together in one room. Young children usually sleep with their parents. However, as they get older, they are likely to sleep in another room with their brothers and sisters until, as teenagers, the boys move into one room with their father and the girls into another room with their mother.

One has to consider these crowded housing conditions in a historical sense, of course, and in comparison with other Asian societies. Housing conditions are no worse, certainly, than they were in pre-Communist days. On the other hand, they are not significantly better than in prewar days, in terms of crowding. Complaints about housing are still the number one complaint about economic living conditions, despite the heavy investment in housing. Improvements have not kept up with people's demands. The regime is bound to feel pressure to meet its promise of a two-bedroom apartment for every family of five or more. Perhaps it sees the best chance of fulfilling that promise by limiting the size of families, thereby limiting the demand for housing, rather than in meeting increased demand with increased housing. That would be in keeping with its general tendency to solve supply-and-demand problems by focusing on (i.e., limiting) the demand side of the equation. Its controls over society make that so much more feasible a solution than is ever possible in Western economies.

20

Education

The North Korean leadership has taken great pride in its free educational system and free medical services. When the Communists came to power in 1946, illiteracy was widespread and less than 20 percent of all Koreans had gone beyond elementary school. From the outset, a high premium was placed on the rapid training of technically oriented personnel crucial to the one-generation industrial revolution being planned.

The Korean War all but shattered the educational system established during the first years of Communist rule. All able-bodied young men were conscripted into the armed forces, while women and children were enlisted in noncombatant supportive roles. Even the students at North Korea's one and only university, Kim Il-song (KIS) University in Pyongyang established in 1948, joined the armed forces, holding seminars in the mountains of northern Korea and forming an esprit de corps reminiscent of Mao's loyal band of followers in the caves of Yunan during the early years of the Chinese civil war. (One of the exhibits at the Revolutionary Museum shows Kim Il-song University students communicating by radio from one cave to another during the Korean War.)

Having lost most of the intellectuals and skilled technicians living in the north in the mass exodus to the south after the war, the regime felt a great sense of urgency to develop a new class of skilled technicians "to accelerate the revolution and promote national construction." Official claims that the educational system has produced "new intellectuals" in unprecedented numbers must be considered in light of the Communists' use of the word "intellectual" as interchangeable with "technician." Kim and his advisers, hardly intellectuals themselves, would seem to have had no real understanding of the word "intellectual" in the Western sense. Their concept of an intellectual is a highly skilled technician.

From such thinking comes their basic concept of education as a linking of studying with work, a kind of on-the-job training through life.

Not until 1956 was it possible for the regime to enforce a program of universal compulsory primary education limited, at first, to four years but later extended to six years, including kindergarten. Emphasis was also given to adult education, in an effort to make the whole population literate. Every *ri* had a night program for farmers, a program that normally operated during the winter months. In 1958 the compulsory educational program was extended to the junior middle school level, providing students with a total of seven years of free education. A major expansion of technical schools and institutes was also undertaken; fifteen two-year colleges opened in 1959 alone. Specialized courses in mining, engineering, mechanics, communications, energy, water, fishing, medicine, law, literature, music, and art were available at these schools. In 1960 the regime claimed that 100,000 students were enrolled in seventy-seven such colleges, as well as KIS University. By 1970 the number of colleges had jumped to 129.

During this period, a full-fledged work-study program was established, involving all students of middle school and above in a work program of at least six to eight weeks a year (without pay) in factories, mines, or construction projects. At the same time, a system of "factory colleges" was created in some of the largest factories as a means of enhancing the skills of workers, thereby improving labor productivity. These were technical colleges in the most limited sense, having nothing to do with creating intellectuals. The colleges operated with factory funds and with factory personnel as teachers. The factory manager acted as the dean of the college with factory scientists, engineers, and specialists serving as faculty members. Classes met in the factory, after work hours. In 1965 there were thirty-seven factory colleges with 12,000 students and 2,294 graduates.

Although a program intended to bring all middle school students into a compulsory nine-year educational system was announced in 1959, the shortage of teachers and school facilities postponed its realization until 1967. Shortly thereafter, in November 1970, at the Fifth Party Congress, Kim announced an even more ambitious eleven-year compulsory free educational program, involving two years of kindergarten, four years of primary school, and five years of middle school. He acknowledged that it would probably be 1976 before most students were receiving the benefits of this full program.

It was much more difficult to expand the number of years of free compulsory education in the 1970s than it had been during the 1950s and 1960s because of the relatively small size of the student enrollment during those early years due to the low birthrate during the Korean War and immediately afterward. Primary enrollment dropped from 1.5 million in 1956–1957 to 960,000 in 1960–1961, and total school enrollment rose from 2.5 million in 1959–1960 to only 2.6 million in 1967–1968. Meanwhile, college enrollments fell from 300,000 in 1967–1968 to 200,000 in 1970–1971. Of the combined school enrollment of 2.6 million students in 1968, 1.8 million were reported to be attending 9,200 primary and secondary schools; another 700,000 were in high schools, higher technical schools and colleges.

There was a substantial increase in the number of school enrollments at all levels in the 1970s. School enrollment jumped from 2.6 million students in 1968 to 8.6 million, or roughly half the population, in 1980. Some 6 million of these students were reported to be in primary, middle, and high school, leaving 2.6 million in college and university, including those enrolled in factory colleges and correspondence courses. Existing colleges were expanded and other new institutions for the study of automation, shipbuilding, agriculture, and economic planning were founded. In 1976 officials reported a total of over 140 two-year colleges and more than 500 "specialized high schools" and higher technical schools, evenly distributed around the country.

Each province had at least one industrial, agricultural, medical, teachers', and party college. Altogether, there were ninety engineering, medical, and agricultural colleges, thirty teachers' colleges, ten party colleges, two or three economic colleges, the same number of foreign language colleges, one music school, one fine arts school, a general arts college, a drama college, and an athletic college. By 1980 the number of colleges had grown to 170, of which 25 were in Pyongyang. Enrollment in these colleges had increased, from a low of 200,000 in 1970, a drop from the 300,000 students enrolled in college in 1962, to a new high of 350,000 in 1980. Attendance at factory colleges, night schools, and correspondence course was also at an all-time high, suggesting no lessening of the emphasis on adult education as a consequence of the expanded effort in other directions. The number of factory colleges was said to have increased from twenty in 1960 to thirty-seven in 1965 to eighty-five in 1981.

Today, there is typically one primary school in each *ri* and one middle school in each district made up of two or three *ri*. Normally, a middle school in a city accommodates about 1,000 students and a rural middle school about 500 or 600 students. Defectors estimate the size of an average class to be about thirty students, with a teacher/student ratio of about 1:20. Because of limited classroom facilities, many schools operate in two shifts, an early shift from 9:00 A.M. to 5:00 P.M. and a later shift from 1:00 P.M.to 9:00 P.M. The afternoon overlap is accommodated by non-classroom activities such as physical education, militia training, and study hall.

Boys and girls receive essentially the same education in coeducational institutions through middle school. Upon completion of this eleven-year compulsory program, at the age of sixteen or seventeen, most girls in the cities go to work, either on farms or in local factories. Most males begin their eight years of obligatory military service after middle school. Approximately 30 percent of all male students, usually the sons of high-ranking government and military officials, however, are exempted from military service to continue their education through high school and college or, possibly, university. Kim Chong-il, for instance, never served in the army but went straight from middle school to high school to KIS University. After completing their military duty, about 5 percent of former military draftees enter a one-year preparatory course for college or university. Admission to college or university from the army is somewhat easier than it is directly from middle school. There seems to be a tendency to favor this school-to-army-to-college career progression. The army decides which of its "graduates" will go on to college and which will be placed in construction jobs.

The regime has released no detailed statistics on state expenditures on education. Western economists have tried to estimate expenditures in an effort to gain some insight into the relative priority of education, health, and housing; however, the estimates are at best rough approximations. There is the problem of converting won into dollars or some other meaningful exchange rate. Finally, so much of North Korea's investment in construction, be it the building of schools, hospitals, or apartments, has involved volunteer labor outside the monetary system. It is all but impossible to calculate the monetary value of these non-monetary expenditures.

The regime has said that it spends an average of 10,000 won to educate one child from nursery school through high school, or almost 1,000 won per year of education. Using statistics on the average number of admissions to high school from middle school, one can posit an enrollment of about 2.5 million in primary schools, another 2.5 million in middle school, and about 1 million in high school. That would suggest that some 6 million children and young people are receiving education at state expense at an expenditure in the neighborhood of 6 billion won. This does not include expenditures for the almost 3 million college and university students, including those in factory colleges and correspondence courses. If we use the average cost of educating primary and secondary school pupils of 1,000 won per student per year, on the assumption that the higher costs of a college education are balanced by the lower costs of a factory college education, we arrive at total state expenditures for education in the neighborhood of from 8.5 to 9 billion won. These figures, while tentative, would suggest a relatively high priority of education in North Korea.

It is unclear, however, exactly what the regime includes in its calculations of the cost of education; for example, does it include the cost of subsidized student clothing (which might properly be included in other consumer categories), or the costs of food provided free of charge to students, or government stipends to certain students to cover miscellaneous expenses? Considering the low level of economic expertise and the built-in distortions of a Communist statistical reporting system, it is doubtful that the regime is any better able than Western economists to sort out the strictly educational expenditures from other related state expenditures on students, which probably explains its reluctance to release aggregate expenditures on education.

In short, official statements on education are likely to give a very misleading impression of the progress to date. Moreover, none of the quantitative measures accurately reflects the qualitative changes under the Communists, changes which include improvements in mass education and a thoroughgoing indoctrination of the people at the cost of a decline in higher education. One cannot weigh these relative gains and losses in any net assessment, especially not one expressed in quantitative terms. It is far better to try to get some feeling for the strengths and weaknesses of the system without relying on quantitative measures.

The results of the Communist efforts to train technicians have been impressive, indeed. Over 600,000 technicians and specialists were trained between 1970 and 1976, bringing the total number of trained technicians in North Korea to over 1 million, up from 22,000 in 1953, 133,000 in 1960, and 497,000 in 1970. In terms of the percentage of the estimated total workforce, this represented an increase from under 1 percent in 1953 to 3 percent in 1960, over 8 percent in 1970, and 15 percent in 1980. Graduates of college and higher technical institutes, in

1980, accounted for about 10 percent of the labor force, and the average worker had seven or eight years of education, compared to four or five years in 1970.

There is no question that technical proficiency has increased, but foreigners still remain unimpressed with North Korean technical skills. Western technicians who have supervised the construction and bringing into production of plants imported from the West have despaired of North Korean engineering incompetence, their disregard of safety procedures, their careless maintenance and repair procedures, and their stubborn refusal to accept advice.

Moreover, the deficiencies in the educational system may outweigh the gains made in technical skills. One is brought up short, every now and then, when one learns, for instance, that the North Koreans had to postpone a visit by three Harvard professors when a Food and Agricultural Conference was meeting in Pyongyang because there were not enough English interpreters. Similarly, the government had to cancel the visits of other foreigners while the International Ping-Pong Meet was under way when again enough interpreters were not available.

The critical shortage of foreign language linguists has affected North Korea's economic development in many areas. The pressing need to know foreign languages to learn foreign technology led Kim to stress the teaching of foreign languages at all levels. Recognizing the United States to be the most technologically advanced country, Kim reportedly made the study of English compulsory in higher middle schools in 1978. Prior to that, students in middle school were required to study Russian; after 1978, both English and Russian were mandatory. English, French, and other Western languages had been introduced as optional courses in middle and high schools in the early 1970s, but there was nowhere near the same push to study foreign languages then that there has been since 1978. In a crash program to train English-speaking technicians and party and government officials, North Koreans were sent to special language training programs in Japan, Guyana, Yugoslavia, and Iraq. Apparently, the International Ping-Pong Meet, held in Pyongyang in 1979, dramatized the acute need for translators in many different languages. Shortly thereafter, the School of Foreign Languages broke away from Kim Il-song University to become a separate institute.

Most serious of all the deficiencies in the educational system is the relative absence of a true higher education and of a truly educated, intellectual class in North Korea. Fifty years after its founding in 1948,

Kim Il-song University is still the only four-year university in the country. Its 12,000 students represent less than 0.01 of the population.

Each year the regime has allocated additional resources to improve the facilities of Kim Il-song University. The main campus library boasts over 3 million volumes and 1,200 seats, but, according to foreigners who have toured the campus, the elaborately furnished library rooms have no one studying in them. Many different editions of Kim's collected works, bound in leather, adorn the bookshelves, but no one seems to be reading them. A separate file (which takes up one whole room) indexes Kim's every speech, with cross reference by date, location, subject, and key words and thoughts in each speech. But, again, no students appear to be using the files. While the grounds and buildings of the university grow ever more splendid every year, there has been little evidence of any significant improvement in the curriculum, except the establishment of a new school of international relations—with the breakaway of the Department of Diplomacy as a separate college from the Law College—which teaches international politics and languages.

Students usually enter KIS University when they are nineteen or twenty years of age. The maximum age is reportedly twenty-five, and the average age is twenty-three. About 80 percent of the student body lives in university dormitories; the others live at home in Pyongyang. Tuition, room, and board are 30 won per month. As at all schools and colleges, textbooks, school supplies, and uniforms are provided at government subsidized prices.

There are usually a few foreign students studying at the university. In the early 1960s, there were thirty or forty Japanese students and about forty-five others from the Soviet Union and Eastern Europe, most of whom were studying Korean history and language. In recent years, the number of Russian students has dropped and the number from Third World countries has grown. At one point, a whole dormitory was reportedly occupied by Vietnamese students.

Graduates of KIS University constitute the true educational elite. Kim Il-song's son, Kim Chong-il, apparently first wanted to go to school in the Soviet Union or Eastern Europe but decided to attend KIS University to underscore North Korea's *chu'che* (national self-identity) philosophy. He is reported (quite naturally) to have been an outstanding student, excelling in public debating and "original political thinking."

In one respect, and perhaps only in one respect, Kim Il-song University is like every other school in North Korea—its emphasis on political indoctrination. From nursery school on, students are taught the national ideology as part of every subject, be it math, reading, or social studies. Young children become used to thanking Kim Il-song for their every meal, for their school supplies, for their teachers, for the schools themselves. A popular nursery school song expresses their thoughts in the refrain, "Thank you Marshall Kim Il-song, for bringing us up as future pillars of society." In reading, students read about Kim's guerrilla exploits; in math, they learn to count by counting the number of American soldiers killed or the number of tanks destroyed in the Korean War; in history, they study the Communist revolution in Korea; in music, they sing Kim's marching songs; and in drama, they reenact his life story. The emphasis on the political never diminishes.

Kim Il-song University students in the social sciences are required to spend almost half of their time in ideological study. Students in the science departments can spend more time on scientific studies, devoting only about 20 percent of their time to Kim study. At the College of Economic Management, roughly a third of the course offerings are concerned with ideology and political matters. As students become more sophisticated, in college or university, they necessarily have to spend more time studying Kim's teachings and expend more energy in public observance of the Kim cult. Their studies are increasingly marked by the intrusion of political affairs into education.

From all reports, there is considerable dissatisfaction with the limited opportunities for higher education. While the regime may have made notable progress in expanding mass education at the lower levels, it has not made commensurate gains at the higher levels. Many students who want to go on to high school or college and are well qualified to do so are barred, either because of *songbun* or because of the limited number of schools of higher learning. The system is structured to provide the necessary training for productive labor, but then people are expected to go to work. Only about 30 or 40 percent of middle school graduates go on to high school, less than 10 percent of high school graduates go on to college (two-year) or university (four-year), and only some 5 percent of military draftees go back to school. Competition for admission to Kim Il-song University is intense; only one student out of every five or six applicants is accepted; in some departments, only one out of ten applicants.

Imbalances in the curriculum constitute another serious deficiency of the educational system. Sciences predominate, while the social sciences are all but neglected, except for the study of Marxism-Leninism and the Communist revolution in Korea. According to one former student, more than three out of four classrooms at KIS University consist of laboratories for the study of biology, chemistry, geology, communications, and related practical subjects. Foreign visitors, on the other hand, have been singularly unimpressed with the laboratories at the university.

North Korean defensiveness about their academic program of studies in the social sciences is evident in the unwillingness of officials to allow visiting foreign social scientists to meet with social science professors. U.S. social scientists who have specifically requested scholarly exchanges with their counterparts in North Korea have been allowed to talk only with North Korean government experts on the United States, not university professors. The regime has also been very reluctant to send social scientists to international meetings, presumably for the same reason: fear of exposing their academic limitations.

Whether these limitations are primarily due to the poor academic qualifications of the instructors or the politization of education is difficult to determine. Many of the problems are doubtlessly the result of the system. The intimidating effect of the *songbun* system on teachers who might otherwise demand high academic standards of students who can afford to adopt a lazy, indifferent attitude toward their studies because of guaranteed success in life due to good *songbun* has already been discussed. Once admitted to Kim Il-song University, students are virtually guaranteed of graduation. University officials boast of having had "no failures." Students who are having difficulty are helped by other students in their study group until they "show good school records."

Teachers and students are quick to realize what really matters. In a system that puts a premium on political loyalty, over and above everything else, the bright and ambitious cultivate their political skills and worry less about academic proficiency. In such a system, educational standards inevitably fall victim to political pressures. As much as it may hope to raise educational standards, the regime is ultimately faced with the basic contradiction between many aspects of its national ideology and the pursuit of higher learning. A U.S. scholar of Korea was struck by the regime's deliberate efforts to "maintain a relatively unsophisticated technological level in rural areas" to promote Kim's "local self-sufficiency concept." An extension of this can be seen in North Korean workers' refusal to accept advice from Western technicians, knowing the advice to be sound but fearing some abnegation of Kim's cherished chu'che philosophy.

Some of the problems are due to the shortage of teachers and materials. Teachers of primary grades in rural areas, in particular, are most often new graduates of middle school, barely seventeen years old. School supplies, other than textbooks and paper and pencils, are simple. Maps, charts, pictures, and other materials are usually made by the teachers and the students themselves. There is much rote memorization, a time-honored Korean tradition, but it is carried to the extreme in the memorizing of Kim's long speeches and the countless dates and other trivia of his life.

Students, like teachers, are generally overworked. They attend school, on the average, from thirty-five to forty hours a week, thirty-five to forty weeks out of the year, but also perform from twelve to twenty hours of volunteer labor each week in addition to their daily contribution to work chores on campus, their involvement in militia training two or three times a week, and their required attendance at political indoctrination sessions three or four nights a week.

Limitations in terms of the quality of teachers, the quantity and quality of school supplies and equipment, and the time and attention students can devote to their studies are all overshadowed by the one basic problem that affects the quality of education—the conflict between the pursuit of "truth" and the Communist insistence on its own brand of the "truth." The quality of North Korean education can never be any better, or any closer to the truth, than the official party line. That has been a given in all Communist countries, but in a country like North Korea, more isolated from the world and more cut off from reality than any other Communist country, the truth can be distorted to an almost unbelievable degree, with little chance of its being challenged by North Koreans.

Consider the fact that North Koreans grow up today with no knowledge of U.S. involvement in World War II in Europe. They are taught that the United States bombed Japan, late in the war, with the intention of occupying it for its natural resources. They believe that the Soviets, not the Americans, are primarily responsible for the defeat of Japan. Until he left North Korea on a diplomatic assignment abroad, one very well-educated North Korean had never known that the United States and England, and not just the Soviet Union, fought Germany and Japan. The average North Korean, in other words, knows little history except Korean history and the history of Marxism-Leninism.

Even the study of Korean history is tainted by Communist analysis of the "class struggle" and "exploitation of the poor by the rich." There is no study of the world's religions. Visitors to North Korea, who may get a favorable impression of the buildings of KIS University or the musical versatility of North Korean students, rarely get any insight into such behind-the-scenes realities.

One can get a good idea of the level of North Korean studies from reading its scholarly journals, such as they are. There are only about ten or twelve periodicals that could be considered remotely scholarly, and even that would be stretching the definition. These journals are in the fields of chemistry, physics, geography and the other natural sciences, linguistics, history, and archaeology. Since few of these journals are available outside North Korea (none in translation), the worldwide familiarity with North Korean academic studies must be considered virtually nil.

Most publications, which deal with the natural sciences, reveal a low level of research and experimentation. Western scientists have found no original ideas or research techniques of any real merit. Illustrative of this, perhaps, is the fact that no North Korean scientist—in fact, no North Korean scholar in any field—has any international standing.

The North Koreans have done some good archeological work; some of their digs have produced significant finds. This is one area in which the regime apparently feels comfortable in sending its "scholars" to international meetings. Some research is being done in linguistics on different Korean dialects. At various times, the regime has published classical Russian literature and even some classical European literature, with accompanying analytical comment. However, the average North Korean has no knowledge of world literature other than Korean literature. Even the most educated North Koreans have never heard of Homer, Chaucer, Shakespeare, Milton, any famous Russian or Chinese writers, or any modern European authors of note. The average North Korean is not even exposed to traditional Korean literature; he is likely to have read nothing but Communist revolutionary literature written since 1948.

Advanced students in music are exposed to classical Western music to perfect their technical skills and, apparently, to impress foreigners. Visitors to North Korea are often treated to impressive performances of Bach, Brahms, or Chopin by music students who could reasonably be considered virtuosos on the piano or other musical instruments. The average North Korean has never heard of such composers, however. By and large, North Koreans know only the revolutionary music sanctioned by the regime for the masses. It is the only music played on the radio or television. The elite in Pyongyang may attend musical concerts featuring classical Korean music, and, of course, the older generation remembers such music, but they do not hear it often.

In short, with one or two exceptions (archaeology and linguistics), the level of academic studies in North Korea lags far behind the general industrial level of the country, indeed, far behind the level of academic studies in most underdeveloped countries at a lower industrial stage than North Korea.

One striking decline in educational standards has been the abandonment of the study of Chinese characters, one of the Communists' first actions in the late 1940s, when the regime was primarily concerned with eradicating illiteracy, a goal that was aided by a switch from the use of Chinese characters to the use of the Korean phonetic *hangul*. The short-term gains in reducing illiteracy were accomplished at the long-term costs of abandoning a classical education in Chinese characters. In China and Korea, the mark of an educated man has always been his knowledge of Chinese characters; so it is today in Communist China, Taiwan, and South Korea, but not in North Korea. Only a very few North Koreans who study linguistics or ancient Korean history still know Chinese characters. Most people do not even know the Chinese characters in their names. Nothing could better bespeak the drop in educational levels under the Communists. Some observers of the Korean scene see this as one of the major difficulties in a future reunification of the two Koreas. At a minimum, it typifies the gulf between the two countries. In a key sense, North Korea has separated itself from its cultural heritage, a heritage that China, Taiwan and South Korea still share, despite their contemporary political differences. Having lost a major cultural heritage that would be very difficult to regain at this point, after a break of more than a generation, the DPRK not only has lost an important link with other Asian countries but also has suffered an inestimable decline in prestige in the eyes of these countries. Whatever the Communist successes in mass education, they must be weighed against these losses in higher education.

In short, the regime has educated a whole generation of North Koreans in Kim Il-song's image, more sophisticated than he in the technical, scientific, and economic areas but essentially practical-minded people interested in solving immediate issues at hand. North Koreans have had little in the way of a truly intellectual experience. They have

certainly not been engaged in a "quest for the truth" or had any experience "playing with ideas." They are technically trained bureaucrats, imbued with Kim Il-song's teachings. Continued isolation on the world
scene guarantees the continuing unsophistication of a country that sacrifices educational standards to practical necessity and simplistic political ideologies. More than the Communists probably realize, their
educational policies are likely to prove counterproductive to their other
efforts to establish North Korean prestige in the world today and break
out of the long years of isolation from the world scene.

Intellectuals who remained in North Korea after the partition of
Korea were coerced into menial jobs that fit into Kim's concept of
productive labor. Few of their stories have reached the Western world,
but some are known to have committed suicide in despair at being
sent to collective farms "to clean chicken yards." Along with former
landowners and other classes of people who were deemed to be "enemies of the state," these intellectuals educated before the war are
thought to have composed a group of dissidents who remained thoroughly opposed to the regime but powerless to do anything about it.
They have all passed from the scene by now, and with them has died a
whole cultural inheritance.

The loss of a highly educated elite has long-term implications, not
only for North Korea's domestic economic development, but also for
its political, social, and cultural interchange with the rest of the world.
Corrections in an educational system require years to show results.
Even if the North Koreans were to begin now to make some of the
needed changes, it would be decades before the basic problems were
solved. Since these problems derive from the political system itself,
there is really no hope so long as Kim Il-song's teachings survive.

21

Health Care

Another consumer sector of crucial importance to North Koreans for which the regime has assumed full responsibility is health care. Government expenditures for health, like education, are almost impossible to estimate, given the paucity of data released by the regime. The best one can do, again, is to get some feeling for the priorities of the health program, its progress to date, and consumer satisfaction or dissatisfaction with the services provided.

In assuming full responsibility for the health of its people, as well as the costs involved, the regime has given priority to preventive medicine as the surest and cheapest way to good health. Much less emphasis is given to medical treatment of diseases. These priorities suggest a somewhat callous concern for keeping people healthy for productive labor and far less concern for the treatment of the disabled and medically ill.

The Communists have instituted nationwide regular medical checkups that might be the envy of Western doctors preaching preventive medicine. It is this feature of the DPRK's health program, plus the practice of cleanliness, that most impresses foreigners with the excellence of medical care in North Korea. Medical checkups are provided on a routine basis to every school (including nurseries), factory, cooperative farm, office, and military unit. People are given a complete check-up once a year but, in addition, are required to have monthly check-ups for the treatment of minor conditions such as colds. In some cases, doctors come to the schools and factories; in other cases, people go to the local clinic. There is no way to avoid these periodic checkups but, then, there is no way of being denied them, either. It is impossible to hide a medical condition from one's employer; the state knows everything about everyone's health just as it knows almost everything else about everybody.

Because of the organizing of health care around people's place of work or school, members of the same family do not see the same doctor. There is no such thing as a family doctor. Children see the doctor at school and parents see the doctor at their respective places of work. Needless to say, there is no choice of doctor. As doctors are reassigned from one clinic to another, people have no choice but to see a new doctor. They are used to changing doctors as they move from school to school, in and out of the army, and from one job to another. In short, there is no continuity of medical care in North Korea, with children seeing the same pediatrician for years and adults seeing the same internist for years. However, there is continuity in medical records; one's lifetime "health card" is automatically forwarded to one's new health clinic every time one moves.

In keeping with its emphasis on preventive medicine, the regime has been very aggressive in attacking epidemic diseases, including typhus, smallpox, cholera, and encephalitis. In the early 1960s the Communists instituted national inoculation programs against these diseases. According to Dr. Han Ung Se, director of North Korea's Public Health Department, "In prewar days, superstition was a big obstacle to combatting contagious diseases. Everyone used to think that a child could only become a man after he had contracted the measles, so grandmothers would take their grandsons to children suffering from the measles. Needless to say, a large number of children died as a result."

Today, all children are inoculated against smallpox, measles, diphtheria, and whooping cough. Adults are regularly inoculated against tetanus, typhoid, typhus, hydro-fever, Japanese encephalitis, and cholera. Chlolera is a particularly dreaded disease; in 1970, there was an epidemic of cholera and people were reportedly "lined up for blocks waiting for their inoculations." Hydro-fever, a disease with flu-like symptoms that is caused by drinking nonpotable water (especially during the rainy season in July) or swimming in dirty water, is also common. All serums against this and other diseases, which are of North Korean origin, have been developed by the Institute of Microbiology in Pyongyang. Some, like the encephalitis serum, are apparently in chronic short supply; people often have to wait many months for a scheduled shot. Nevertheless, North Korea has been quite successful in preventing the infiltration of Japanese encephalitis.

Many doctors are engaged in epidemic prevention work in epidemic prevention units in every hospital down to the *ri* level. Several times a year, these doctors make a tour of the area under their jurisdiction, order sterilizers, and see to it that disinfectants are sprayed wherever necessary. They are responsible for spraying public places, such as trains, buses, restaurants, and hotels with DDT and other insecticides. Foreigners report such spraying of trains after every stop. Members of the Epidemic Prevention Centers also give lectures on the prevention of disease and demonstrate various procedures for using different medicines; they distribute posters and direct student volunteer labor in support of epidemic prevention work.

The prevalence of tuberculosis is generally blamed on malnutrition and hard work. Physicians in outlying areas such as Sinuiju have been adamant about the need to improve food supplies if the disease is ever to be eradicated. Large numbers of workers, particularly miners, are reported to be suffering from tuberculosis. The government sends medical teams to treat these people, but physicians apparently use every possible means to avoid the assignment. People are encouraged to give blood for tuberculosis patients; public recognition of "heroic service" is given to those who do. There has been significant progress in combating tuberculosis, despite its continued prevalence. (About 10 percent of the population is reported to suffer from tuberculosis.) At one time it was the leading cause of death; today it ranks much farther down the list. Cancer, heart disease, and strokes are now the leading cause, in that order, with digestive and respiratory ailments also accounting for a significant number of deaths. Together, cancer and heart disease are reported to account for roughly four out of ten deaths. According to government sources, life expectancy is now seventy-three years (seventy years for males and seventy-six for females), compared to forty-six years in 1945. Sources at the United Nations, however, put the figure at sixty-one years for men and sixty-five years for women. According to the regime, the death rate has been reduced to one-quarter of its pre-1945 rate, probably an exaggeration but suggestive of the significant medical advances made since the early 1950s.

Major causes of hospitalization, as distinct from deaths, are gastric disorders and malnutrition, reflecting both the diet and the level of tension in the society. Hard work and constant political indoctrination are reported to take their toll in the relatively high incidence of neurosis among the population, but reliable information is lacking.

There is apparently a low incidence of influenza in North Korea and the regime has taken precautions that foreigners do not bring the disease into North Korea. According to one source, during a worldwide epidemic, all visa applications from countries experiencing a flu outbreak were canceled. The regime encourages people to wear gauze masks over their mouths and noses if they have a cold or the flu. These masks, which are common in Communist China, used to be even more common in North Korea than they are today. One does not see them as much in the cities as in rural areas, where people are less sophisticated and apparently less reluctant to wearing them. Nonetheless, people in cities are annoyed if someone who is not wearing a mask coughs or sneezes in a bus or on the subway.

Apparently much of this derives from Kim Il-song's obsession with germs. The few American visitors who were granted an interview with Kim were required to have a medical checkup before seeing him. According to several sources, North Koreans submitted to a similar medical checkup before being admitted to Kim's inner offices. Procedures went well beyond the normal health precautions, suggesting an abnormal fear of germs on Kim's part, reminiscent of Joseph Stalin in his later days.

From all reports, Kim enjoyed exceptionally good health until his sudden death from a heart attack at age eighty-two in 1994, perhaps thanks to these elaborate efforts to protect him from every contagious disease. His one conspicuous medical problem, which mystified Western observers for years, was the large growth at the back of his neck just above the collar. The growth swelled and shrank over the years, or at least appeared to do so as well as Western observers could tell, given North Korean photographers' best efforts to photograph him only from angles that did not show the growth and given Kim's easy way of keeping on the right side of foreign visitors so they too could not see the growth. There is a story—perhaps apocryphal—that it never occurred to Kim that he had a tumorous growth; he simply assumed that it was related to his changing weight. According to a reliable source in North Korea's Foreign Ministry, he never heard any discussion of the lump in all his years in North Korea, illustrating the extreme restraint of North Koreans in discussing personal matters relating to their "great leader." It is almost inconceivable that they did not notice the growth. Some have suggested that Asians, accustomed to seeing goiters of various types on people's faces and necks, take a disinterested attitude about such things. It seems more likely that their sense of propriety—exaggerated in the case of Kim Il-song—simply ruled out any discussion of the subject. It is interesting, in any case, that a subject that garnered so much attention in the West was simply dismissed by North Koreans.

One area of preventive medicine that has received increased attention in recent years in the West but which, for obvious reasons, has been virtually ignored in North Korea is nutrition. Underdeveloped countries, struggling to improve the basic diet of the people, can hardly afford to emphasize the nutritional requirements of good health: a varied diet, or high protein diet, with fresh fruits and vegetables, all of which are lacking in North Korea. Compared to Americans, North Koreans do not appear to worry as much about their health or the quality of the medical care they are getting. This is not to say that they have no gripes about the medical system, only that they are not as health sensitive as Americans or as upset by poor-quality medicine.

As in education, there has been significant progress in medicine in terms of the number of doctors, nurses, and hospitals. Before "liberation" there were no state-owned hospitals in North Korea and only ten private clinics with a total of from 200 to 300 beds. There were fewer than 100 doctors. Today, there are 6,700 hospitals, clinics, and rural health centers and some 30,000 doctors (or approximately 1.7 doctors for every 1,000 North Koreans). As one of its first priorities, the regime sought to train more doctors at the established six-year medical colleges in Pyongyang, Hamhung, Ch'ongjin, and Sariwon and also at newly established medical junior colleges located in every province. In terms of the number of doctors and hospitals per capita, North Korea ranks high in the world today. It is unclear just how well trained these doctors are, however.

Medicine is definitely not a prestige profession. As noted earlier, medical doctors, lawyers, professors, and other intellectuals of prerevolutionary days were denounced as enemies of the state and sent to collective farms and, with their descendants, relegated to the lower classes. Medical school, which is not eagerly sought after, involves a lot of training, relatively low wages, and no prestige. Many young men choose not to go to medical school; therefore, almost three-quarters of North Korea's doctors are women. Nurses, all of whom are women, are technically called "nursing workers." There are no nursing colleges in North Korea. Girls with a high school education or less are qualified to become nurses.

As in education, the question of quality of medical care must be considered apart from the gains in the number of doctors, nurses, or medical facilities. There is a tremendous difference in the quality of medical care; some of North Korea's hospitals have the most modern equipment, high-quality medicines, and better-trained physicians, and others are poorly equipped and inadequately staffed. There are the so-called central hospitals in Pyongyang, like the Red Cross Hospital and the Pyongyang Medical College Hospital; city and provincial hospitals; like the Pyongyang Hospital and the Haeju Hospital; county or ward hospitals; factory hospitals; and rural health centers. Generally, factories with 7,000 or more employees operate their own hospital for their employees, while factories with 300 or more employees have clinics, similar to the rural health centers which serve cooperative farmers. The Munnakpyong Clinic, for instance, serves the twenty-one households of the employees of a cable shop of the Kapsan mine. Clinics are operated not by doctors but by nurses or midwifes. They have no beds and give only first-aid treatment. During the 1970s there was a big push to turn these rural clinics into people's hospitals at the *ri* level. A *ri* hospital would normally have one doctor and two nurses. Apparently some of the clinics were simply renamed village hospitals, with no upgrading of personnel.

Because of the limited number of medical personnel, patients often have to wait a long time to see a doctor or nurse at these clinics, although the situation may have improved somewhat in recent years given the increase in the number of doctors and the new emphasis on rural medicine.

Seriously ill patients are not treated in rural clinics or *ri* hospitals but are sent to county hospitals, or, possibly, provincial hospitals. If they cannot be treated at the provincial hospital, they are sent to central hospitals in Pyongyang, although admission to these hospitals is difficult to obtain. Serious cancer and heart disease patients are sent to the Red Cross Hospital in Pyongyang which specializes in these two diseases. One of the largest hospitals in North Korea, the Red Cross Hospital serves 1,400 patients with a staff of 600 doctors and 200 interns. Its annual operating budget is said to be about 10 million won. Only residents of Pyongyang can receive treatment at a central hospital like the Red Cross Hospital without first going to a city hospital. North Korean officials have told U.S. visitors that all eye surgery is done in the central hospitals in Pyongyang. Patients needing cataract or other eye surgery must be brought to Pyongyang, suggesting the relatively limited amount of surgery done in the countryside. When one observes the modern operating rooms and equipment in central hospitals in Pyongyang, one is observing not only the best, but, in some cases, the only facilities for certain kinds of operations or cancer treatment.

There is no question about the good medical care given at the Red Cross Hospital and other central hospitals in Pyongyang. The doctors, North Korea's best, have received training in the former Soviet Union, East Germany, Hungary, and Romania; the medical equipment is good; the hospitals are spotless; and the hospital food and medicines are more than adequate.

The Pyongyang Maternity Hospital, the country's showcase hospital, has become a regular stop on the VIP tour of Pyongyang since its opening in late 1980. Its modern equipment imported from Sweden, its well-furnished rooms, and its internal television monitoring system are impressive. There is no other medical facility like it in North Korea. Although most babies in North Korea are born in a hospital, there is a world of difference in having a baby in the Pyongyang Maternity Hospital and elsewhere. Many mothers in rural areas still prefer to have their babies at home, in which case, the baby is delivered by a doctor, with the help of a midwife. The result has been an impressive lowering of the infant mortality rate to one of the lowest in the Far East. Fewer than ten newborn babies out of every 1,000 born die, which is a major accomplishment compared to the prewar mortality rate of 350 deaths out of every 1,000 babies born. Also, many fewer women die in childbirth, compared to prewar days.

Except for a few pediatric hospitals, tuberculosis sanatoriums, and the rare exception like the Pyongyang Maternity Hospital, most hospitals are general hospitals with an x-ray department, pathology lab, internal medical clinic, surgical clinic, orthopedic clinic, herb medicine clinic, dental clinic, ophthalmic clinic, pediatric and obstetric clinics, and an ear, nose, and throat clinic.

A typical hospital, like the Tongui Central Hospital, has about 100 to 150 beds. There are a few rooms which accommodate only two patients and several more which accommodate four patients, but most rooms accommodate from ten to fifteen patients each. Most of the beds are filled most of the time. The majority of the patients are surgical patients. The most common operations are for appendicitis, tonsillitis, boils, and abscesses. Only the beds in the most modern hospitals have mattresses; most are wooden-board beds. Patients apparently bring their own quilts from home. A seaman hospitalized in the Cho'ongjin

National Hospital reportedly borrowed a quilt from one of his North Korean roommates. An injured member of the USS *Pueblo* crew who spent forty-four days in a hospital in Pyongyang also had to borrow a blanket from his North Korean hospital roommate. The North Koreans finally brought him blankets from the USS *Pueblo* because of the acute shortage of blankets at the hospital.

Hospital patients are not issued hospital clothing, and there are many patient complaints about being cold. Even with a borrowed blanket, the seaman reported being "tormented by the chilly gusts of wind blowing in from the windows." For some reason—probably to clear the rooms of germs—windows in hospitals seem to be kept open regardless of the weather outside. Many foreign visitors have noted the open windows, even in operating rooms during operations, and the lack of air-conditioning.

Generally, patients are restricted to their hospital rooms, except when they have visitors, whom they meet in a special visiting room. If they are not ambulatory, they cannot have visitors; no visitors are ever allowed in patients' rooms in North Korean hospitals. The Pyongyang Maternity Hospital has an inside television system that allows visitors to see and talk with patients on television. It is clear that the rules isolating hospital patients from other people are strictly enforced throughout the country.

While they are in the hospital, patients must submit their food ration card and eat only hospital-provided meals. The seaman who was hospitalized in Ch'ongjin in 1968 was given conspicuously better meals than those provided his four North Korean roommates; even at that, "all three meals each day consisted of a bowl of brown, unpolished rice and a side dish of fish." He grew tired of the same menu three times a day and asked for bread at least once a day, to be provided at his own expense. His request was complied with only once. Thereafter, he was refused bread on the grounds that "bread and other bakery products are not sold in Ch'ongjin." Another foreigner hospitalized in the Ch'onghin Hospital at a later date was also given the same meal every day. His consisted of "a bowl of unpolished rice, soybean paste soup, two fried eggs, and a small piece of pork." The menu never changed during the eight days of hospitalization, although he was given apples, in addition, on four different occasions. His North Korean roommates "took turns peering at the sunny-side-up eggs and pork that were served to him every day. They said they had never eaten such food." During his hospitalization, he was strictly prohibited by his doctor from leaving his room. He was also forbidden to smoke or drink alcoholic beverages. Apparently, there are strict rules against smoking and drinking in all North Korean hospitals.

The North Koreans made an exception in allowing the injured crew of the USS *Pueblo* to smoke in the hospital. They did not fare very well as far as food was concerned, however. "Hospital food consisted primarily of an onion-and-potato soup with meat, usually pork or ham. The pieces of meat were usually rotten, and the soup usually cold. There was also a bowl of sweet milk, some hard bread which tasted like wax and three apples every day." On one occasion, one of the crew was feted with a table full of apples, peaches, cake, soup, and salami, which he ate, only to find out that it had been arranged strictly for propaganda photography.

One can certainly appreciate North Koreans' resistance to going to the hospital. It is not a comfortable experience in any sense, with the strictly enforced rules against smoking, visitors in patients' rooms, and special gifts of extra food. Most depressing of all are the crowded conditions, with so many patients in one room, the discomfort of the beds, especially for surgical patients, and the mediocrity of the food. Hospitals, being considered "relatively unimportant agencies," are given a low allocation of fish and vegetables, resulting in low-quality side dishes being served to patients. Seriously ill patients do apparently receive some dispensations. According to one source, very sick patients in the Pukchong-gun General Hospital, a county hospital, were given an egg every meal. Daily rations for other patients consisted mainly of vegetables, with a fish stew served twice a week and a meat soup served twice a month. There were no recreational facilities, such as movies, televisions, or radios, no barbershop or shower facilities. Typical Korean outdoor latrines were used by ambulatory patients. Other patients cleaned their own bedpans.

Getting to the hospital can be a painful experience, especially for seriously ill patients or those who live in the country and need to be taken a considerable distance to the nearest county hospital or, possibly, provincial hospital. North Korean–made jeep trucks of the Kaengsaeng-69 type serve as ambulances and, by all accounts, a trip in these trucks over county roads is memorable. One of the injured members of the USS *Pueblo* crew was driven through the countryside, over rough, frozen roads, in a canvas-topped jeep-type vehicle, accompanied by two doctors.

A handful of showcase ambulances, presumably imported from the Soviet Union or Eastern Europe, have been shown off to visiting VIP dignitaries. One American reporter was shown "an ultramodern ambulance" at the Red Cross Hospital in Pyongyang equipped with the latest emergency heart attack equipment. Although he was told that there were twelve more ambulances like it in Pyongyang, the reporter never saw them, "if they exist. . . . What I did see were wooden trucks, painted white with a red cross, that appeared to serve as ambulances." Foreigners who have lived in Pyongyang for months and, in some cases, years have reported never seeing an ambulance. It may be that it is difficult to recognize a hospital truck, serving as an ambulance, with the lack of identifying marks. Clearly, there is a shortage of trucks or ambulances, if that is what they are called, for taking people to the hospital, judging from firsthand accounts of people being seriously injured in traffic accidents in Pyongyang and being carried off to the hospital "by hand" (in the arms of friends or passers-by), with no sign of an ambulance or hospital truck. A foreign visitor in Pyongyang in July 1975 witnessed the tragic drowning of three North Korean ice skaters who fell through the ice of the Potongong River in Pyongyang. After their bodies were recovered, they were carried off with no sign of an ambulance or other vehicle. If this is true in Pyongyang, imagine what it is like in the country!

There are three "first-aid posts" in Pyongyang: one for heart attack victims, one for apoplexy, and the third for broken limbs, knife wounds, and other accidents. Each of these is manned around the clock by a doctor and a nurse. Each of these first-aid stations is supposed to be equipped with three ambulances to rush victims to the hospital after initial treatment. Judging from firsthand accounts of accidents, however, ambulance service is not what the authorities suggest.

The epitome in medical care is provided to high-ranking government officials at the Government Hospital in a suburb of Pyongyang. Kim and other top officials used to go to the Pyongyang Medical Hospital, but in January 1968 Kim instructed the Ministry of Health to build a modern hospital to provide exclusive medical treatment for the top party and government officials. The hospital which opened in February 1971, is officially named the Government Hospital, but it is better known as the Ponghwa Clinic after the name of the village where it is located, just outside Pyongyang, near the Executive Apartments, where government ministers live.

The clinic employs about thirty doctors, thirty interns, and fifty nurses. Most of the doctors were formerly professors at the Pyongyang Medical College. Only people with the best professional skills and intact political reputation work in the Ponghwa Clinic. No foreigners have ever been employed there. Dr. Ch'oe Ung-sam, the director of the clinic, who was Kim's longtime chief personal physician, graduated from a Japanese medical school and later served as dean of Ch'ongjin Medical College. In addition to the clinic, he operated a special medical service providing twenty-four-hour medical care for Kim on a house-call basis and other special services for cabinet ministers and top NKWP officials.

As might be expected, Director Ch'oe had a chauffeur-driven Mercedes Benz. Less important clinic doctors use Volga, Toyota, and Nissan automobiles. The clinic is reported to have one ambulance and several Kaengsaeng jeeps. Unlike most hospitals, it has a central heating system. Each room has a radiator, air-conditioner, sofa, two armchairs, and coffee table. Its elite patients look out over a floral terraced courtyard.

Most North Koreans are not aware of the existence of the Ponghwa Clinic, just as most Soviets did not know about the Kremlin Clinic in Moscow. Both leaderships have kept such prestigious facilities under wraps. Foreign visitors have never been taken to the Ponghwa Clinic despite North Korean interest in showing off its premium facilities. However, if one were to go near the Ponghwa Clinic, one would notice the government cars parked out front, a scene reminiscent of the Kremlin Clinic in Moscow, where knowing Soviets were quick to point out the limousines and chauffeurs waiting for the government leaders receiving special medical care inside the clinic. North Koreans are not in a position to see the Ponghwa Clinic, however. Like other secret elite facilities, it is located in an isolated area, set off from the main road and approachable only by a private road guarded by security guards at the gates of the walled enclosure that hides the whole facility from public view.

On a much lesser scale, members of the privileged class, though not of the elite, receive superior medical care at the central hospitals if they live in Pyongyang, or from "special sections" of other hospitals. Local party chiefs in rural areas would not have to wait hours before seeing a doctor, as other people would; nor would they be denied medicines that might be in short supply. The average citizen is probably aware of these differences in medical care, but they are not glaring enough to cause widespread public dissatisfaction.

Medical care is one area in which the regime seems to have satisfied the people's expectations. They have been pleased with the genuine advances made in the fight against traditional epidemic diseases and the improvement in medical care and treatment of curable illnesses, especially those involving surgery. The provision of medical care, free of charge, is considered one of the regime's most impressive accomplishments. Like Soviet citizens, North Koreans view their freedom from crippling medical bills as one of the great pluses of the Communist system. They have been told that medical care is a luxury in South Korea and in the West only the rich can buy it. By and large, they are convinced that "North Korea is a utopia compared to South Korea in this regard. They can see that in the DPRK, under state medical care, every citizen is entitled to free medical care. Gone are the days when people had to worry about medical bills." On the whole, they regard their system as a superior one. That is not to say that they do not see the problems in the system. Their chief complaints are the lack of interest of doctors in their patients, the lack of care for the chronically and terminally ill, the unpleasantness of hospital care, the difficulty in getting a medical excuse from work for relatively minor but nonetheless debilitating conditions (such as colds and minor injuries), and, worst of all, the shortage of medicines.

A worker can get sick leave only with a medical certificate from a doctor or nurse. Since this usually involves some inconvenience in getting to a clinic plus waiting around to see a nurse or doctor, many North Koreans prefer to go to work rather than expend the effort to get authorized sick leave. Anyone wishing to see a doctor must first obtain permission from his work team leader. The leader notifies the local clinic that he is sending a patient. Since the clinic has a list of all residents in its jurisdiction, presentation by the patient of his ID card suffices to complete all necessary formalities at the reception desk. But the patient may wait a long time to see the doctor.

Workers' reluctance to obtain authorized sick leave is probably due to their fear of not being considered sick enough, since anyone found not to be genuinely sick but feigning illness is subject to a reduction in food rations. Even with medical proof of illness, they get reduced sick pay, reported to be about 60 percent of their regular pay with less than five years on the job, 70 percent of their salary with five to ten years on the job, and 80 percent after ten years of service. Their concerns about a reduction in pay probably also tend to keep them on the job despite medical reasons for taking sick leave. It is interesting to speculate on the effect of this situation on labor productivity in North Korea. In the long run, labor productivity probably suffers more than it would if the regime adopted a more enlightened view toward sick leave.

By far and away the most persistent complaint about the North Korean medical system concerns the shortage and extremely high price of medicines, especially antibiotics, which are in great demand. North Korea produces virtually all the antibiotics available to the general public; tetracycline is the most commonly used. Pharmaceutical imports from Japan, the former Soviet Union, and China are reserved for the elite. The regime is proud of its new pharmaceutical industries, such as the penicillin factory at Sunch'on, but it is clear that domestic supplies do not begin to satisfy consumer demand. North Korean pharmaceutical factories of the late 1940s in Pyongyang, Hungnam, and Ch'ongjin were destroyed during the Korean War. Until 1955, when these pharmaceutical factories were rebuilt with Soviet and Chinese aid, North Korea was totally dependent on imports for medical supplies. Imports have become much less important since the Sunchon Pharmaceutical Factory went in full production.

Control over scarce supplies is exerted by doctors who are authorized to prescribe only those medicines that are available, in amounts that can be filled. Most modern drugs can only be procured directly from doctors; they are not sold on the open market, which explains why visitors are so often surprised by the lack of pharmacies or drugstores selling medicines. Even commonly used medicines like iodine and calcium, iron, and vitamin tablets must be procured from hospital dispensaries with a prescription from a doctor. Only certain traditional medicines are available at special drugstores. It is sometimes difficult to buy them, as well as certain items associated with personal hygiene, such as sterilized, surgical, absorbent cotton or wool cloth. Some medicines may involve a special charge, similar to the special charge for gold teeth made by dentists. With these exceptions, all other medical supplies and services are free.

Black-marketing of medicines may be the most pervasive form of black-marketing in North Korea. North Koreans will pay extravagant prices for medicines brought into North Korea. North Korean businessmen, guides, and hotel employees constantly ask foreign businessmen traveling to North Korea for drugs. There are reliable reports of the large-scale smuggling of Chinese medicines across the China–North Korea border. Among the known cases of corruption in the society are cases of doctors illegally taking medicines from hospitals

and selling them through middlemen, so great is the demand for virtually all types of medicines.

Foreign medicines are in demand not only because of the limited
supply of domestic medicines but also because of their superior quality.
The Pon'gung Medicine and Drug Plant and the Ch'ongsu Chemical
Factory produce very poor-quality drugs. There is no reliable information as to whether North Korean production of tetracycline and penicillin meets generally accepted international norms. North Korean
medicines are poorly packaged, however. The pills, which are very often
large, are difficult to swallow, and many medicines taste terrible. As
mentioned earlier, traditional medicines are still very much used and, in
some cases, preferred. The great majority of patients treated at local
clinics are still treated with folk medicines; modern drugs are usually
distributed by doctors at the larger hospitals.

North Korean pharmaceutical industries produce mainly traditional
medicines. For instance, the Pyongyang Pharmaceutical Factory produces a tiger bone liquor that is used in the treatment of articular diseases and neuralgia. It was supplied to North Korean troops suffering
from these ailments. The Singyang Pharmaceutical Factory produces
more than forty different traditional medicines for treatment of colds,
stomach ailments, and poor circulation. The Ch'ollima Chonch'on
Pharmaceutical factory produces another ten or more traditional medicines for many of these same ailments, plus paralysis and swellings.
Many of the country *ri* hospitals also produce traditional medicines
that are used locally, a relatively new practice intended to provide the
local self-sufficiency in the production of medicines that the regime has
pushed as a major feature of its whole program to achieve neighborhood self-sufficiency.

It is interesting how much North Korean satisfactions and dissatisfactions with medical care parallel Soviet consumer attitudes toward
the Soviet medical system. In large part, this reflects the degree to
which the successes of the North Korean system mirror the successes
of the former Soviet system and the shortcomings mirror former Soviet shortcomings, suggesting certain basic advantages and disadvantages in the Communist system of centralized control over medicine.
As Hedric Smith described medical care in the Soviet Union in his book
The Russians,

Epidemics have largely been curbed. Infant mortality has come
close to the levels of the fifteen most advanced countries. Life expectancy is up to 70 years. By 1970, the Soviet Union had the

highest ratio of doctors to population in the world—23.8 doctors for each 10,000 persons (compared to 15.8 in the U.S.) and more hospital beds than America (10.6 vs. 8.2 per thousand, though one reason is that Russian doctors hospitalize some kinds of people treated as outpatients in America, such as chronic alcoholics). . . .

Soviet officials never tire of telling that security from financial disaster because of health problems is one of the most important and popular aspects of the system. Russians . . . of modest means and position have obtained, virtually cost-free, health care that would have been inordinately expensive in the West. . . .

But privately, many Russians complain . . . that their health system, like the rest of the consumer sector, is plagued by over-worked doctors, shortages of medicine, poor equipment, and generally low quality service. . . .

[The] one problem that Russians complain about quite openly [is the shortage of medicines]. Even the press periodically chides the drug industry for shortages of such standard medicines or medical ingredients as glycerine for heart patients, tincture of iodine, ammonium hydroxide, novocaine, even first-aid kits and tourniquets, let alone sophisticated antibiotics. . . . [T]here [are] standing instructions for doctors not to prescribe medicines they [know to be] out of stock. . . . [C]ritically needed medicines [are often] unavailable at any price in Moscow. Nonetheless, for most Russians such problems are outweighed by the improvements over the past. They regard the system of free health care as one of the most positive features of Soviet socialism. (1985, 76–79)

The above could well have been written about North Korea.

All this said, there is one thing about North Koreans that seems to strike all foreign visitors and was certainly never said about the Russians: the people all look so healthy. One suspects that this is largely a result of the regime's exceptional efforts to project just such an impression. The North Koreans have gone to greater lengths to accomplish this than most nations would ever dream of doing. Foreigners are not allowed to visit places where sick people would normally be; every effort is made to ensure that the people they meet are the finest examples, including the healthiest, of North Koreans. All the pictures of North Koreans in propaganda magazines contribute to the impression of everyone looking healthy and happy; the people photographed are invariably attractive, healthy-looking, well-dressed, and well-groomed.

A close review of major pictorial magazines strongly suggests that professional models are used for supposedly random photographs of people going about their everyday business. The same men, women, and children (even babies!) appear in pictures of collective farmers, office workers in Pyongyang, factory workers in different cities, and students at various schools and colleges.

One reason why North Koreans may honestly give a flattering impression of good health is their good personal hygiene and the general cleanliness of the country—its schools, factories, homes, and offices, streets, public parks, countryside, hospitals, and clinics. The cleanliness of the country can hardly be emphasized too much; all visitors are struck by it. The regime has preached sanitation and good personal hygiene as the cornerstone of its health program. Despite the tediousness of the message, the campaign has obviously yielded returns. The country celebrates "sanitation month" two or three times a year. Every home, school, and factory is inspected four or five times a year by sanitation officials from the local hospital. They look for lice (there is a fine of five won per louse found inside a home or factory) and check the cleanliness of livestock cages in rural areas. A certificate is issued to those meeting the standards; those failing to pass inspection are criticized for lack of ideological fervor. Every North Korean who travels, checks into a hotel, or dines at a public restaurant is required to carry a sanitation pass verifying that he has had a bath at a public bathhouse within the past week.

Because the people and the country look so clean and healthy, does not, of course, mean that they are healthy. One has only to think of the psychological pressure of constant sanitation checks of one's home, threatening both personal censure and political repercussions, to appreciate the stress and strain on people. There is good reason to think that these pressures take a medical toll that may be hidden behind the surface impression of good health. Certain ailments that defectors speak about appear to be traceable to the stress and strain of life in North Korea—the exhaustion wrought by overwork and political pressures, insufficient rest, and lack of recreation. They are not organic diseases as much as functional disorders of neurogenic origin: gastric problems, excessive smoking, and an unusually high incidence of sterility.

While significant advances have been made in the fight against traditional illnesses, and in raising the birthrate and lowering the death rate, there may be a counter phenomenon at work that raises the incidence of socially produced illnesses. More information is needed before definitive answers can be given to questions of the medical effects of living in a totalitarian society, especially one so tightly controlled as the Communist society of North Korea.

In summary, the application of good common sense, basic rules of sanitation, and relatively simple medical practices have achieved remarkable results. Medical advances are likely to come much more slowly in the future. Improvements in sanitation, personal hygiene, and national inoculation programs against dreaded epidemic diseases have produced dramatic, one-time gains. Future gains will require a much greater investment in expensive modern medical equipment and technology, higher education of doctors and nurses, and more advanced medical research.

The state of medical research, which is far below scientific research in other fields, such as chemistry and botany, will be a serious constraint. North Korea has an Academy of Medical Science, the Research Institute of Clinics, the Research Institute of Oriental Medical Science, and other smaller research institutes, but the only original medical research of any note that has been done is in the field of acupuncture and traditional medicines. Medical researchers are reported to be "cultivating over 10,000 different herbs (some of which) are considered superior to modern drugs for treating arteriosclerosis and angina pectoris." The most famous of these herbs, the koryo insam or ginseng root, is used not only for controlling high blood pressure and diabetes but also other conditions: it "relieves fatigue, makes people feel younger, increases sexual potency, and makes people immune from many diseases." Researchers are also reportedly looking for a special medication to extend life expectancy. They have discovered a so-called never-get-old herb that looks like a mushroom. The people working on the project are reported to be taking the drug regularly; its effect was said to be "ten times better than ginseng."

Including traditional as well as modern drugs, North Korea is still far behind other countries in the variety of medicines available, far behind Communist China, for instance, and Japan. The level of medical training, including surgical training of doctors is equally behind other countries. The only modern eye surgery done in North Korea is performed in the central hospitals in Pyongyang, primarily the Red Cross Hospital. Every patient who needs eye surgery must be brought to Pyongyang. The average person does not get cataract surgery, which confines him or her to a life without reading after the age of fifty or sixty. Among other things, North Korean medical science has not reached the stage of open-heart surgery, and its care and treatment of cancer is not advanced. Most of its operational techniques (for brain surgery and esophagotomy, for instance) were learned from the Soviets and East Europeans in the 1960s and 1970s.

Recognizing the low level of training, the regime has begun a search for foreign medical instructors to train its prospective doctors, much as it is seeking foreign professors in all fields to teach its students at Kim Il-song University. However, North Korea's current isolation on the world scene, greater now after the collapse of its former Soviet and East European allies than ever before, leaves it virtually cut off from the major medical advances made in other countries. Totally dependent on advice and assistance from more advanced countries in practically every field of higher learning, including medicine, it is difficult to see how the DPRK can avoid falling farther behind other countries, particularly South Korea, in the immediate years to come.

The saving grace for the regime has been that the people of North Korea know nothing about the rest of the world, least of all the remarkable advances made in other countries in medicine and other fields. In the cult society of North Korea they know only what Kim Il-song and his son Kim Chong-il have told them, and they have been told—and apparently believe—that things are much worse, not better, in the United States, South Korea, and other capitalist countries. That is the belief that sustains them, that and the belief in a better life to come for them and their children in North Korea.

Epilogue

Kim Il-song had no doubts about the good life he was building for his country and his people. He was proud of the improvements in North Korea during his lifetime and held fast to his dream of better times to come. His genius was in communicating that dream to others and in creating a nation of believers, however ill-conceived and out-of-touch with reality that dream was. It will be interesting to see how long the dream can be sustained without him and his powers of persuasion.

What is truly remarkable about him and is so rarely true of dictators who warp a society to the degree that he warped North Korean society is that the people—most of them, anyway—appear to have revered him as a person, as a father figure, and as the "great leader" of their nation. Their cult worship of him was not simply contrived; it was apparently genuine to an amazing degree.

The people were not prepared for his sudden death on July 8, 1994. Despite various ailments that had plagued him at different times in his life, Kim seemed healthy for a man of eighty-two years, and there was no warning of the massive heart attack that killed him within hours.

The nation was overcome with grief on a scale that few outsiders comprehended or acknowledged at the time. Remembering the shock and sense of grief that Americans experienced at the sudden deaths of Presidents Abraham Lincoln, Franklin Roosevelt, and John Kennedy may suggest something of the national sense of loss and grief. The emotional outpouring of grief over the deaths of respected and beloved international celebrities such as Mother Theresa of Calcutta or Princess Diana, with whom people seem to have identified personally, may convey more of the emotional intensity of their grief. Still it was deeper than that. Kim had been their leader since the birth of most living North Koreans, and most had seen him at close range on countless occasions as he traveled around the country on his on-the-spot inspection tours for almost fifty years. They truly felt they had lost a father as well as their "Great Leader."

Even more than that, they had lost a cult leader whom many revered as a semigod. As members of a cult not dissimilar from some of the extreme cults that we have seen in recent years, some of whose members have followed their leader in death in preference to life after the leader's death, North Koreans found themselves absolutely bereft. It would be hard to exaggerate their sense of vulnerability, confusion, and uncertainty, on top of their grief.

The country's handling of Kim's funeral reflected its state of mind at the time. Foreign dignitaries were not invited to attend the funeral ceremonies, despite the fact that a head of state for almost half a century was being honored. Kim's proud *chu'che* philosophy of national independence may have played some role in the decision to ban outsiders, but the simple explanation seems to have been the people's feeling of a loss too personal and too private to share with others. The moral superiority and defiant aloofness that cult members typically feel towards non-believers may also have militated against the inclusion of outsiders at such an emotional time.

The limited glimpse that the outside world was afforded of the national outpouring of grief, with hundreds of thousands of North Koreans weeping for days, bespoke an honest desire to grieve in private, with no play for international sympathy or support. The unusual sense of propriety and privacy about so newsworthy an event, contrary to most countries' handling of such an occasion, was striking and touching and apparently quite sincere.

Observers of the scene have been perplexed that Kim's son and heir apparent, Kim Chong-il, did not move more quickly to assume the mantel of leadership that was apparently his for the taking. Although no one knows for sure, the answer may lie in his own paralyzing sense of grief at his father's death and a sense of the country's need for time and space to absorb the loss. For more than a year, North Korea truly was a country suspended in grief.

It is unlikely that Kim Chong-il will ever replace his father in the hearts and affections of the people. Efforts to promote him as an extension of his father, as the "Dear Leader," as opposed to the "Great

Leader" as Kim was known, are just that—efforts to keep the Kim cult alive, not to replace it with a new Kim Chong-il cult. Cults are too personal to the founding leader of the cult to be transformed into cults of someone else. They grow up and flourish, at least to the extent that the Kim cult flourished in North Korea, around a unique, charismatic leader. Kim was that. From all accounts, Kim Chong-il is not, however much the regime touts his accomplishments and whatever luster wears off on him as the son of the "Great Leader."

Kim Il-song, not Kim Chong-il, will always be at the center of the national cult of personality in North Korea. Kim Chong-il's succession presumes the continuation of the cult. Subsequent leaders will have the choice of promoting the cult as a loyal follower of Kim Il-song's teachings or destroying it to rule in their own right. Considering the intensity of the people's feelings about Kim Il-song, it is doubtful that any would-be leader would think of challenging the cult at this time. Kim Chong-il has the advantage of being an extension of Kim Il-song himself; the people are better able to accept Kim's death with his son and surrogate in place to carry on the cult. They are likely to prefer him, whatever his deficiencies as a leader, to anyone else, whatever his qualifications, who simply by not being Kim makes them confront the reality of Kim's passing.

The people's devotion to Kim will delay their realization of the evils he created in the society. It will not be easy for them to separate the bad from the good in a charismatic leader who ruled their country for almost half a century, longer than any other leader of the twentieth Century. But in the end, with the birth of a new generation that will not be seduced by his charm, his constant presence in their midst and his legendary heroics in freeing North Korea from the Japanese in World War II and in driving the Americans from their country in the Korean War, North Koreans will recognize Kim Il-song for what he was. The cult of Kim, possibly the most intense personality cult on a national scale of all times (though involving a very small nation) and the longest lasting national cult of this or perhaps any other century will vanish from the scene, probably in a backlash of emotion that will tumble it virtually overnight. With its demise many of the distinctive features of the Communist society that Kim created will inevitably be overturned or at least modified with time.

However, the fascination with the Cult itself, the factors creating it, the momentum sustaining it, and the forces that are likely eventually to destroy it will continue. Hopefully, an appreciation of the cult, as it was practiced in North Korea for almost fifty years, will provide useful insights in dealing with subsequent cult societies, not necessarily on a national scale like the Kim cult, but nonetheless awesome and threatening in their hold over the people under their sway.

Further Reading

Ch'oe, Yong-ho. "Christian Background in the Early Life of Kim Il-Song." *Asian Survey*, October 1986.

Cumings, Bruce. "The Corporate State in North Korea." In *State and Society in Contemporary Korea*. Ithaca, NY: Cornell University Press, 1993.

Gak, Hwani Eui. *The Korean Economies: A Comparison of North and South*. Oxford: Clarendon Press, 1993.

Harrison, Selig S. *Testimony on North Korea before the Subcommittee on East Asian and Pacific Affairs*. U.S. Senate Committee on Foreign Relations, January 14, 1992.

Henriksen, Thomas H., and Jongryn Mo. *North Korea after Kim Il Sung: Continuity or Change?* Stanford, CA: Hoover Institution Press, 1997.

Kagan, Richard, Matthew Oh, and David Weissbrodt. *Human Rights in the Democratic People's Republic of Korea*. Minnesota Lawyers International Human Rights Committee, 1988.

Kim Il Sung. *With the Century*. Pyongyang: Foreign Languages Publishing House, 1992.

Kim Il Sung. *Kim Il Sung Works*. Pyongyang: Foreign Languages Publishing House.

Kim Jong Il, The People's Leader. Pyongyang: Foreign Languages Publishing House, 1983.

Lee, Chong-Sik, and Se-Hee Yoo. *North Korea in Transition*. Institute of East Asian Studies, 1991.

Lee, Mun-Woong. *Rural North Korea Under Communism: A Study of Sociocultural Change*. Rice University Studies, vol. 62, no. 1, Winter 1976.

Oberdorfer, Don. *The Two Koreas: A Contemporary History*. Reading, MA: Addison-Wesley, 1997.

Park, Han S. *North Korea: Ideology, Politics, Eocnomy*. New York: Prentice-Hall, 1996.

Pyongyang. Pyongyang: Foreign Languages Publishing House, 1980.

Savada, Andrea M. *North Korea: A Country Study.* Upland, PA: Diane Publishing Company, 1995.

Scalapino, Robert A. *North Korea at a Crossroads.* Stanford, CA: Hoover Institution Press, 1997.

Scalapino, Robert A., and Chong-Sik Lee. *Communism in Korea.* Berkeley, CA: University of California Press, 1973.

Scalapino, Robert A., and Hongkoo Lee. *North Korea in a Regional and Global Context.* Berkeley, CA: University of California Press, 1986.

Smith, Hazel. *North Korea in New World Order.* New York: St. Martin's Press, 1996.

Suh, Dae-Sook. *Kim Il Sung: The North Korean Leader.* New York: Columbia University Press, 1988.

Suh, Dae-Sook, and Chae-Jin Lee. *North Korea after Kim Il Sung.* Lynne Reinner Publishers, 1998.

Yang, Sung Chul. *Korea and Two Regimes: Kim Il Sung and Park Chung Hee.* Rochester, VT: Schenkman Books, 1981.

Index

About the Author

HELEN-LOUISE HUNTER is an attorney who has engaged in private practice with a large international law firm in Washington, D.C. and has served as Permanent Law Clerk in the U.S. District Court for the District of Maryland. For more than 20 years, she was a Far East specialist at the CIA. In the late 1970s, she served as the Assistant National Intelligence Officer for the Far East.